CHAPTER 156

Battle and Joy

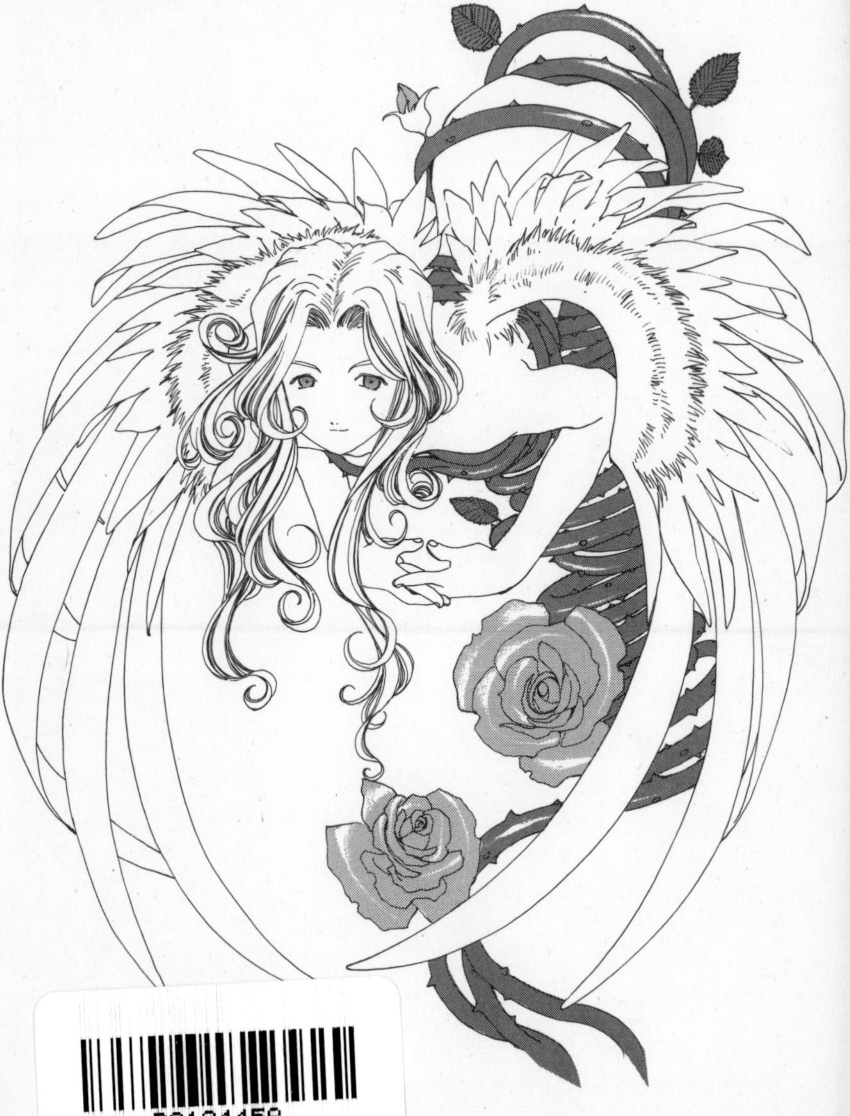

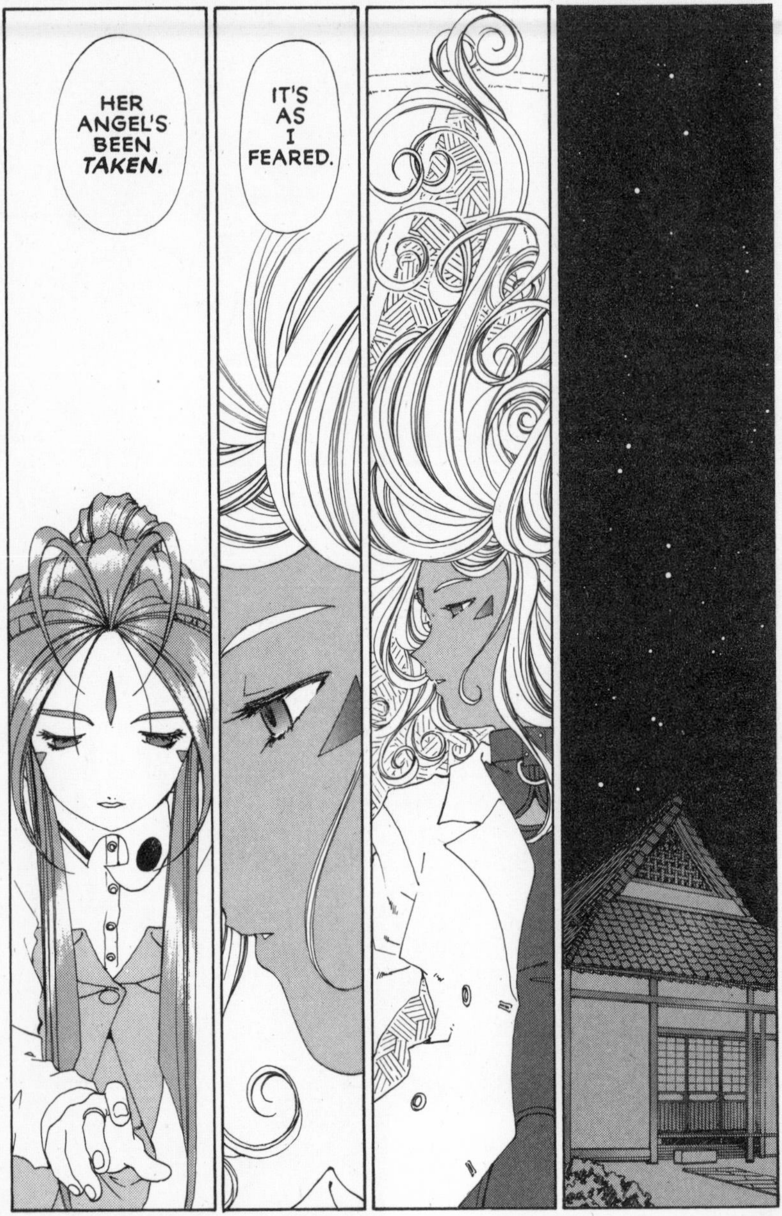
IT'S AS I FEARED.
HER ANGEL'S BEEN *TAKEN.*

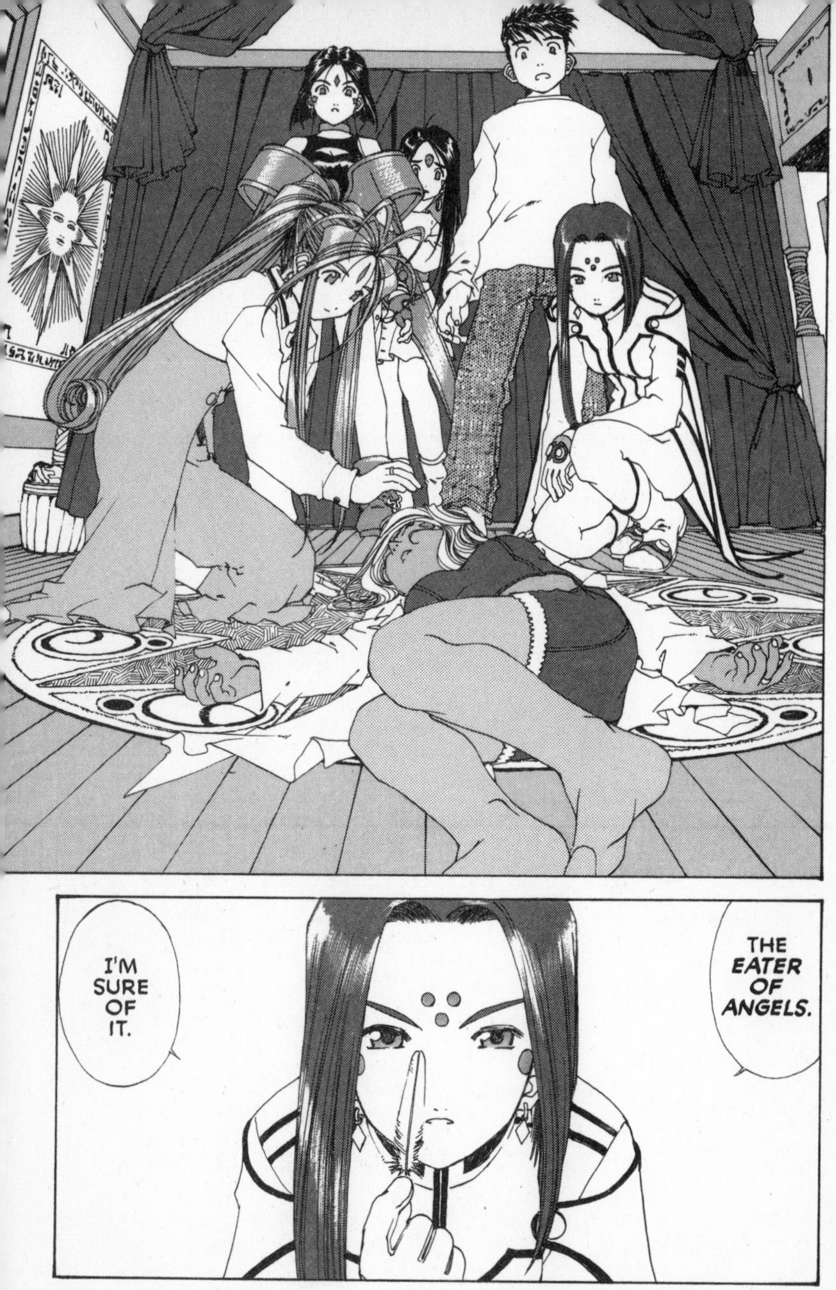
THE EATER OF ANGELS.
I'M SURE OF IT.

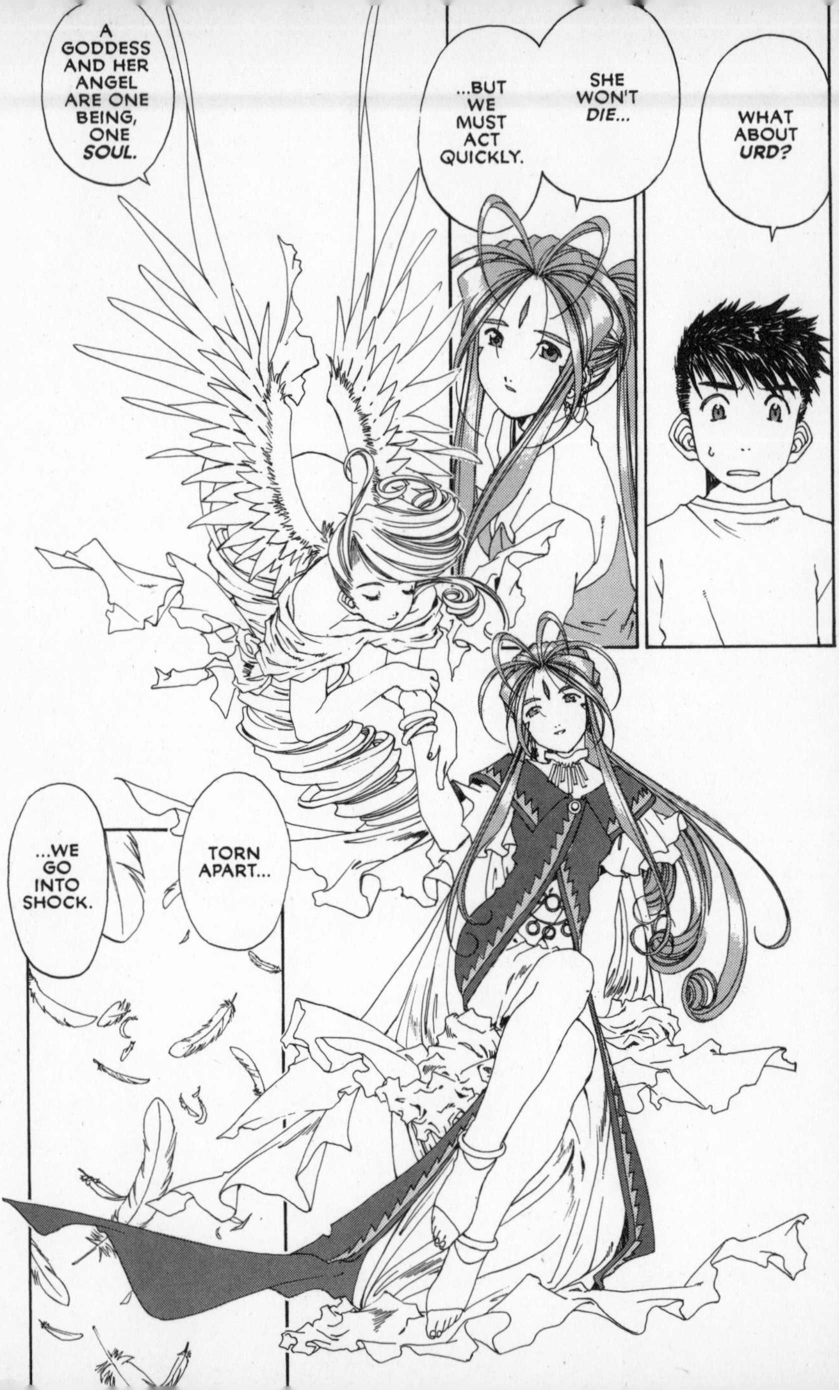
WHAT ABOUT *URD?*
SHE WON'T *DIE...*
...BUT WE MUST ACT QUICKLY.
A GODDESS AND HER ANGEL ARE ONE BEING, ONE *SOUL.*
TORN APART...
...WE GO INTO SHOCK.

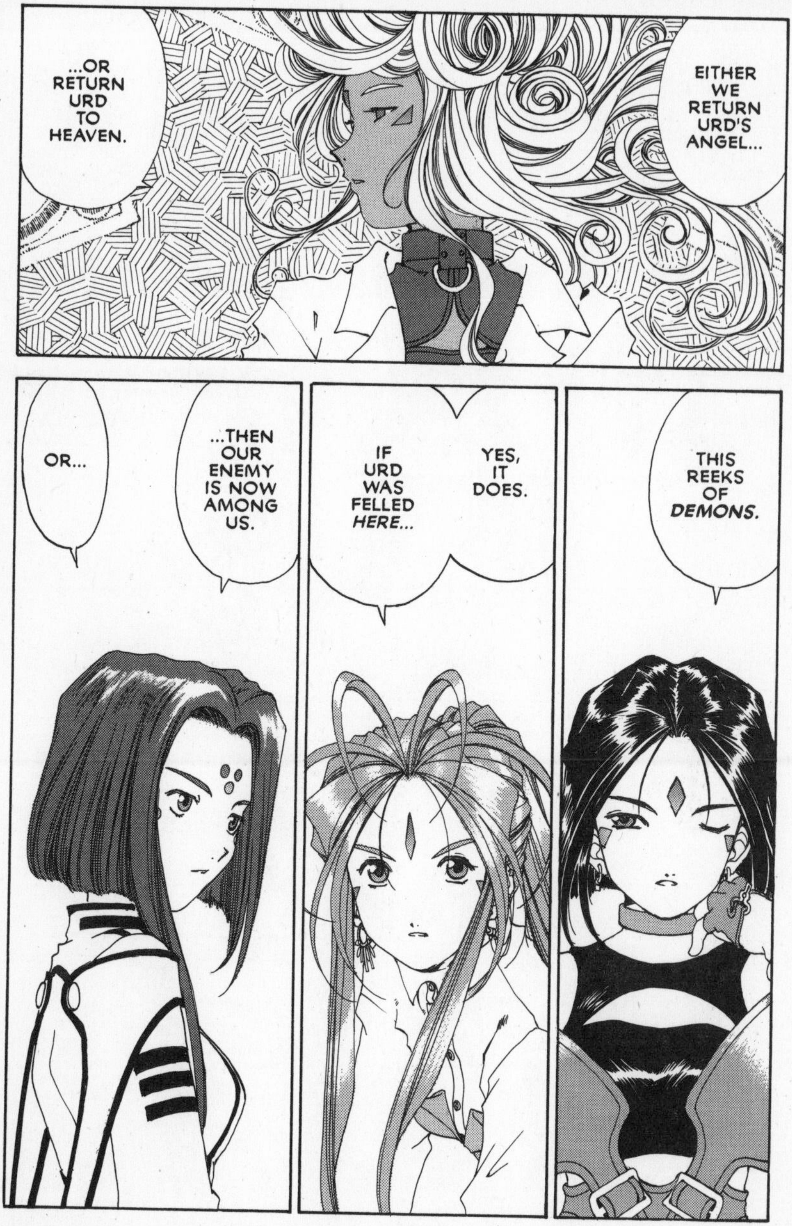

EITHER WE RETURN URD'S ANGEL...
...OR RETURN URD TO HEAVEN.
THIS REEKS OF *DEMONS.*
YES, IT DOES.
IF URD WAS FELLED *HERE...*
...THEN OUR ENEMY IS NOW AMONG US.
OR...

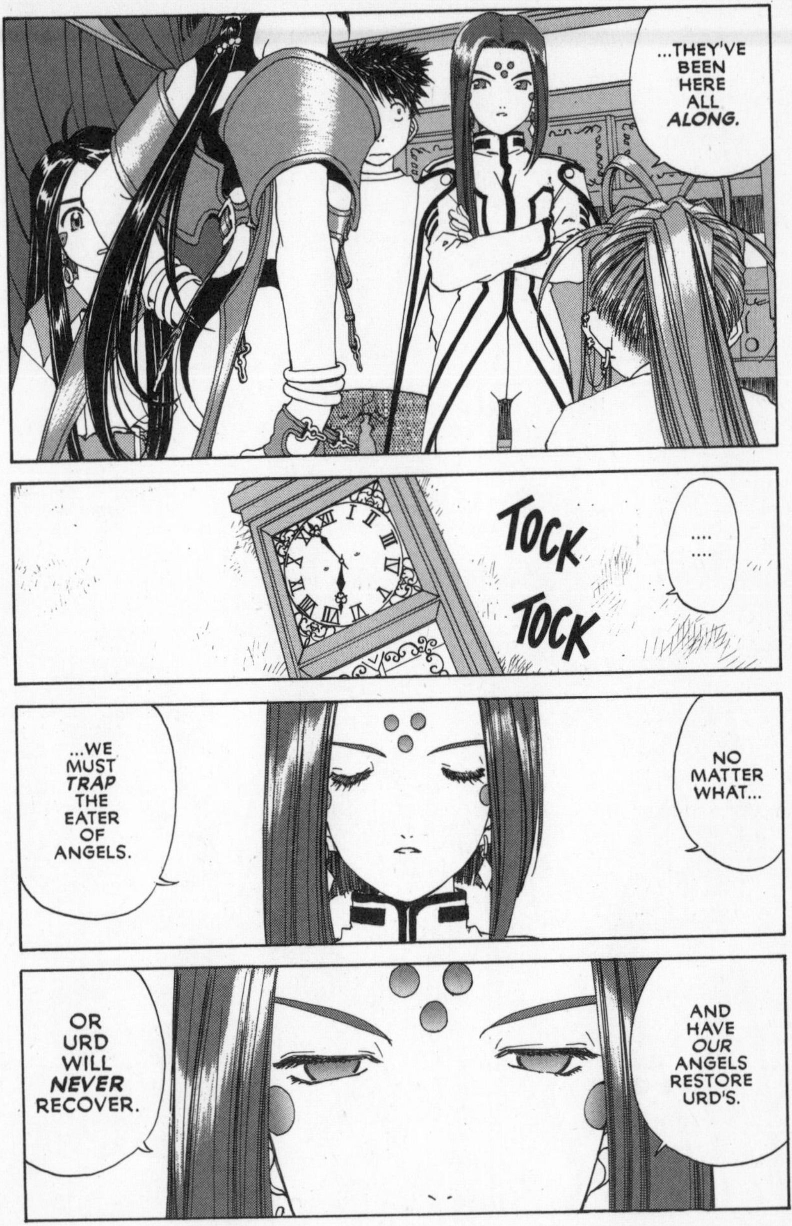
...THEY'VE BEEN HERE ALL *ALONG.*
....
....
TOCK
TOCK
NO MATTER WHAT...
...WE MUST *TRAP* THE EATER OF ANGELS.
AND HAVE *OUR* ANGELS RESTORE URD'S.
OR URD WILL ***NEVER*** RECOVER.

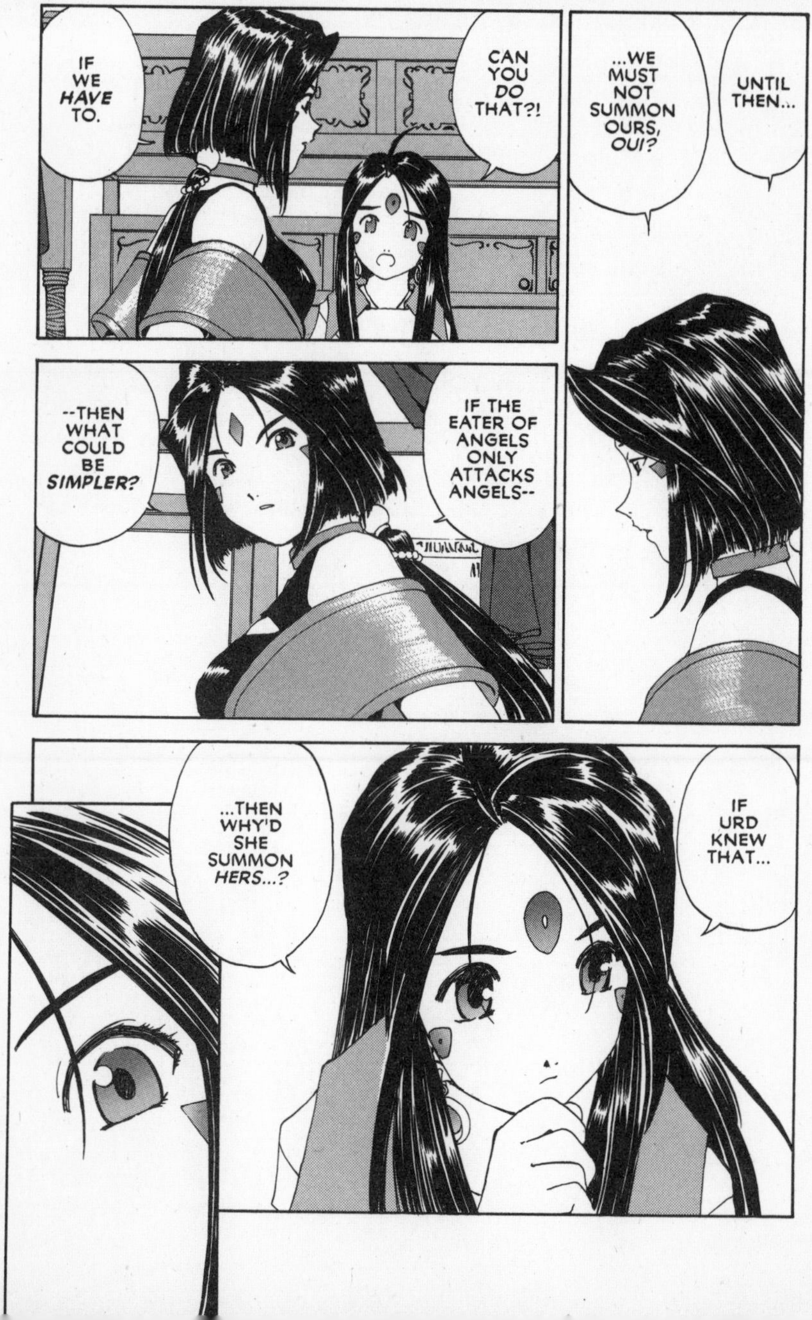
UNTIL THEN...
...WE MUST NOT SUMMON OURS, OUI?
CAN YOU DO THAT?!
IF WE HAVE TO.
IF THE EATER OF ANGELS ONLY ATTACKS ANGELS--
--THEN WHAT COULD BE SIMPLER?
IF URD KNEW THAT...
...THEN WHY'D SHE SUMMON HERS...?

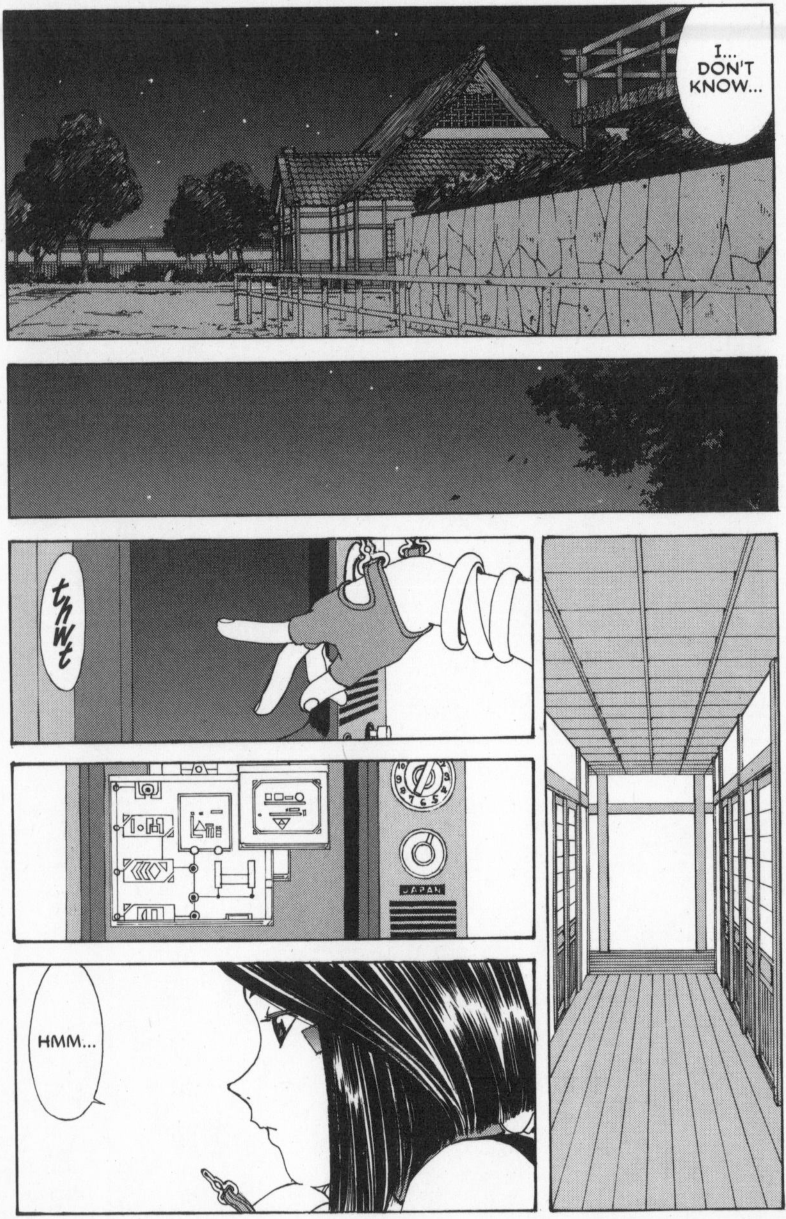
I... DON'T KNOW...
thwt
JAPAN
HMM...

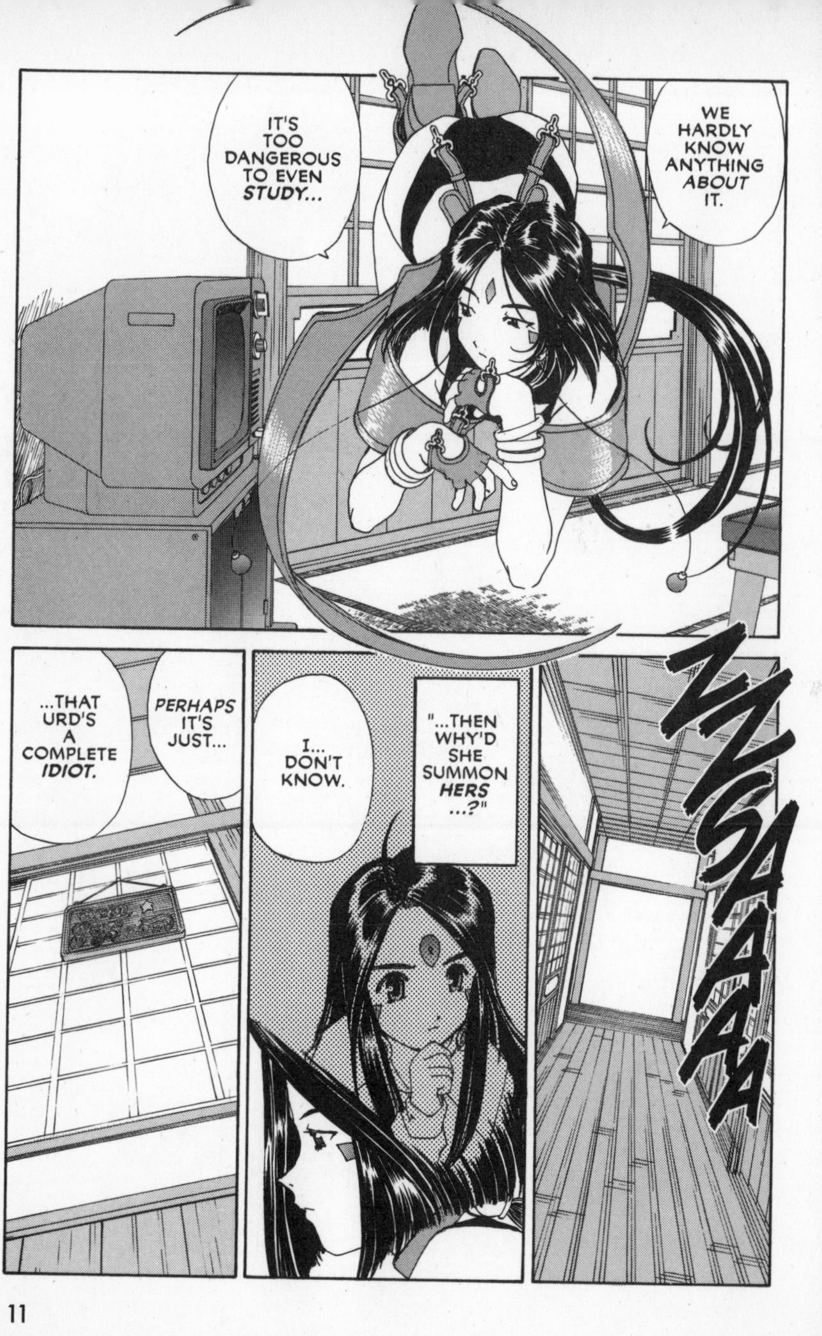
WE HARDLY KNOW ANYTHING *ABOUT* IT.
IT'S TOO DANGEROUS TO EVEN *STUDY*...
MNSAAAA
"...THEN WHY'D SHE SUMMON *HERS* ...?"
I... DON'T KNOW.
PERHAPS IT'S JUST...
...THAT URD'S A COMPLETE *IDIOT*.

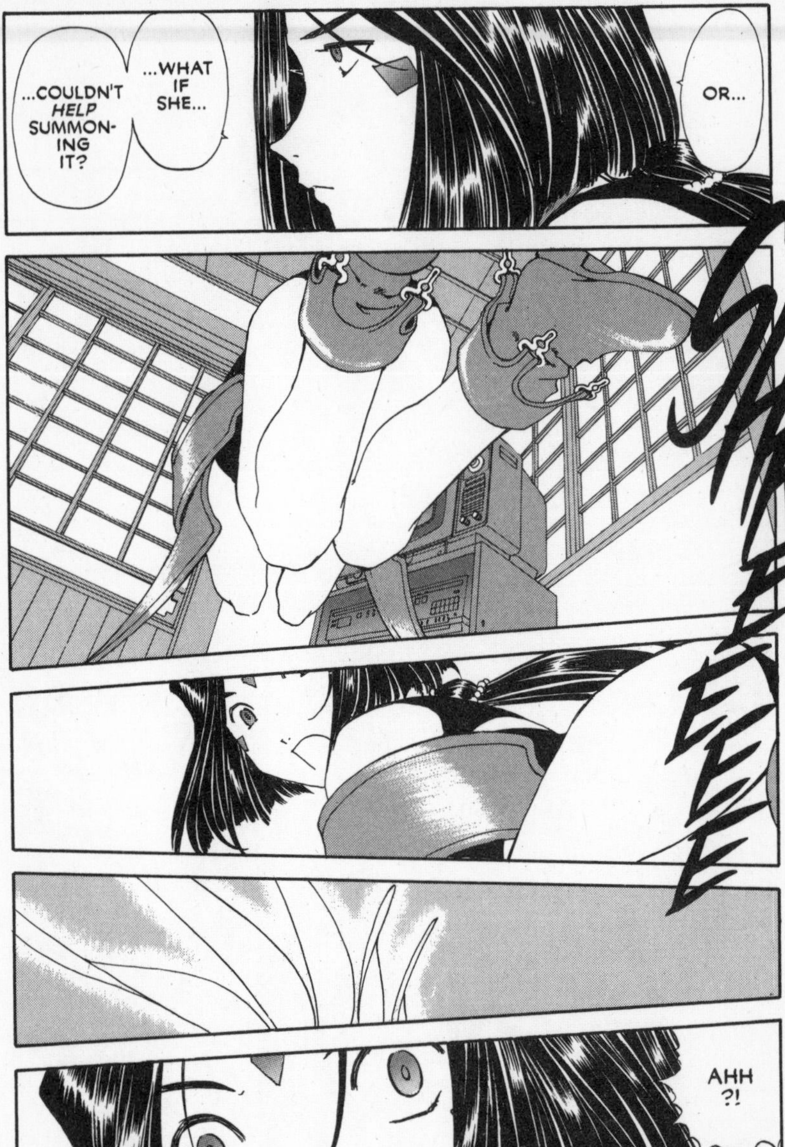

OR...
...WHAT IF SHE...
...COULDN'T *HELP* SUMMONING IT?
SHREEEEEE
AHH ?!

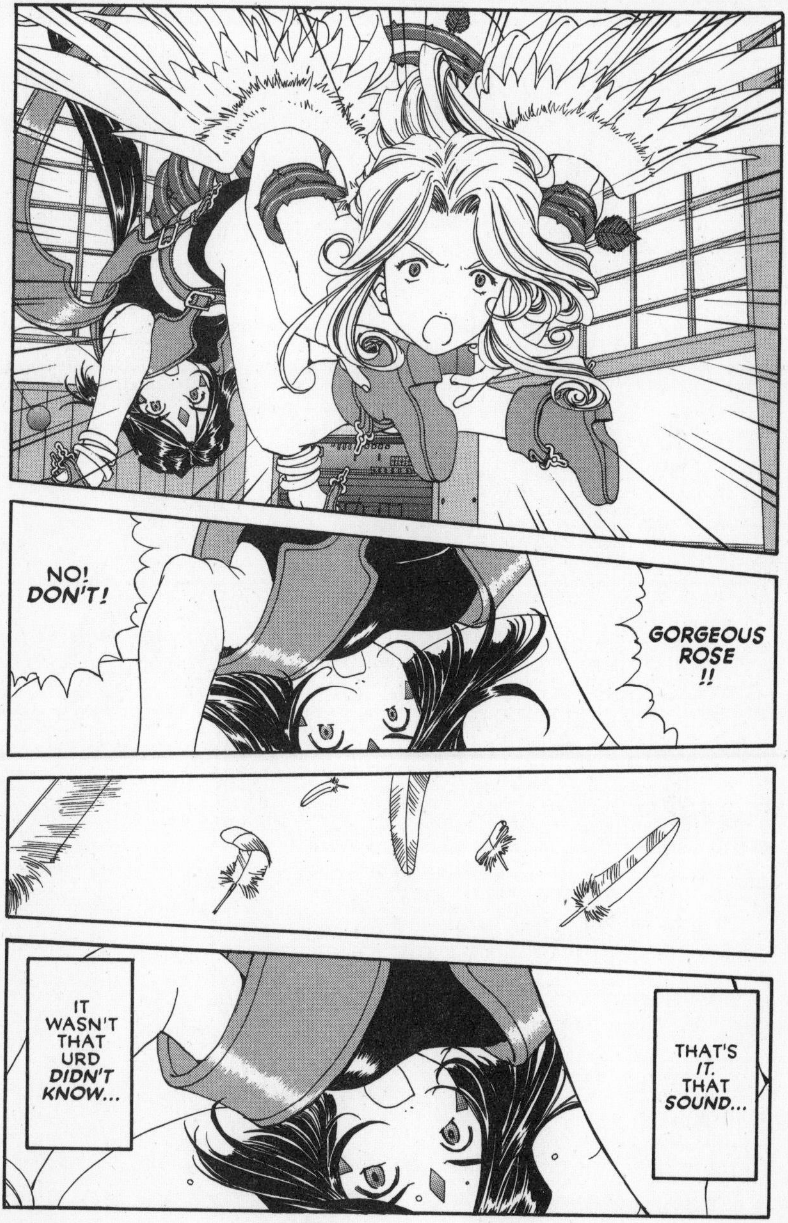
GORGEOUS ROSE !!
NO! *DON'T!*
THAT'S *IT.* THAT *SOUND...*
IT WASN'T THAT URD *DIDN'T KNOW...*

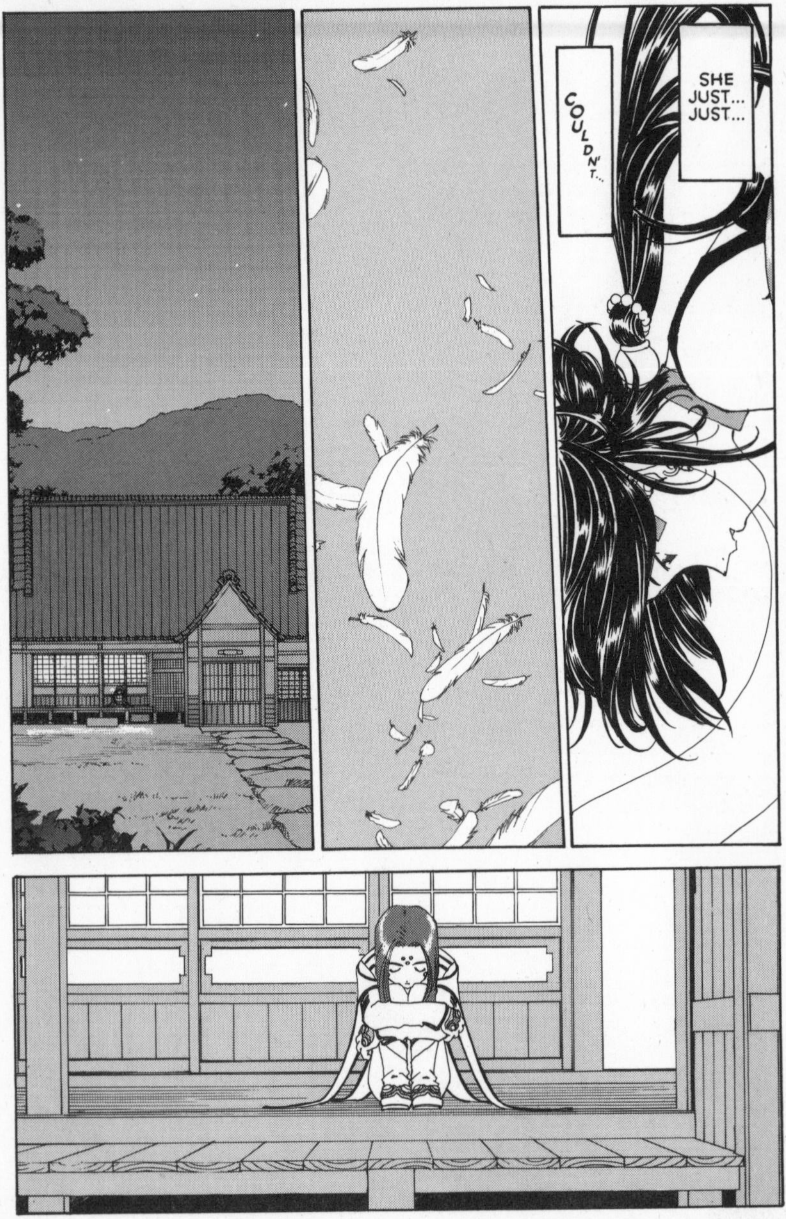
SHE JUST... JUST...
COULDN'T...

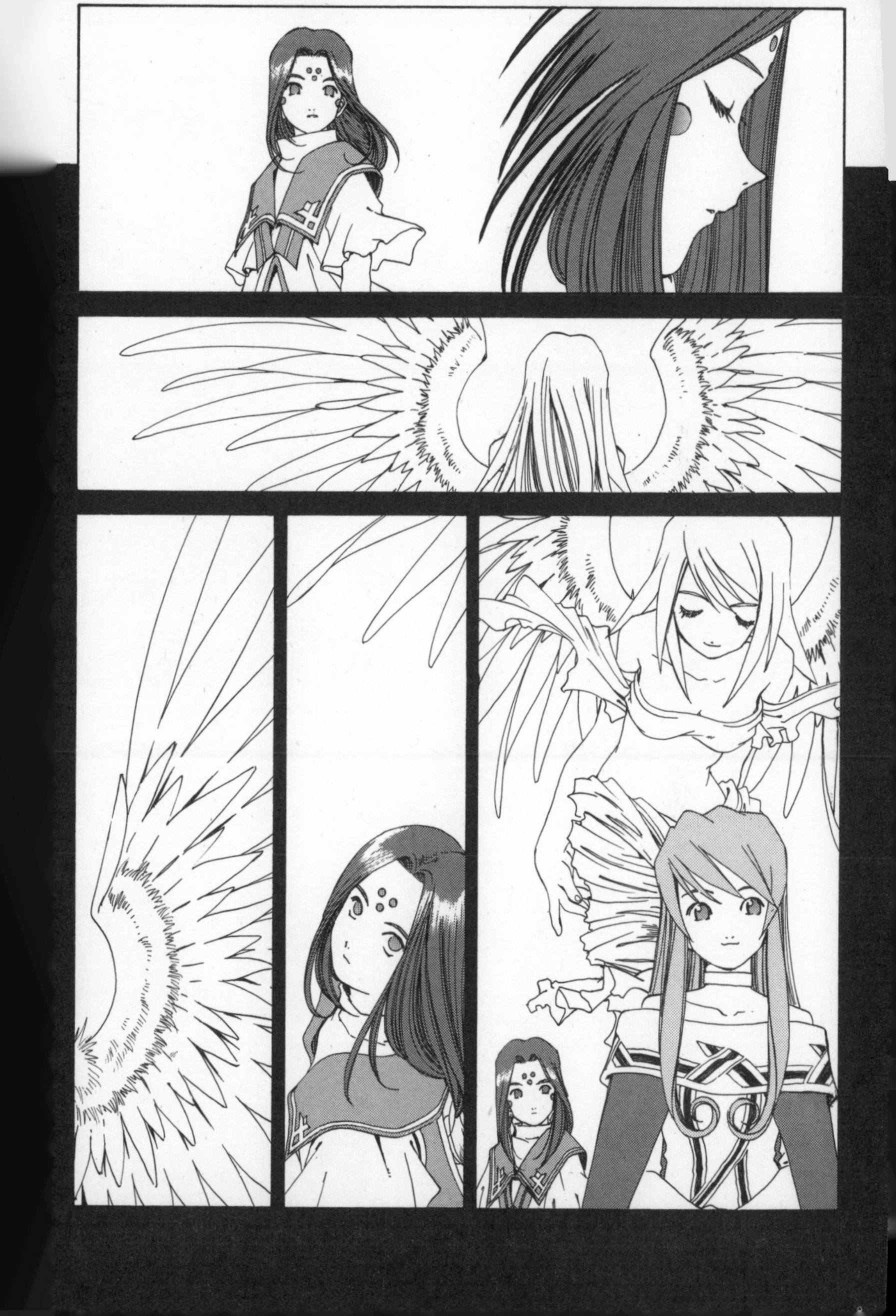

I WANTED YOU TO *MEET...*

--IND?

!

LIND.

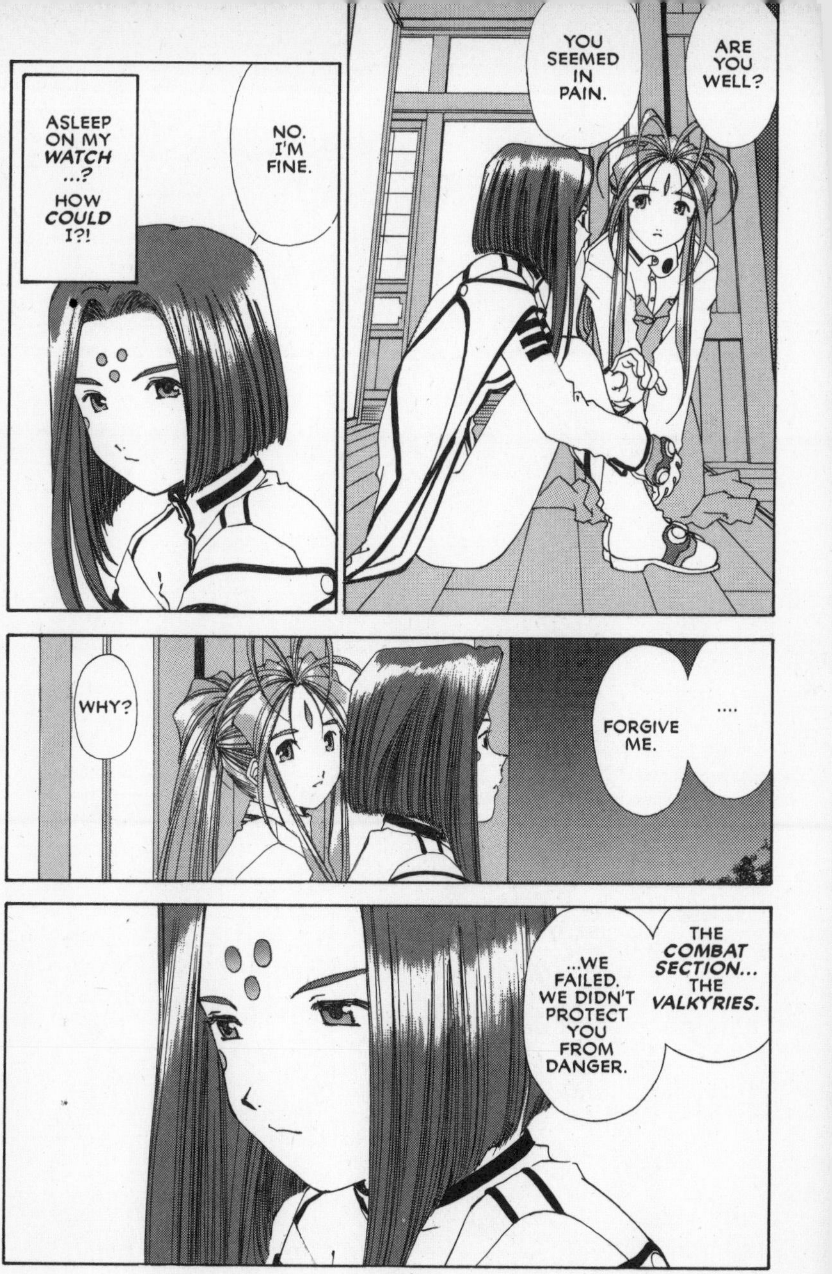
ARE YOU WELL?
YOU SEEMED IN PAIN.
NO. I'M FINE.
ASLEEP ON MY WATCH ...? HOW COULD I?!
....
FORGIVE ME.
WHY?
THE COMBAT SECTION... THE VALKYRIES.
...WE FAILED. WE DIDN'T PROTECT YOU FROM DANGER.

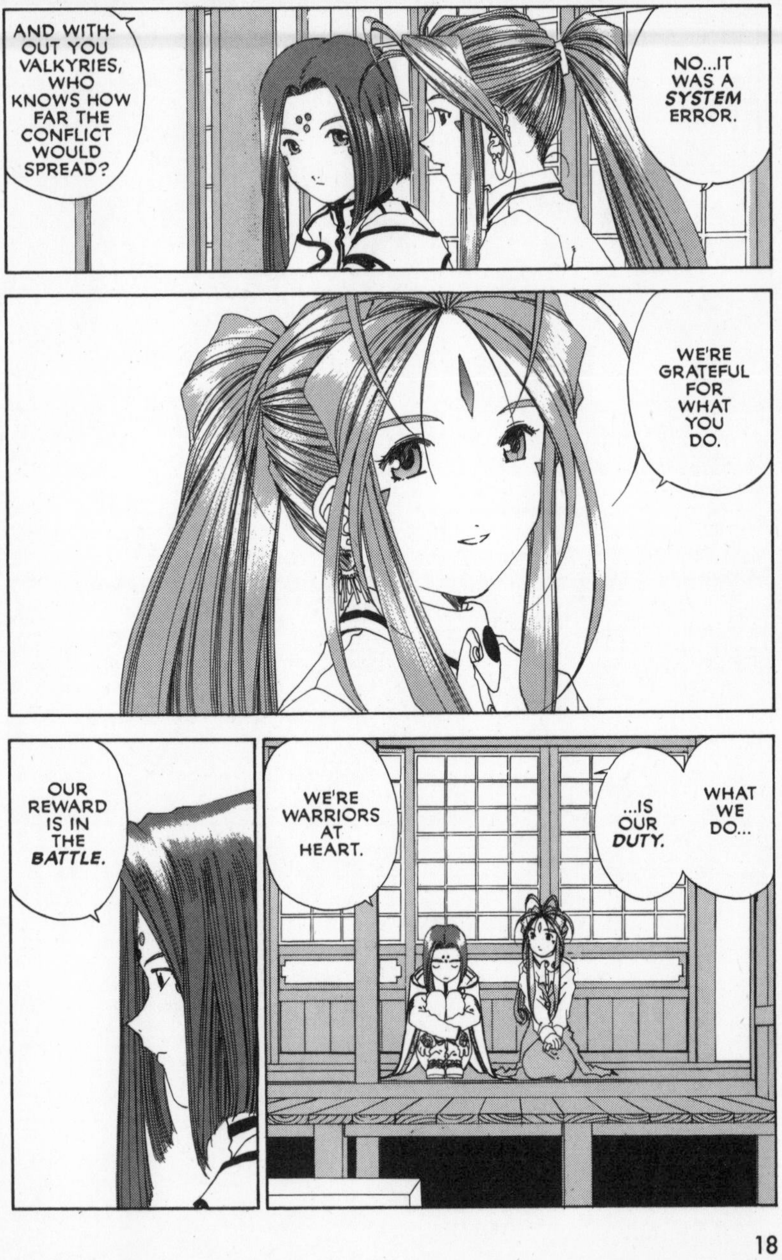
NO...IT WAS A *SYSTEM* ERROR.
AND WITH-OUT YOU VALKYRIES, WHO KNOWS HOW FAR THE CONFLICT WOULD SPREAD?
WE'RE GRATEFUL FOR WHAT YOU DO.
WHAT WE DO...
...IS OUR *DUTY.*
WE'RE WARRIORS AT HEART.
OUR REWARD IS IN THE *BATTLE.*

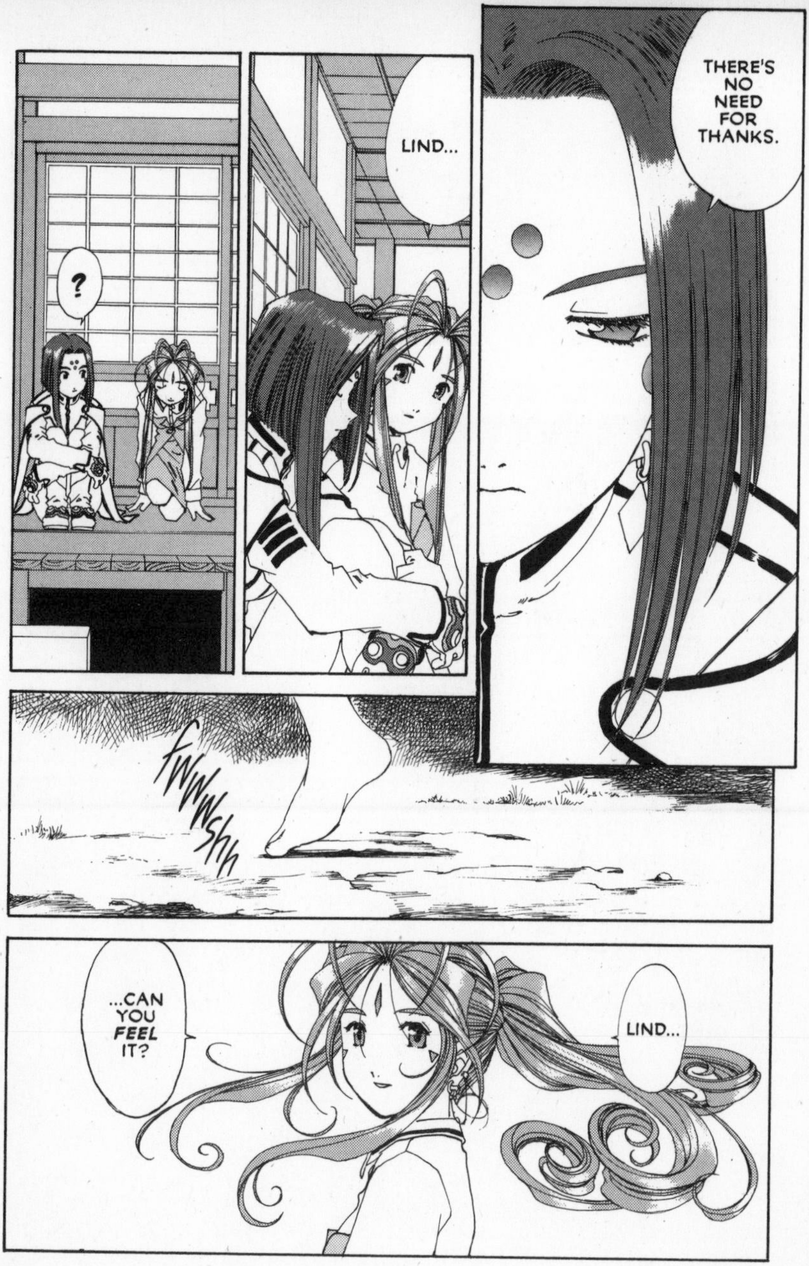
THERE'S NO NEED FOR THANKS.
LIND...
?
FWWWSHH
LIND...
...CAN YOU FEEL IT?

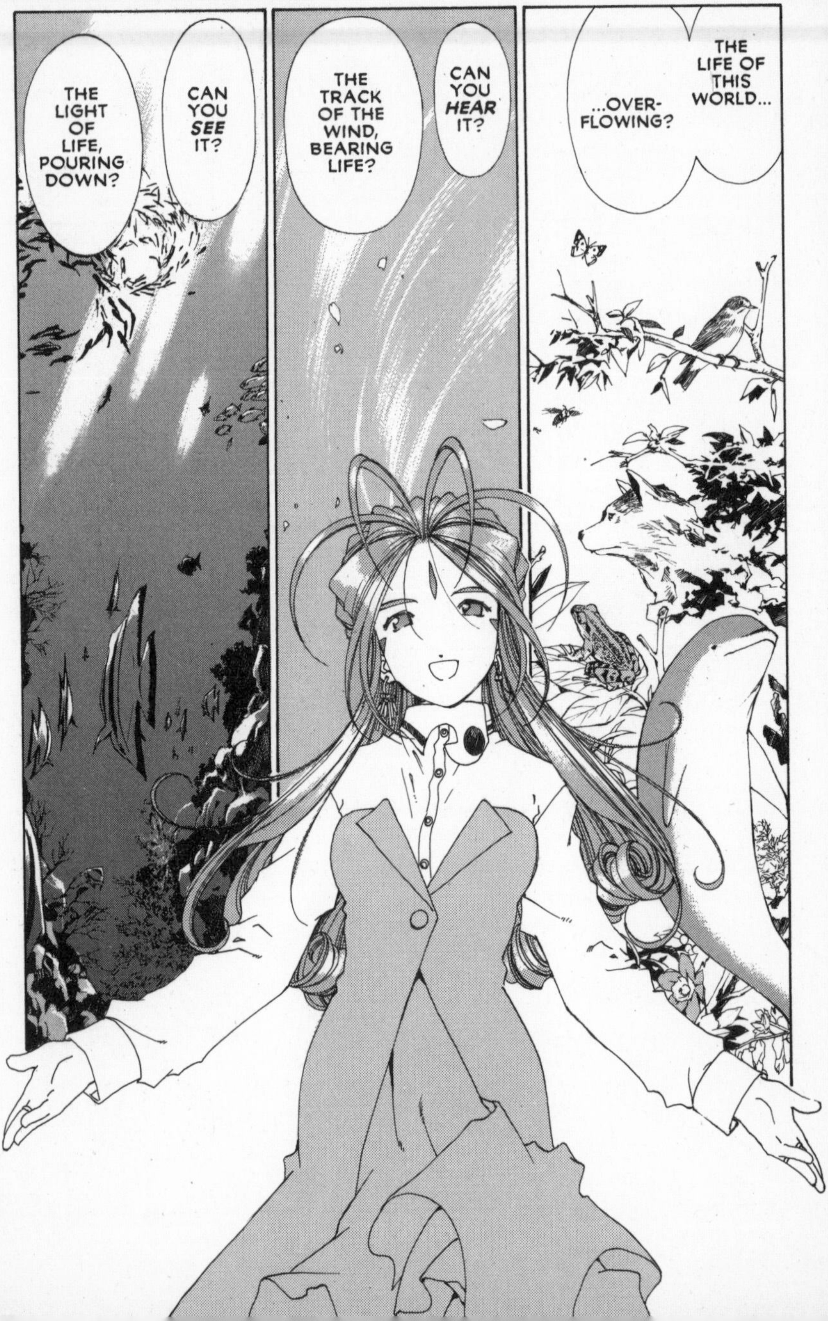

THE LIFE OF THIS WORLD...
...OVER-FLOWING?
CAN YOU *HEAR* IT?
THE TRACK OF THE WIND, BEARING LIFE?
CAN YOU *SEE* IT?
THE LIGHT OF LIFE, POURING DOWN?

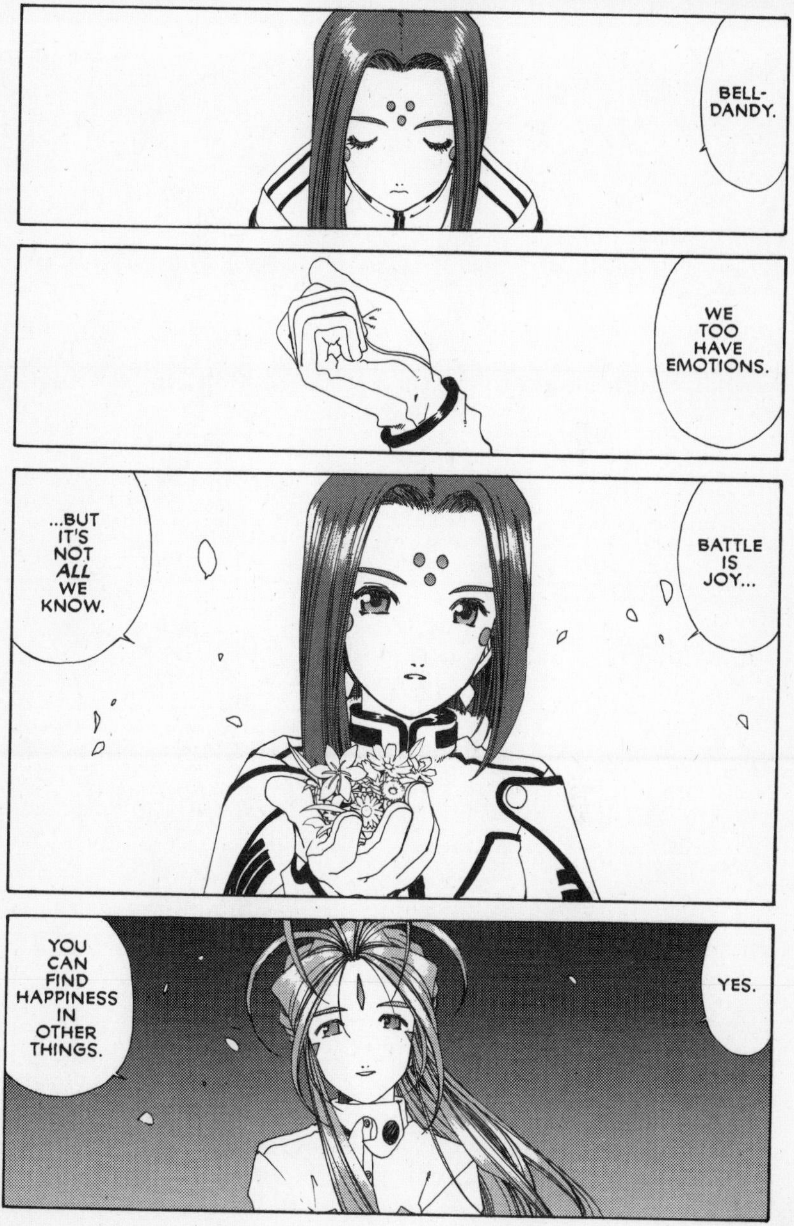
BELL-DANDY.
WE TOO HAVE EMOTIONS.
BATTLE IS JOY...
...BUT IT'S NOT *ALL* WE KNOW.
YES.
YOU CAN FIND HAPPINESS IN OTHER THINGS.

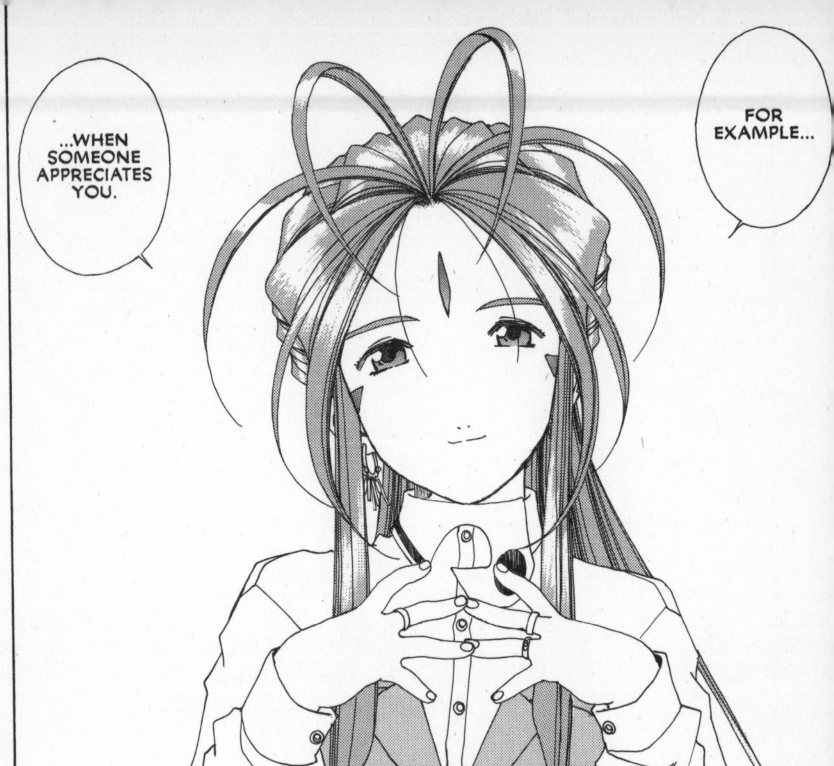
FOR EXAMPLE...
...WHEN SOMEONE APPRECIATES YOU.

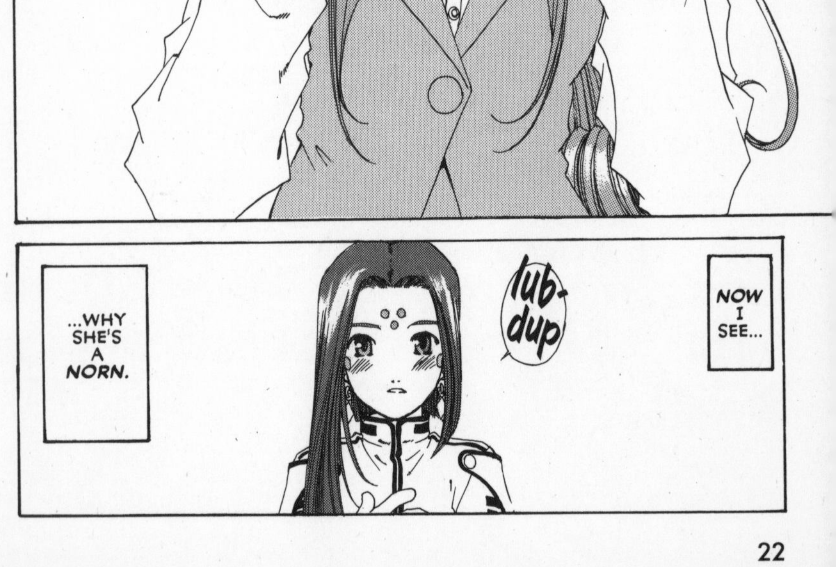
NOW I SEE...
lub-dup
...WHY SHE'S A NORN.

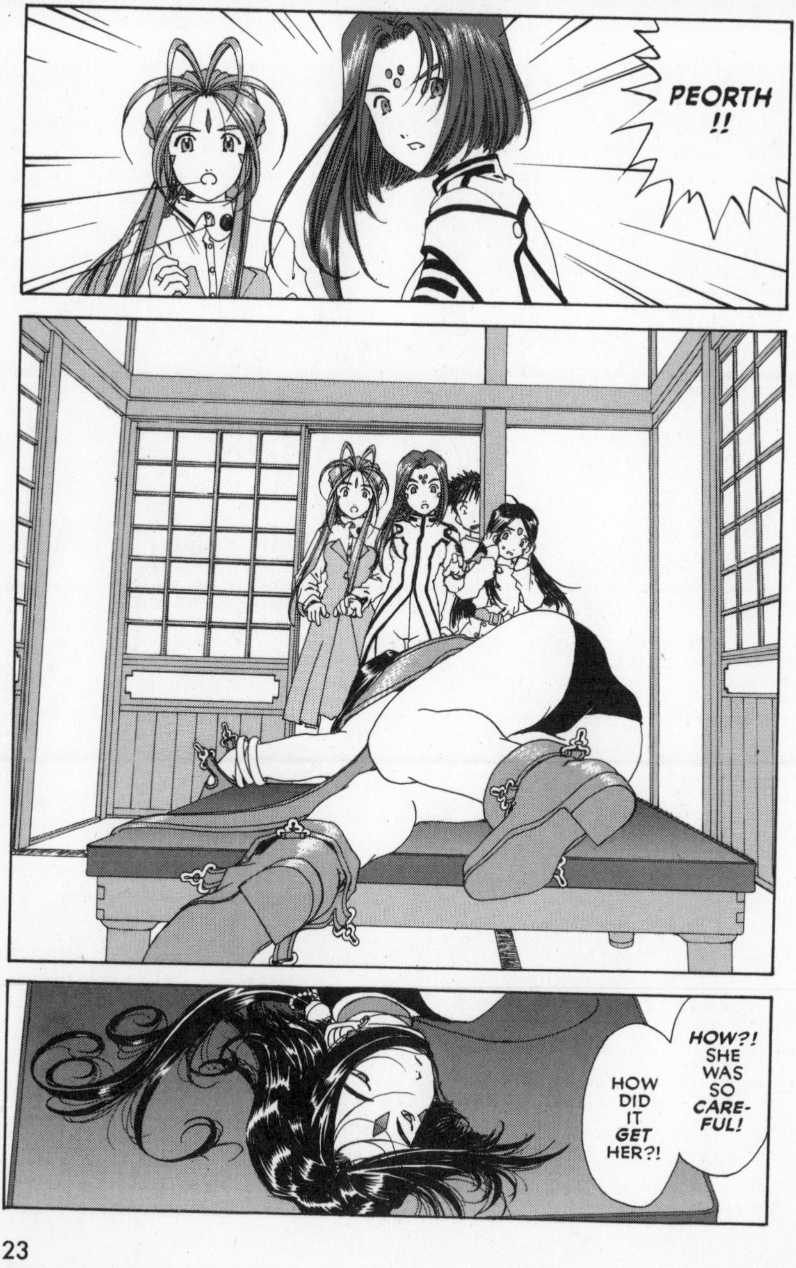
PEORTH !!
HOW?! SHE WAS SO CAREFUL!
HOW DID IT GET HER?!

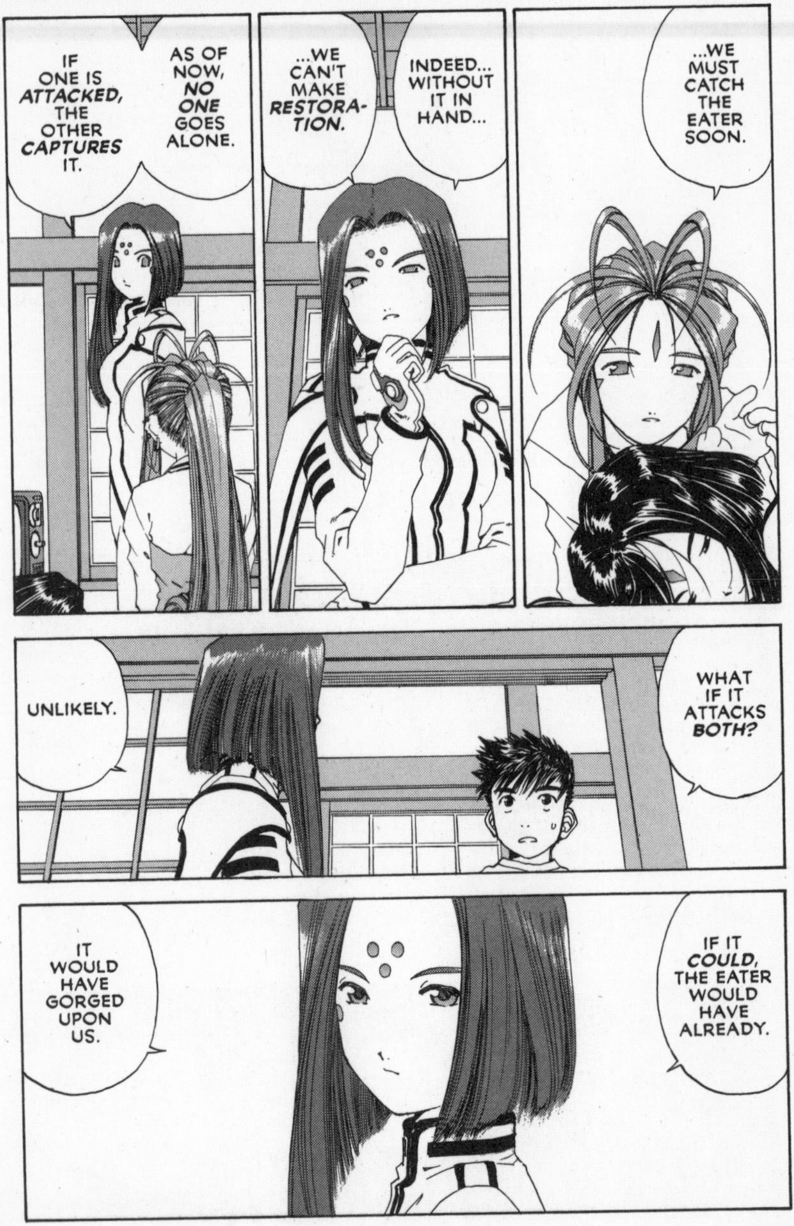
...WE MUST CATCH THE EATER SOON.
INDEED... WITHOUT IT IN HAND...
...WE CAN'T MAKE *RESTORATION.*
AS OF NOW, *NO ONE* GOES ALONE.
IF ONE IS *ATTACKED,* THE OTHER *CAPTURES* IT.
WHAT IF IT ATTACKS *BOTH?*
UNLIKELY.
IF IT *COULD,* THE EATER WOULD HAVE ALREADY.
IT WOULD HAVE GORGED UPON US.

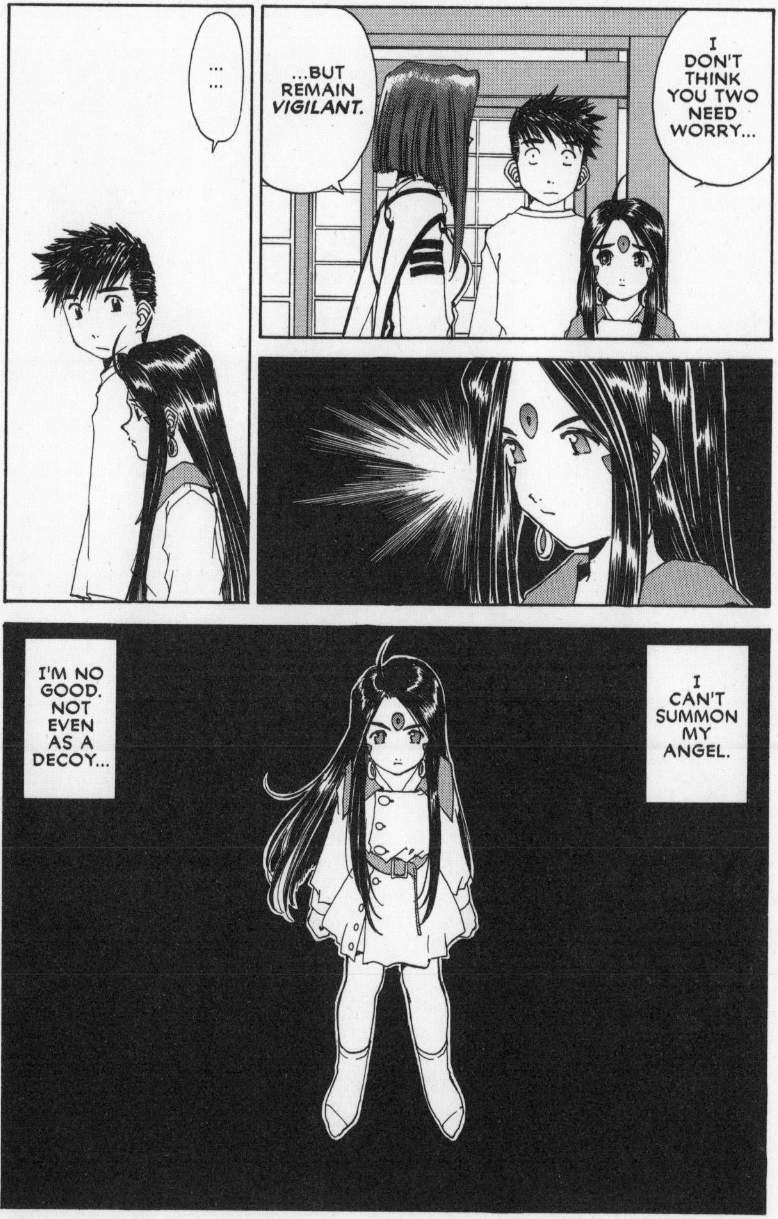
I DON'T THINK YOU TWO NEED WORRY...
...BUT REMAIN *VIGILANT.*
... ...
I CAN'T SUMMON MY ANGEL.
I'M NO GOOD. NOT EVEN AS A DECOY...

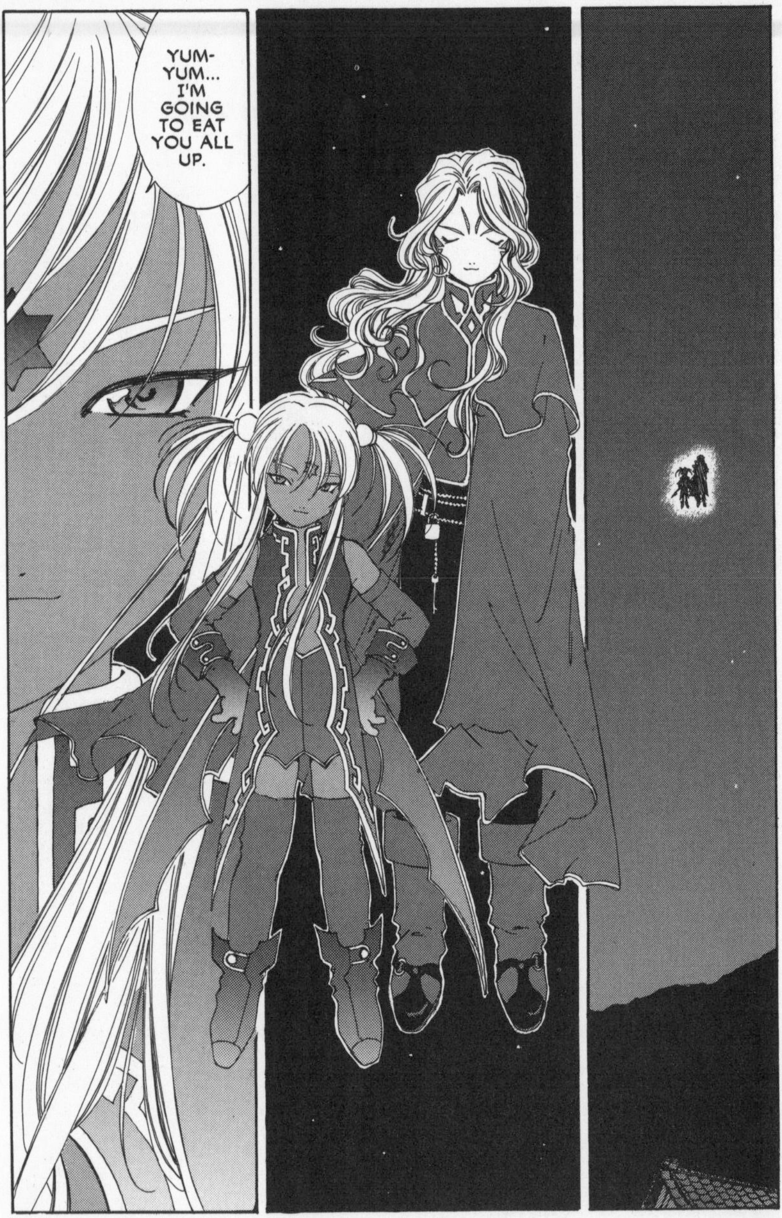
YUM-YUM... I'M GOING TO EAT YOU ALL UP.

CHAPTER 157

A Dance of Feathers

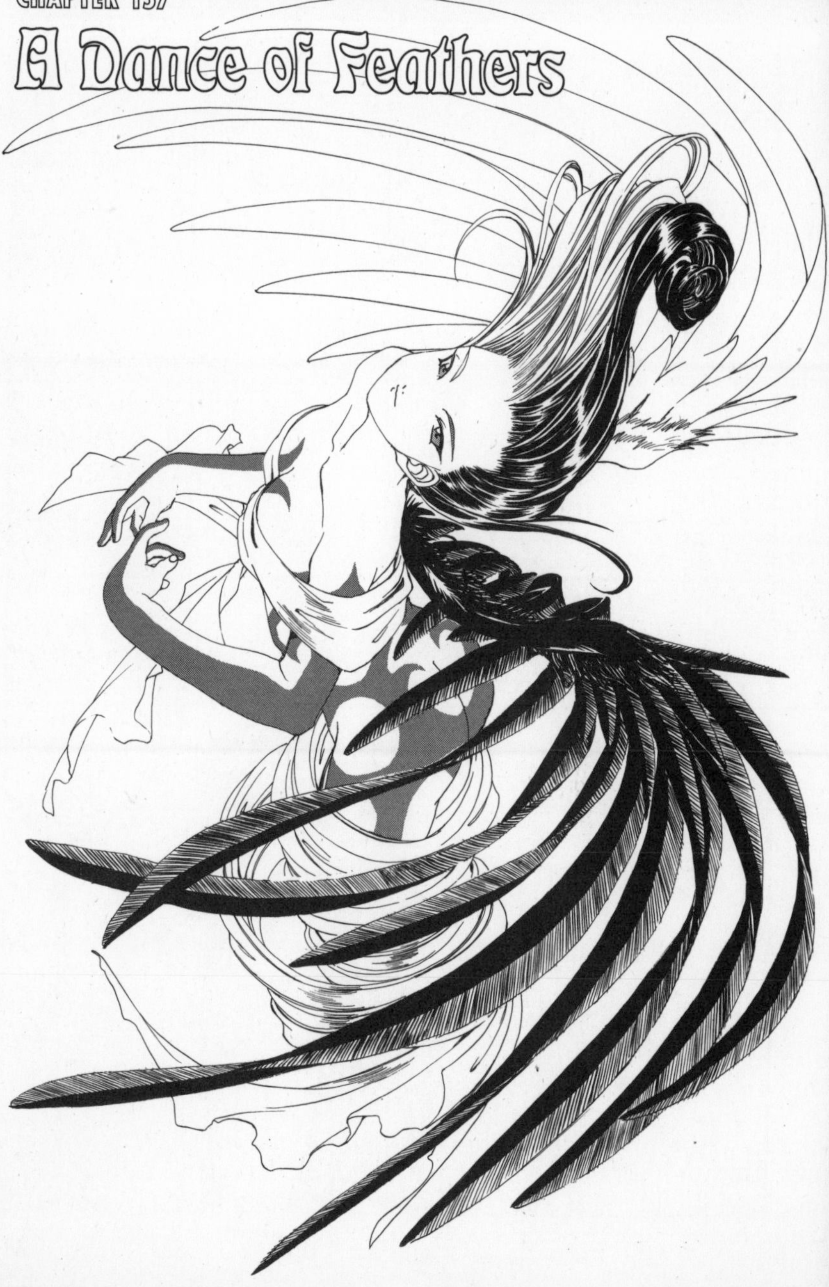

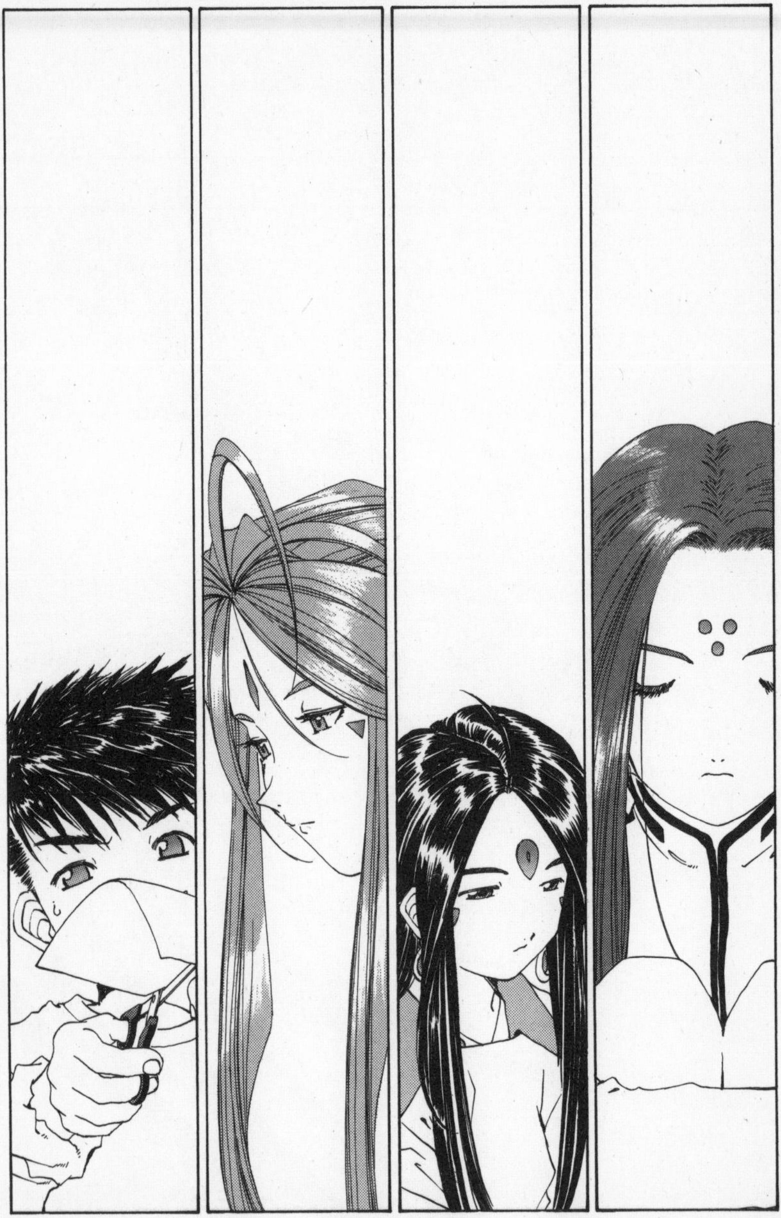

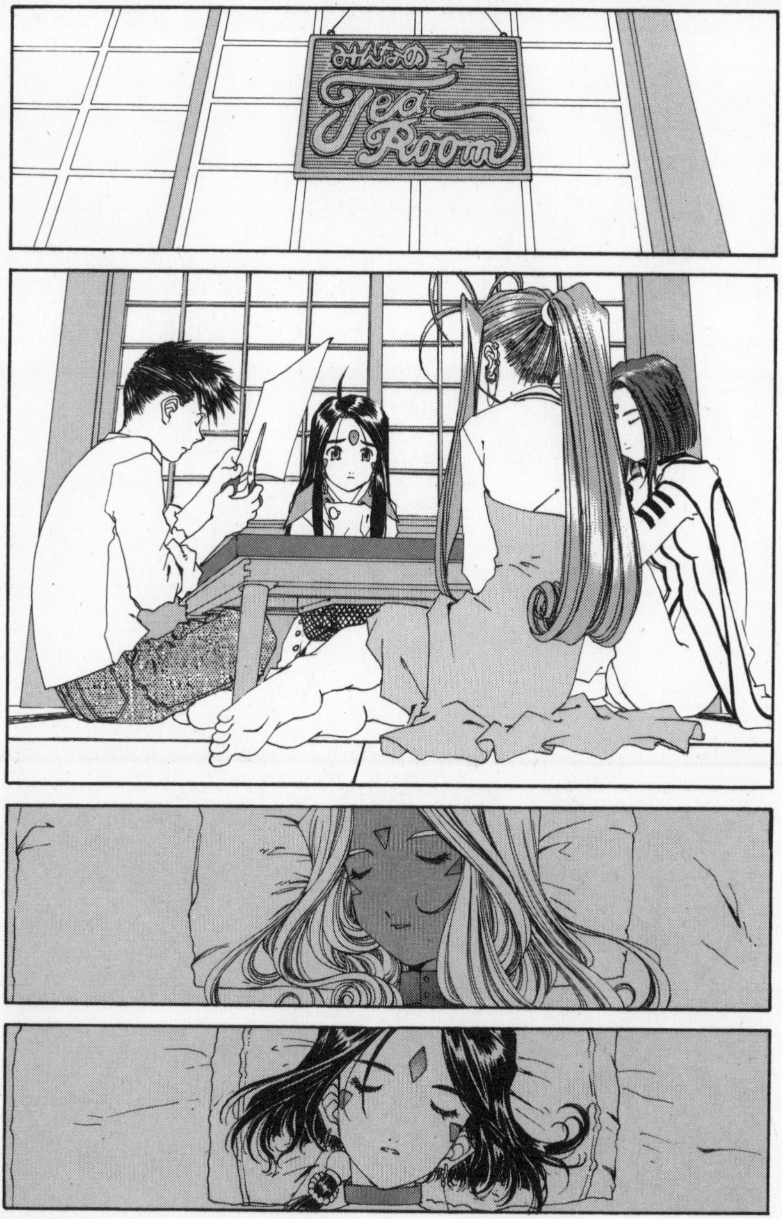
みんなの
Tea Room

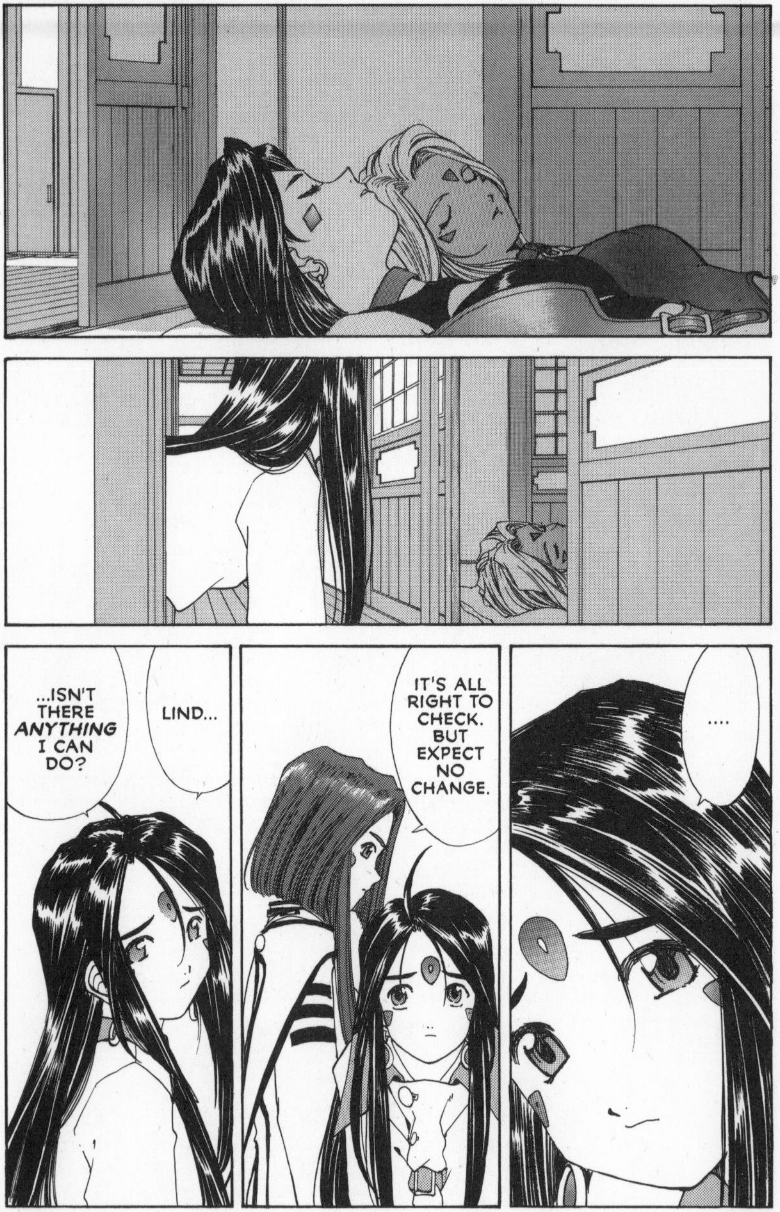
....
IT'S ALL RIGHT TO CHECK. BUT EXPECT NO CHANGE.
LIND...
...ISN'T THERE ANYTHING I CAN DO?

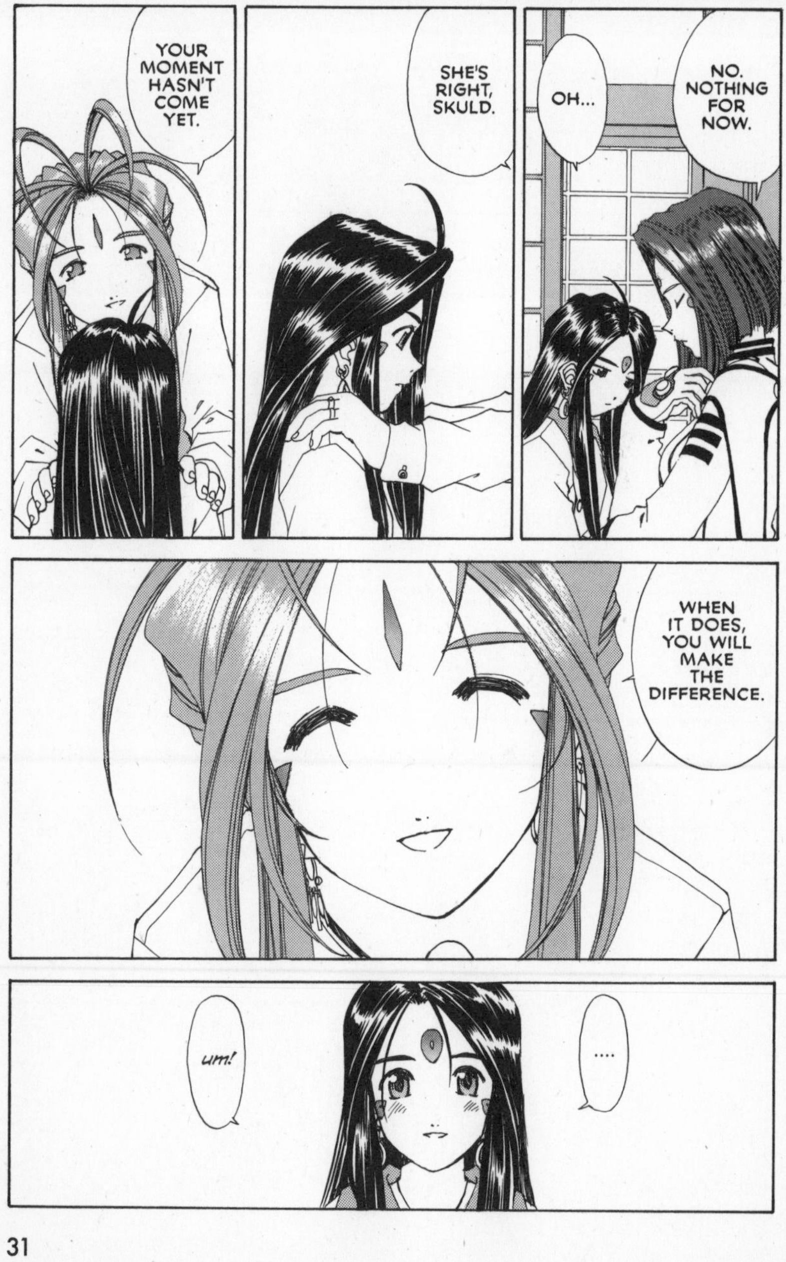
NO. NOTHING FOR NOW.
OH...
SHE'S RIGHT, SKULD.
YOUR MOMENT HASN'T COME YET.
WHEN IT DOES, YOU WILL MAKE THE DIFFERENCE.
....
um!

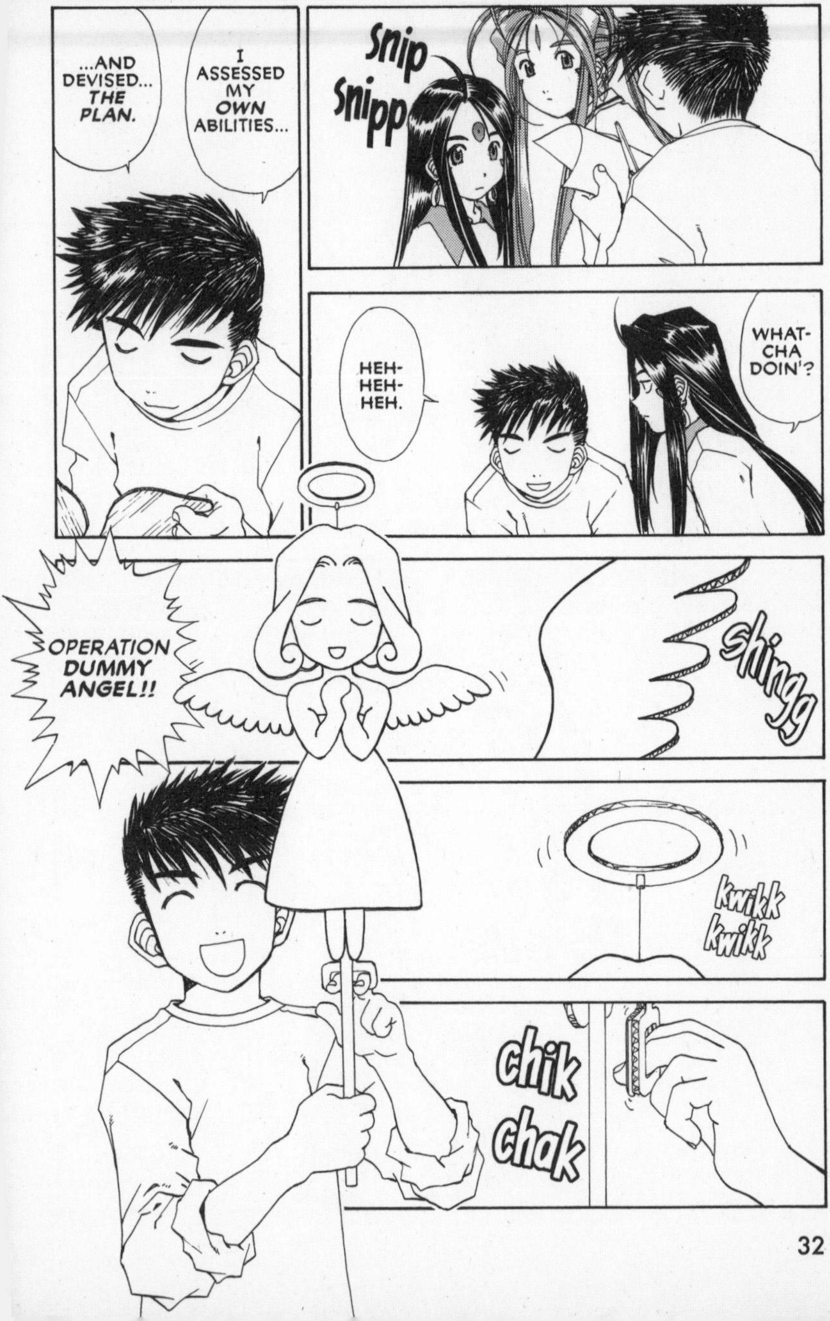

Snip
Snipp
WHAT-CHA DOIN'?
HEH-HEH-HEH.
I ASSESSED MY *OWN* ABILITIES...
...AND DEVISED... *THE PLAN.*
shingg
kwikk kwikk
chik chak
OPERATION DUMMY ANGEL!!

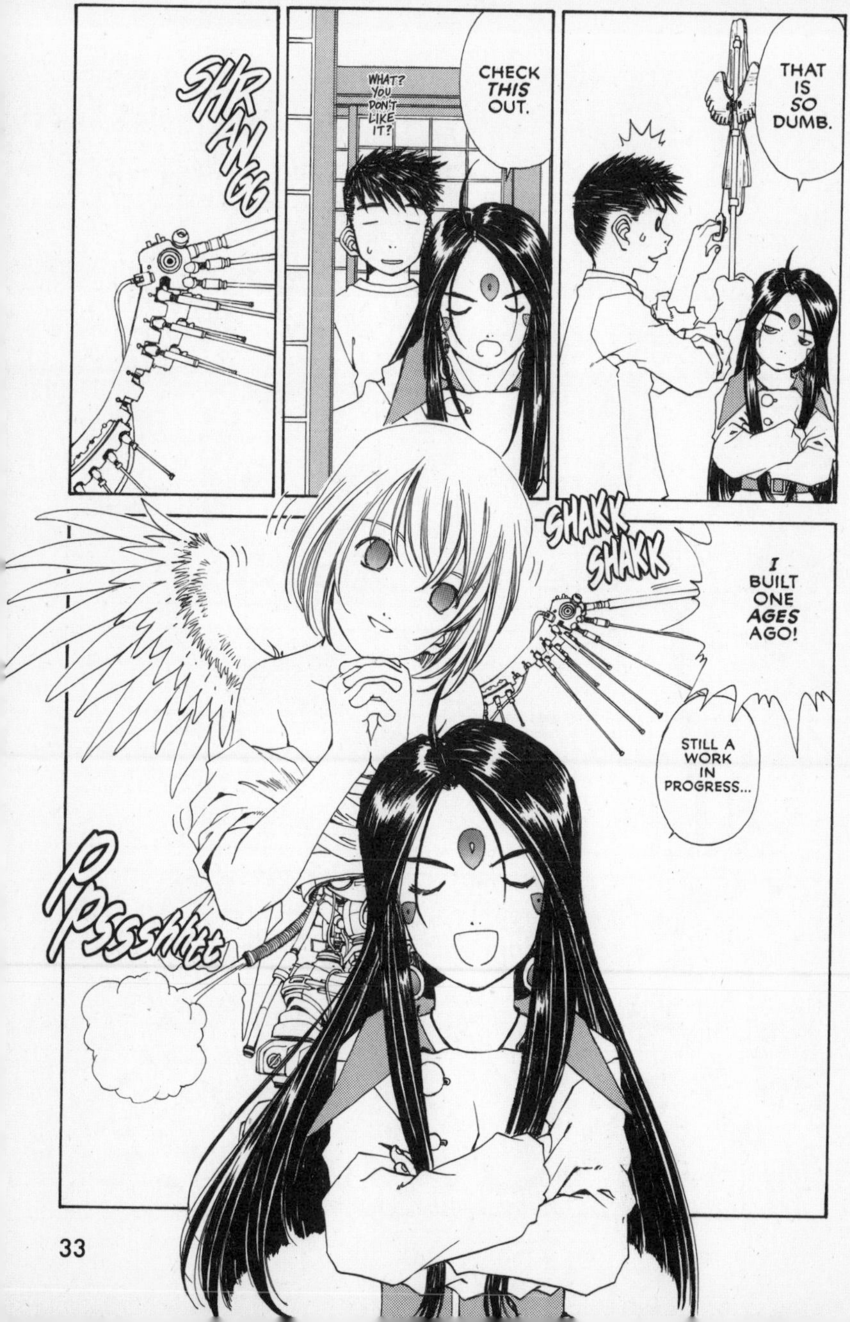
THAT IS SO DUMB.
CHECK THIS OUT.
WHAT? YOU DON'T LIKE IT?
SHRANGG
I BUILT ONE AGES AGO!
SHAKK SHAKK
STILL A WORK IN PROGRESS...
Psssshtt

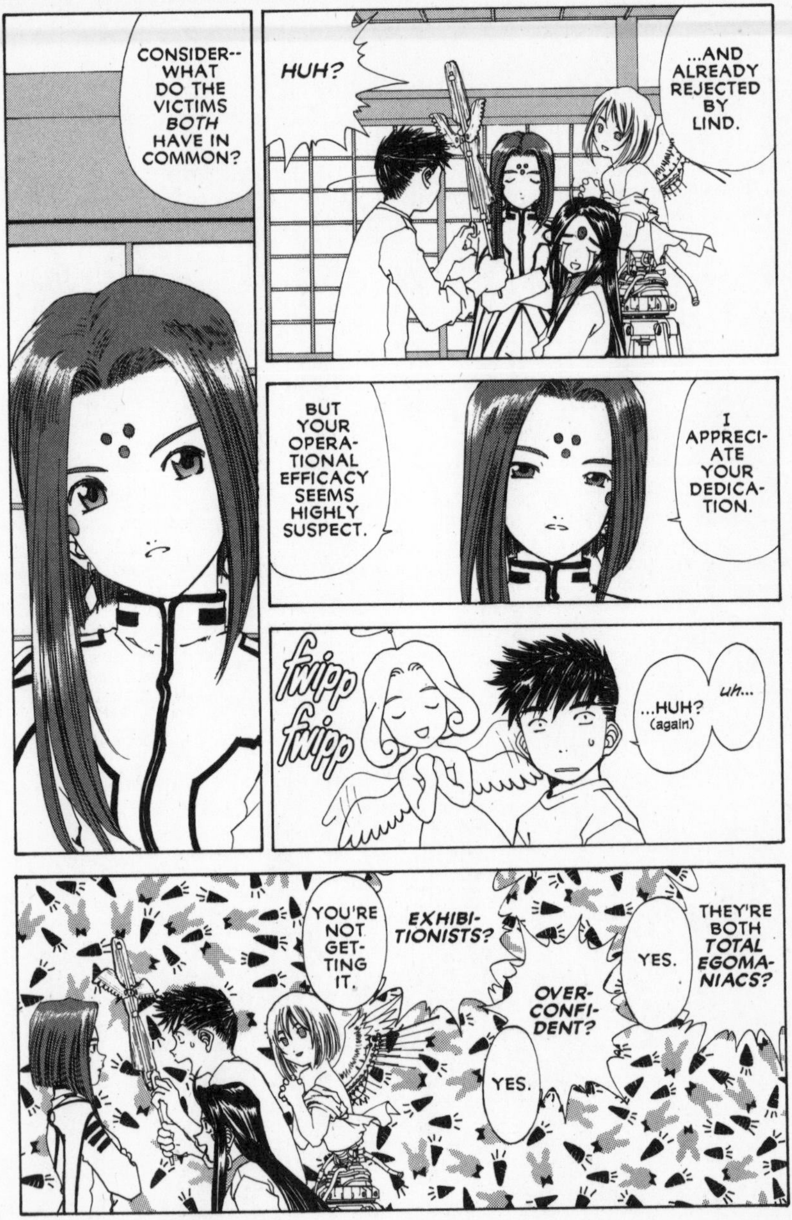

...AND ALREADY REJECTED BY LIND.
HUH?
CONSIDER-- WHAT DO THE VICTIMS *BOTH* HAVE IN COMMON?
I APPRECIATE YOUR DEDICATION.
BUT YOUR OPERATIONAL EFFICACY SEEMS HIGHLY SUSPECT.
uh...
...HUH? (again)
fwipp fwipp
THEY'RE BOTH *TOTAL EGOMANIACS?*
YES.
OVER-CONFIDENT?
YES.
EXHIBITIONISTS?
YOU'RE NOT GETTING IT.

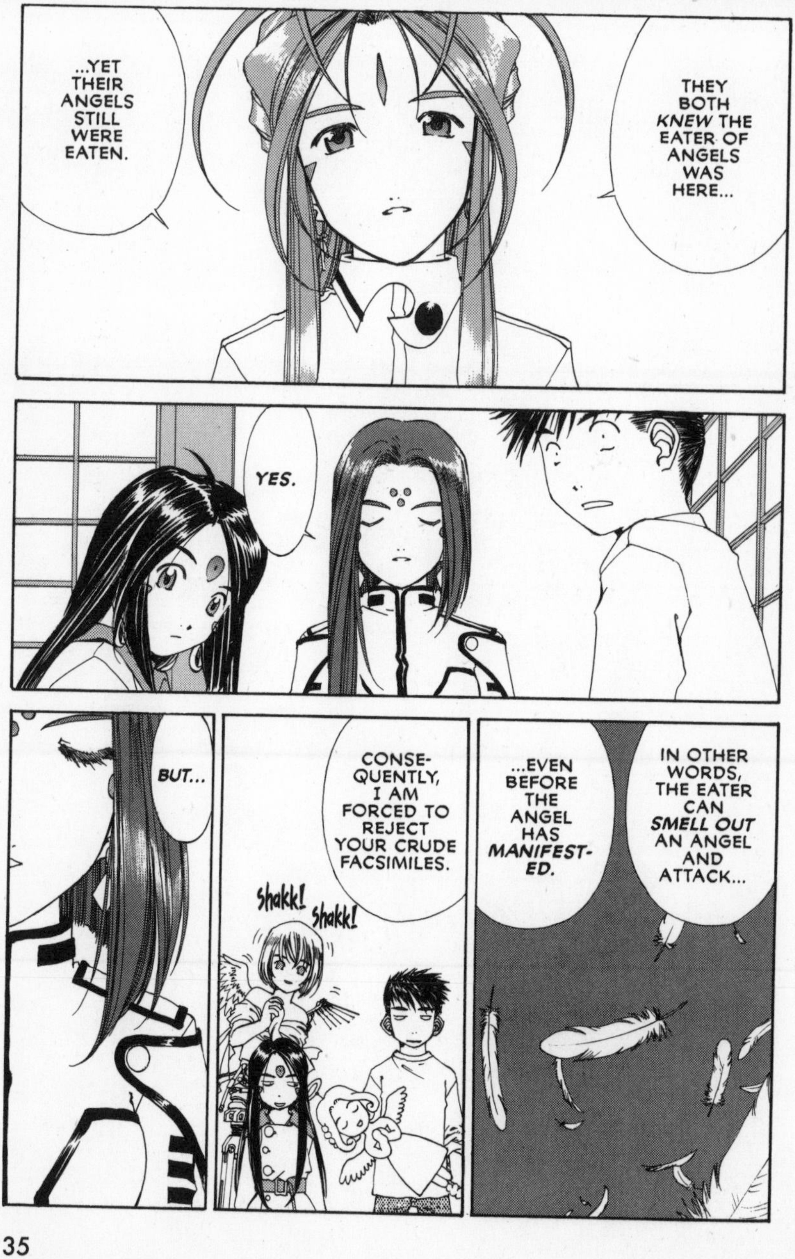
THEY BOTH *KNEW* THE EATER OF ANGELS WAS HERE...
...YET THEIR ANGELS STILL WERE EATEN.
YES.
IN OTHER WORDS, THE EATER CAN *SMELL OUT* AN ANGEL AND ATTACK...
...EVEN BEFORE THE ANGEL HAS *MANIFESTED.*
CONSEQUENTLY, I AM FORCED TO REJECT YOUR CRUDE FACSIMILES.
Shakk!
Shakk!
BUT...

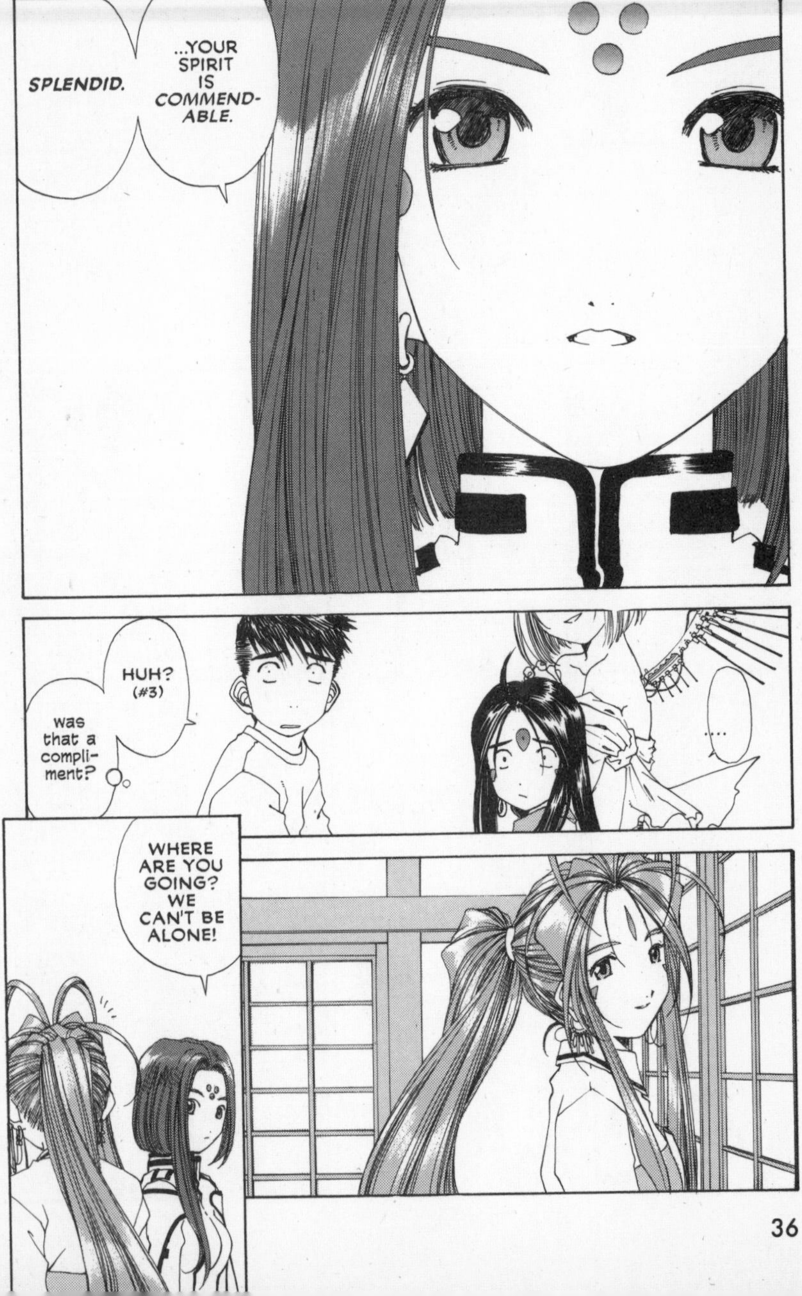
SPLENDID.
...YOUR SPIRIT IS COMMEND-ABLE.
....
HUH? (#3)
was that a compli-ment?
WHERE ARE YOU GOING? WE CAN'T BE ALONE!

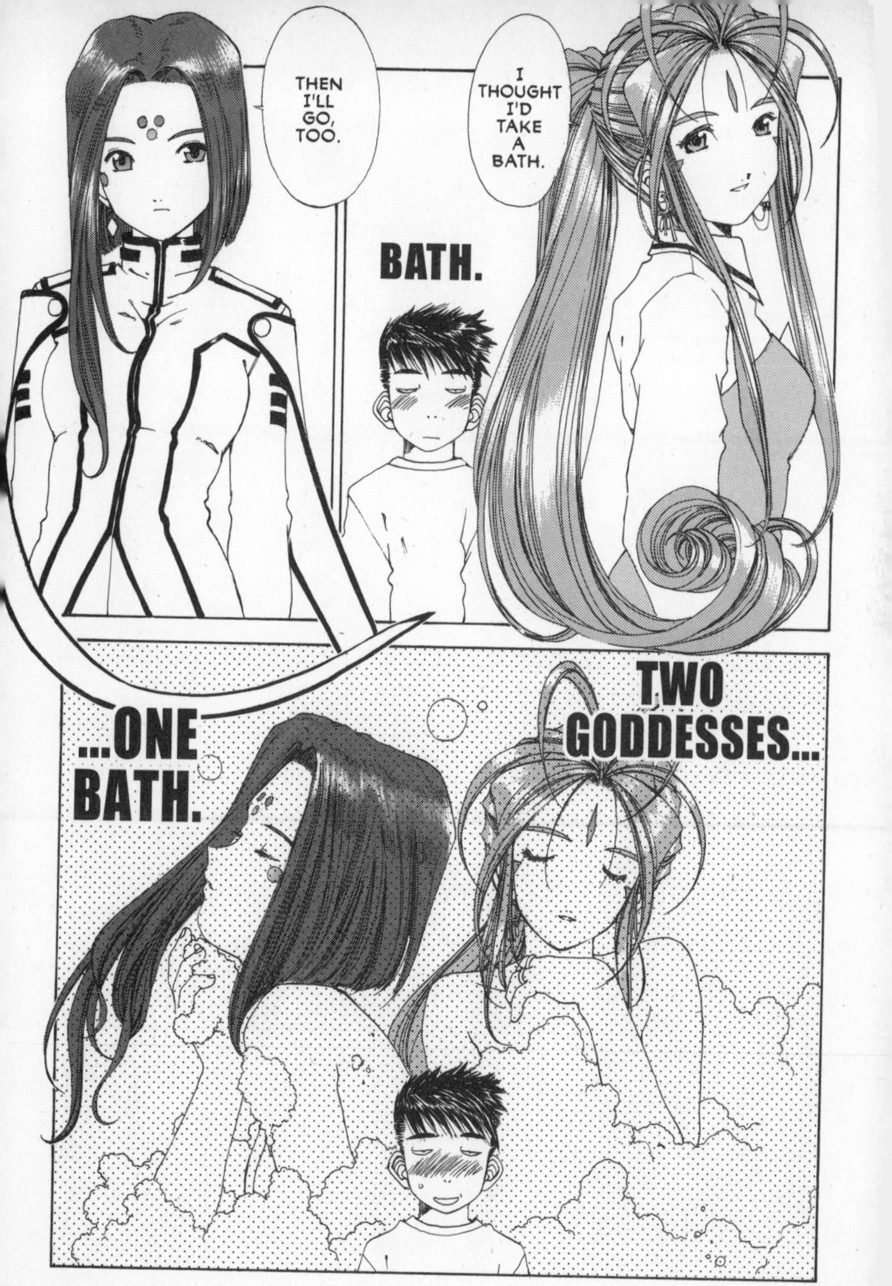
I THOUGHT I'D TAKE A BATH.
THEN I'LL GO, TOO.
BATH.
TWO GODDESSES...
...ONE BATH.

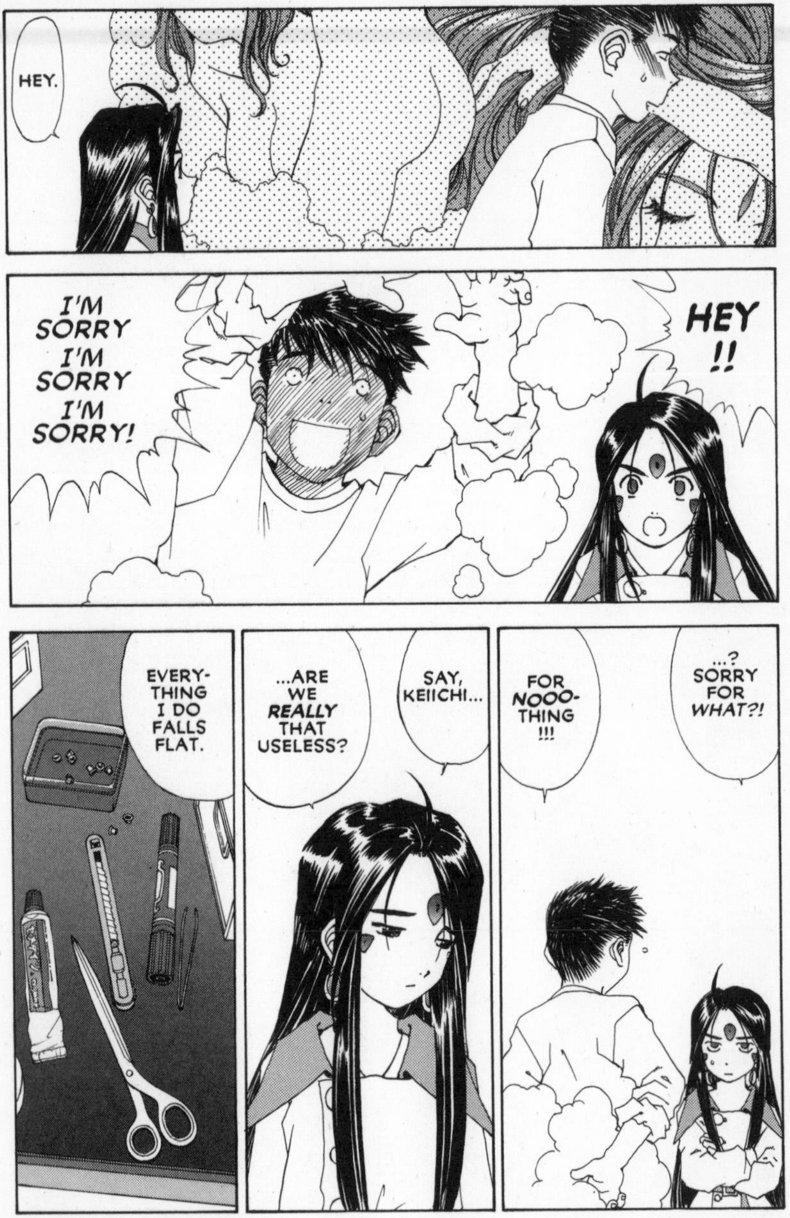
HEY.
HEY !!
I'M SORRY I'M SORRY I'M SORRY!
...? SORRY FOR WHAT?!
FOR NOOO-THING !!!
SAY, KEIICHI...
...ARE WE REALLY THAT USELESS?
EVERY-THING I DO FALLS FLAT.

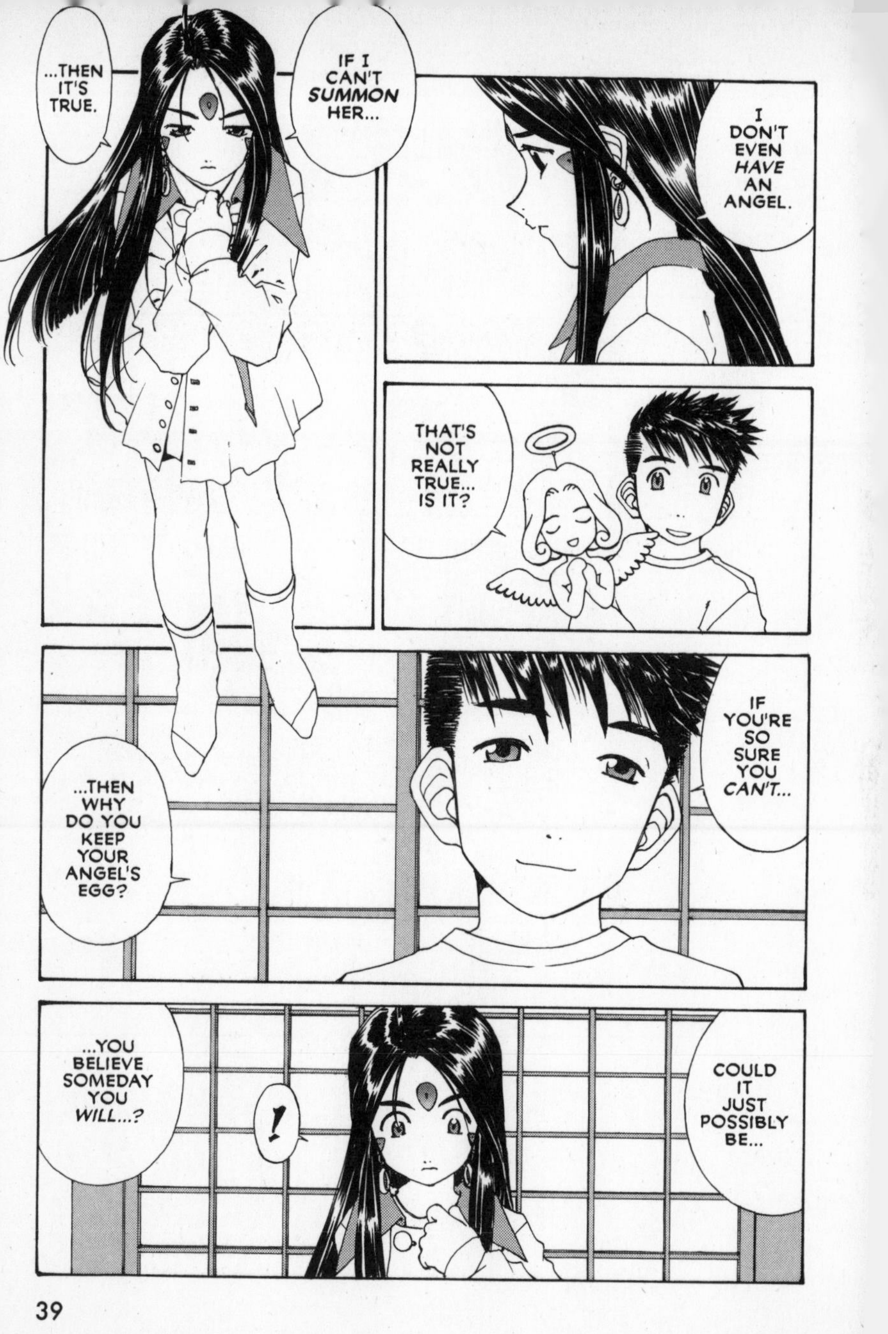
I DON'T EVEN *HAVE* AN ANGEL.
THAT'S NOT REALLY TRUE... IS IT?
IF I CAN'T *SUMMON* HER...
...THEN IT'S TRUE.
IF YOU'RE SO SURE YOU *CAN'T*...
...THEN WHY DO YOU KEEP YOUR ANGEL'S EGG?
COULD IT JUST POSSIBLY BE...
!
...YOU BELIEVE SOMEDAY YOU *WILL*...?

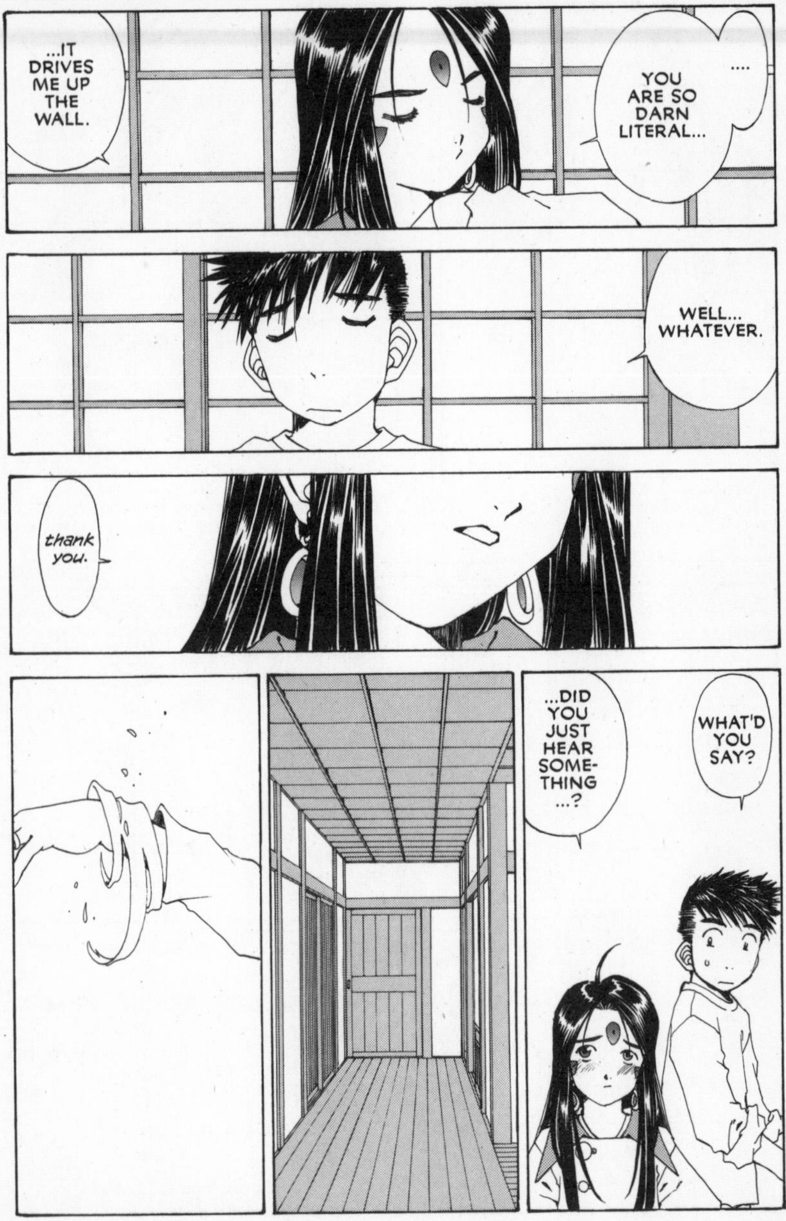
....
YOU ARE SO DARN LITERAL...
...IT DRIVES ME UP THE WALL.
WELL... WHATEVER.
thank you.
WHAT'D YOU SAY?
...DID YOU JUST HEAR SOME-THING ...?

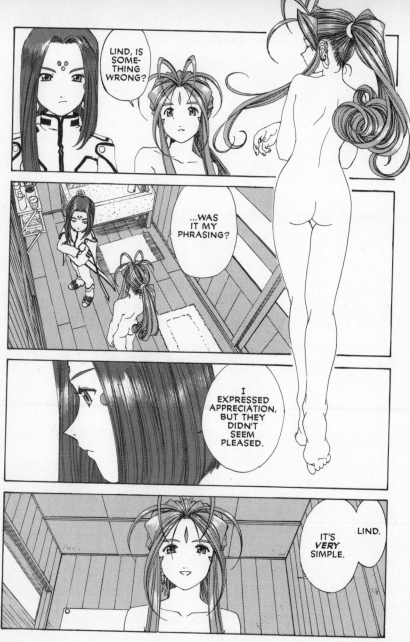

LIND, IS SOMETHING WRONG?

...WAS IT MY PHRASING?

I EXPRESSED APPRECIATION, BUT THEY DIDN'T SEEM PLEASED.

LIND.

IT'S *VERY* SIMPLE.

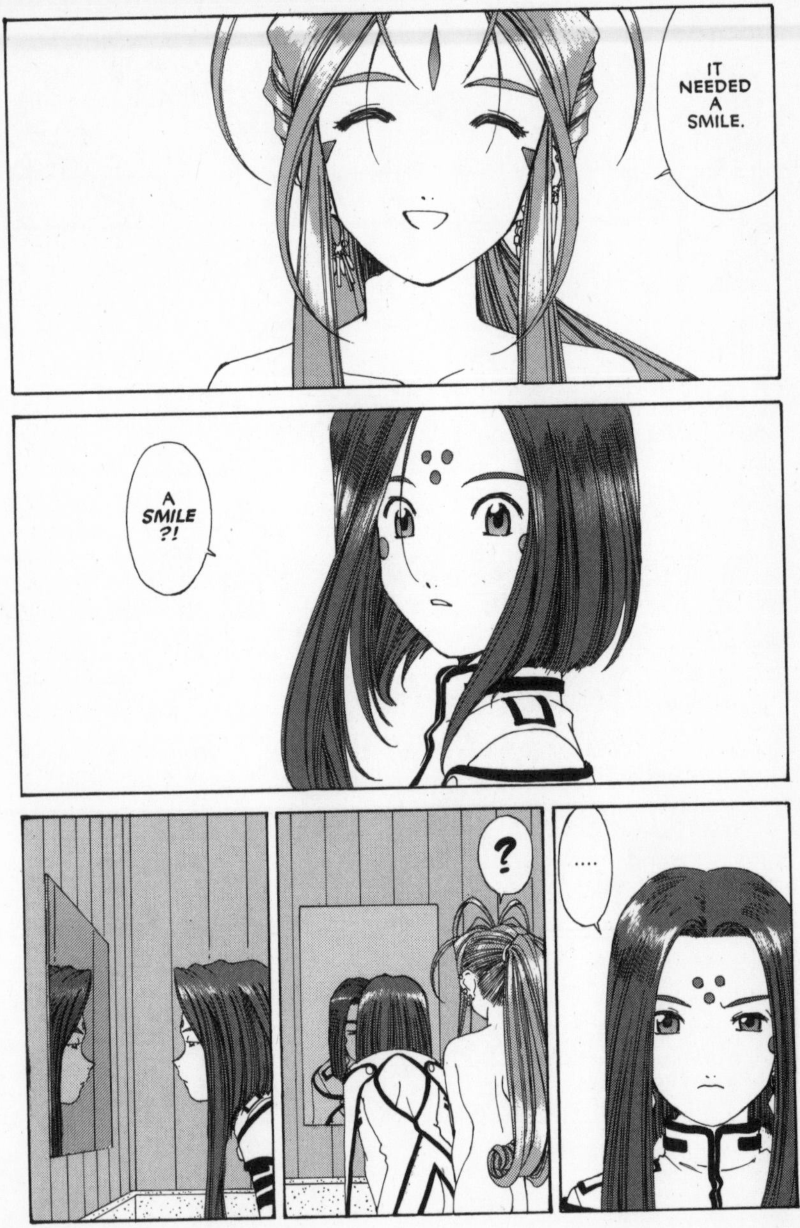
IT NEEDED A SMILE.
A SMILE ?!
....
?

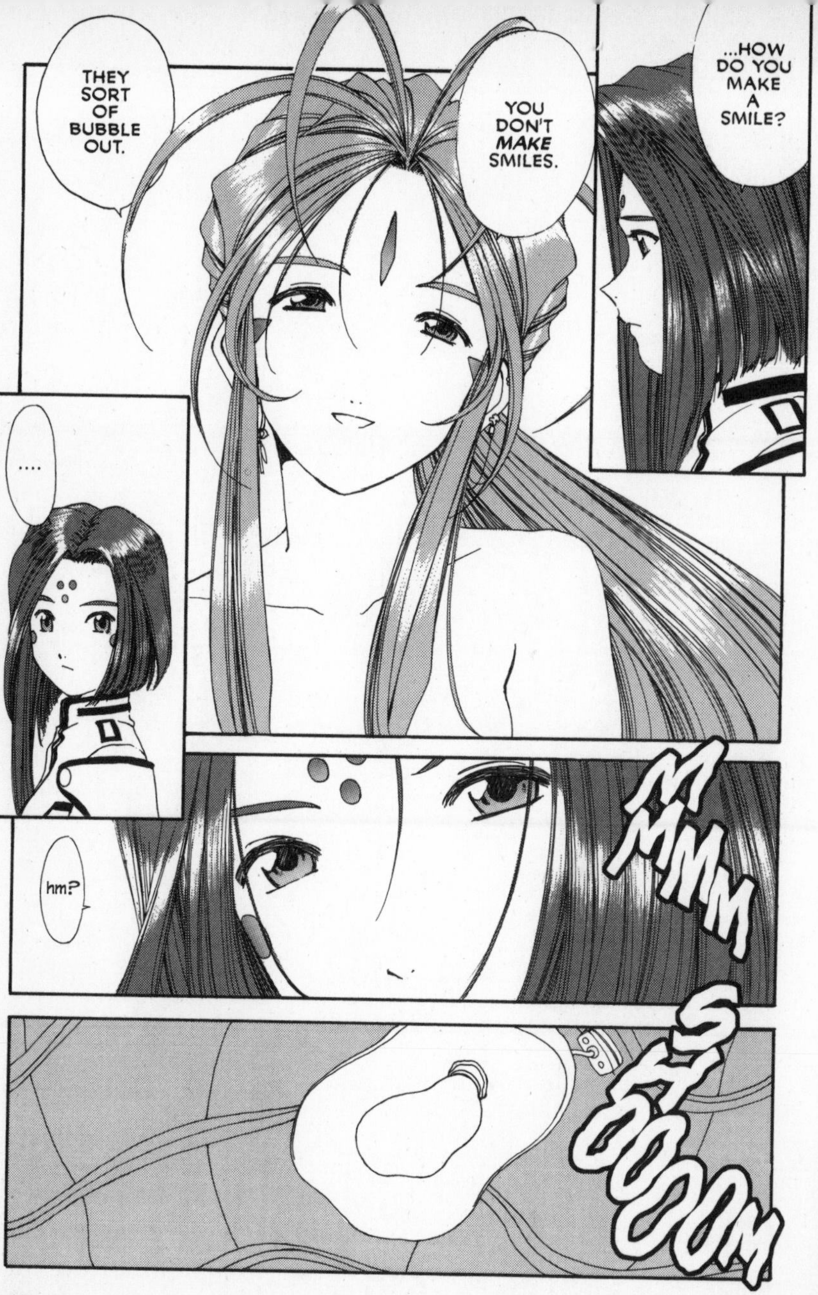
...HOW DO YOU MAKE A SMILE?
YOU DON'T *MAKE* SMILES.
THEY SORT OF BUBBLE OUT.
....
hm?
MMMM
SHOOOOM

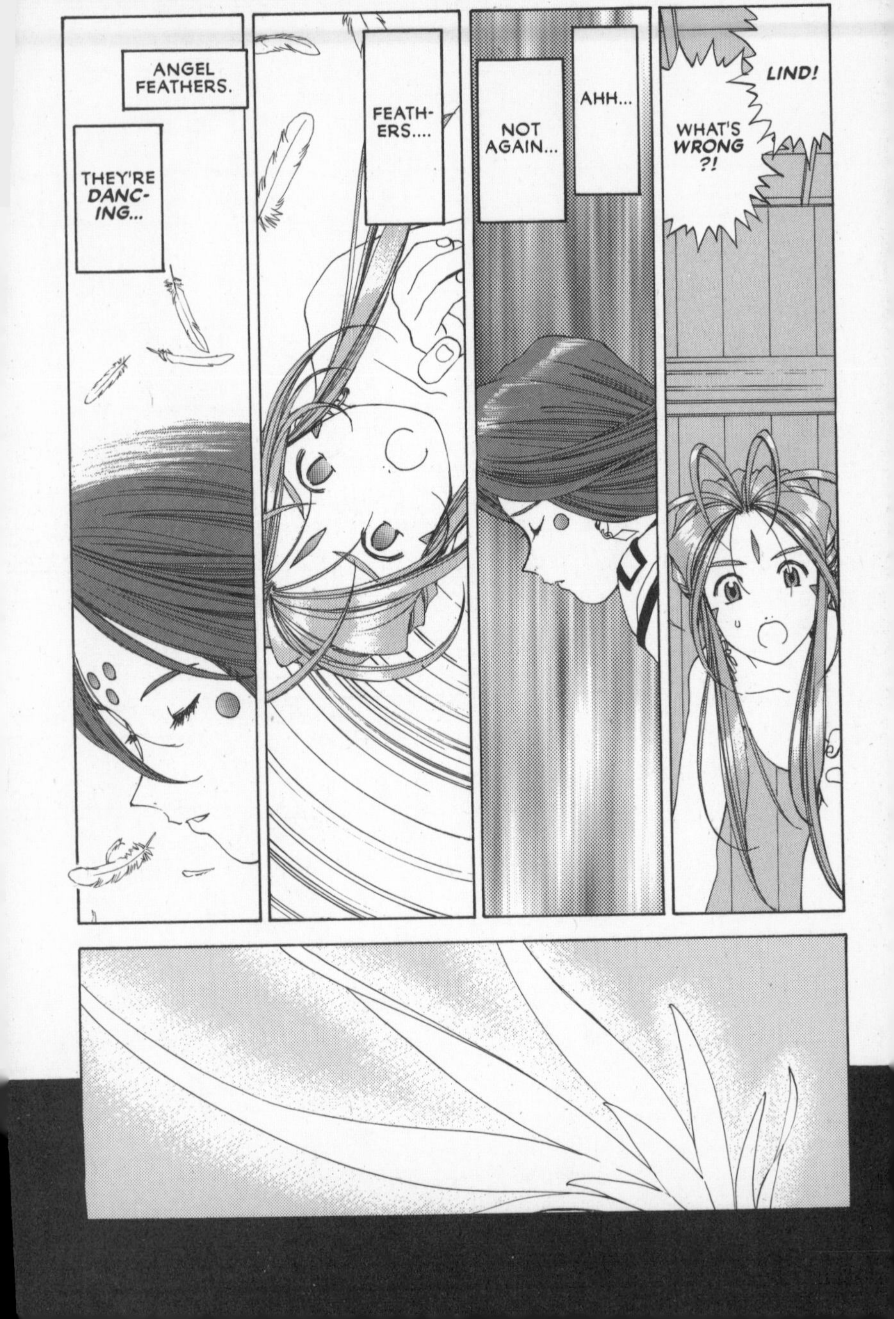
LIND!
WHAT'S WRONG ?!
AHH...
NOT AGAIN...
FEATH-ERS....
ANGEL FEATHERS.
THEY'RE DANC-ING...

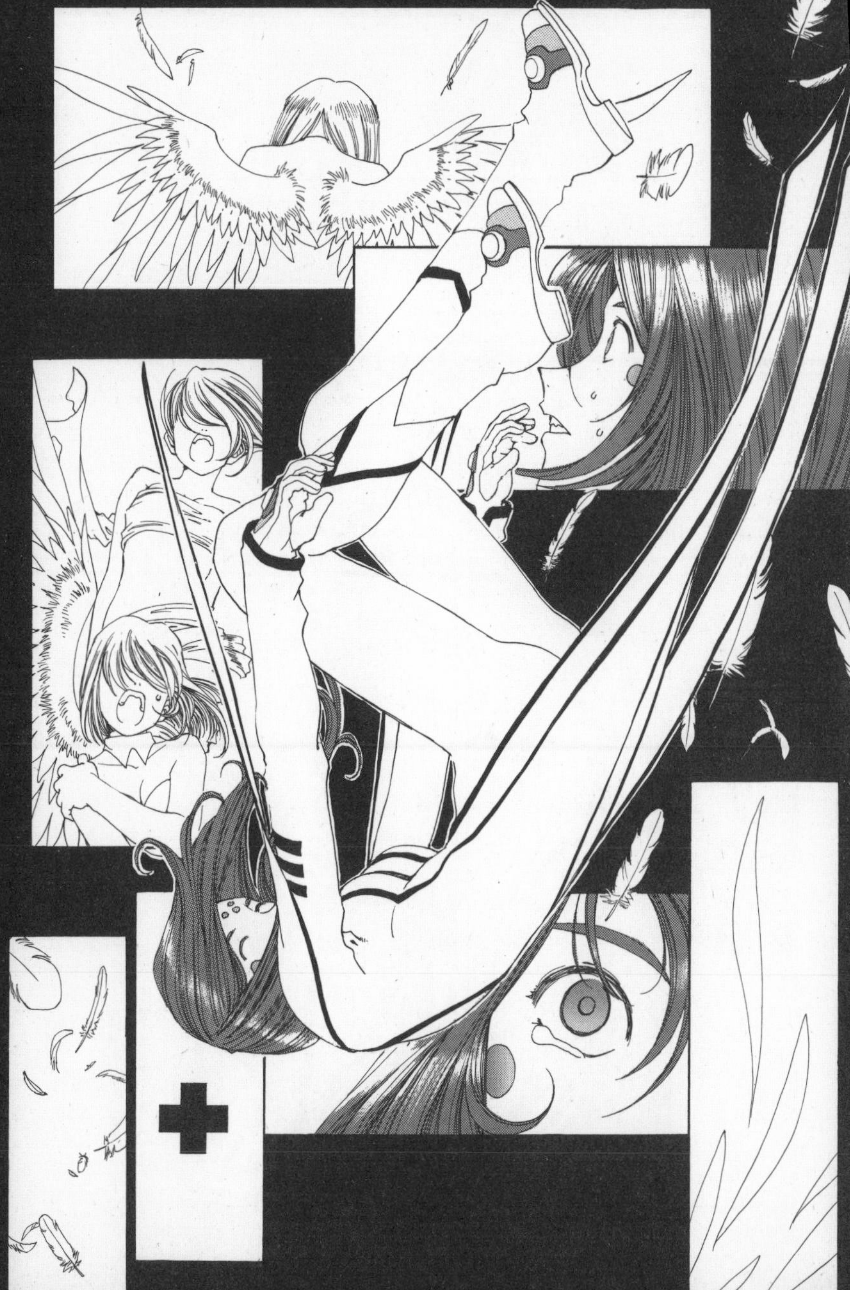

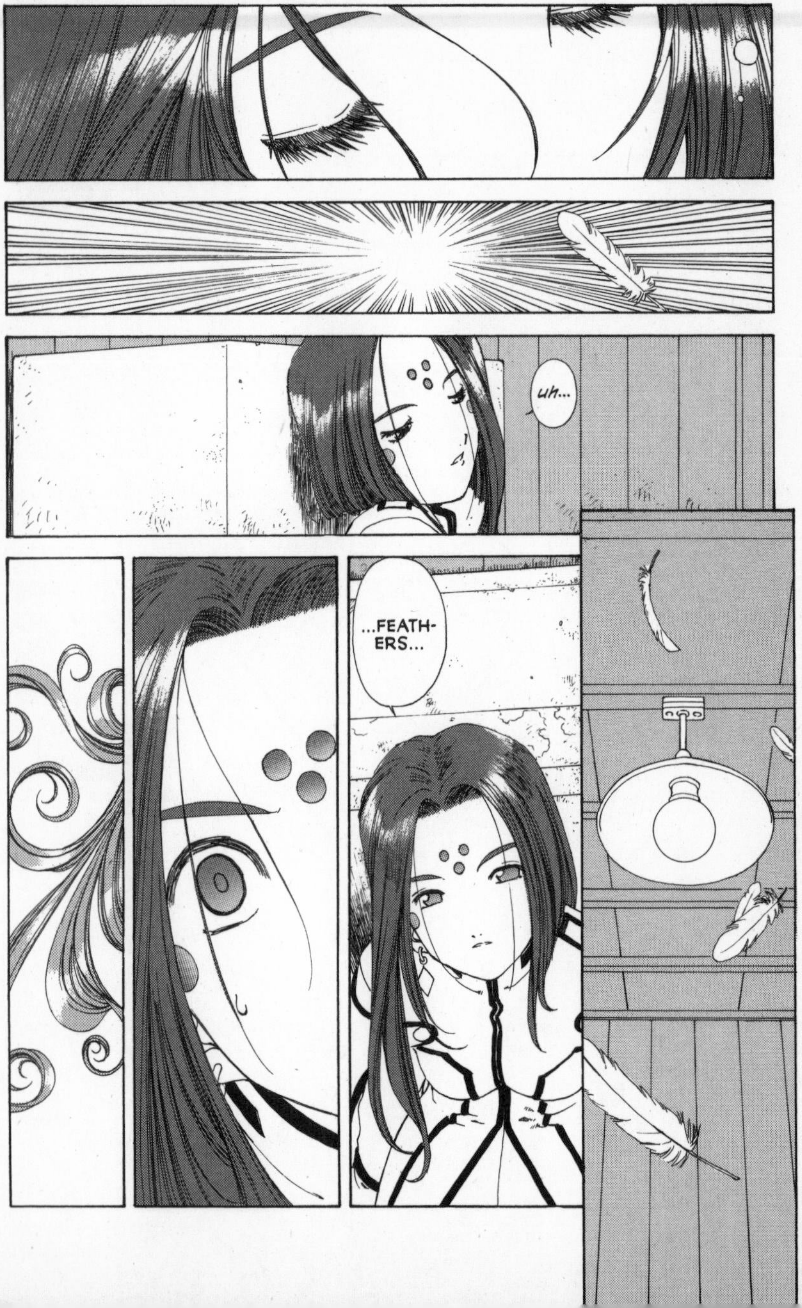
uh...
...FEATH-ERS...

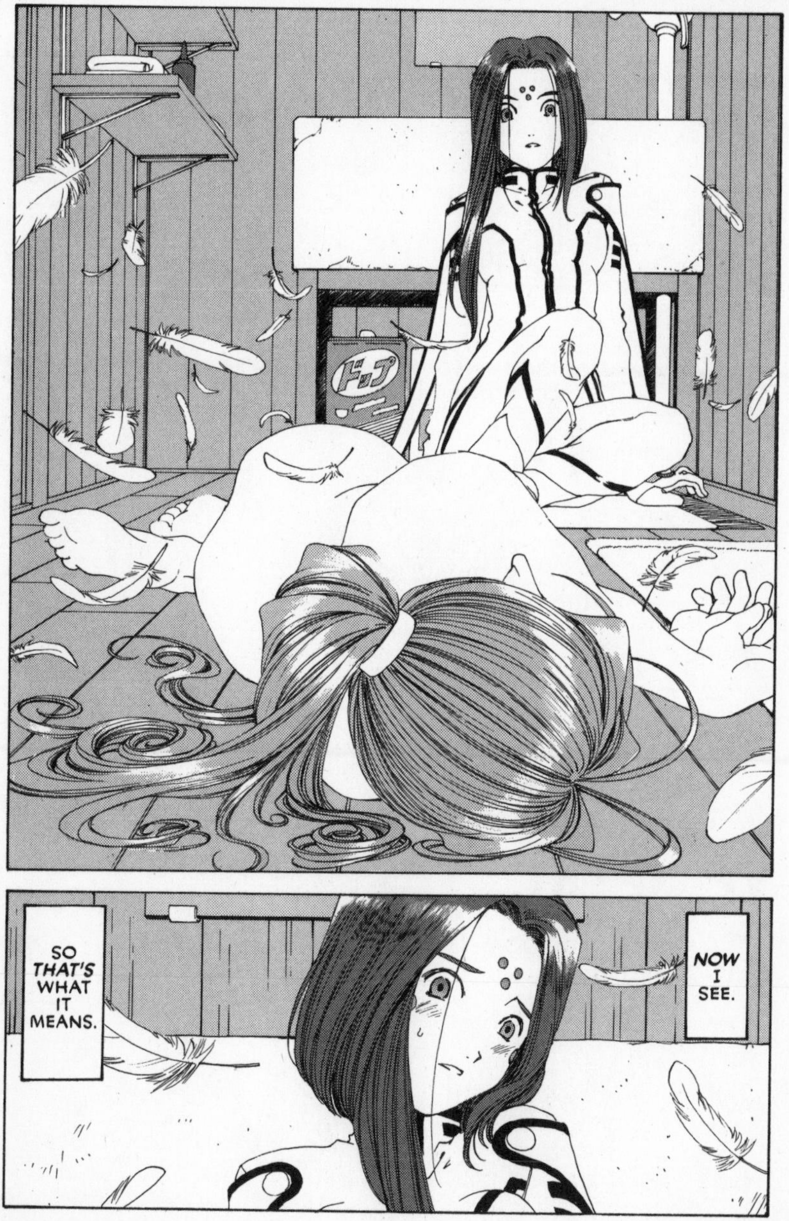
NOW I SEE.
SO THAT'S WHAT IT MEANS.

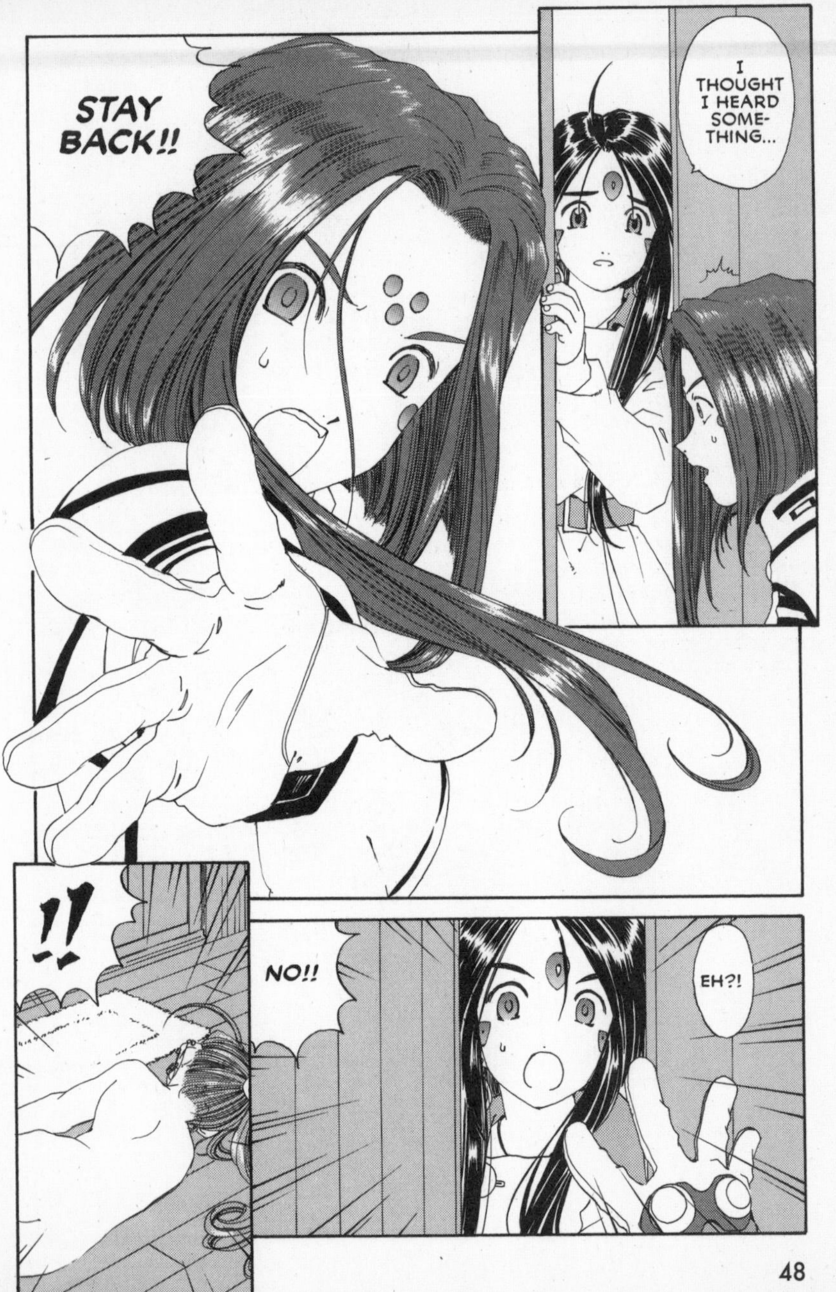
I THOUGHT I HEARD SOME-THING...
STAY BACK!!
EH?!
NO!!
!!

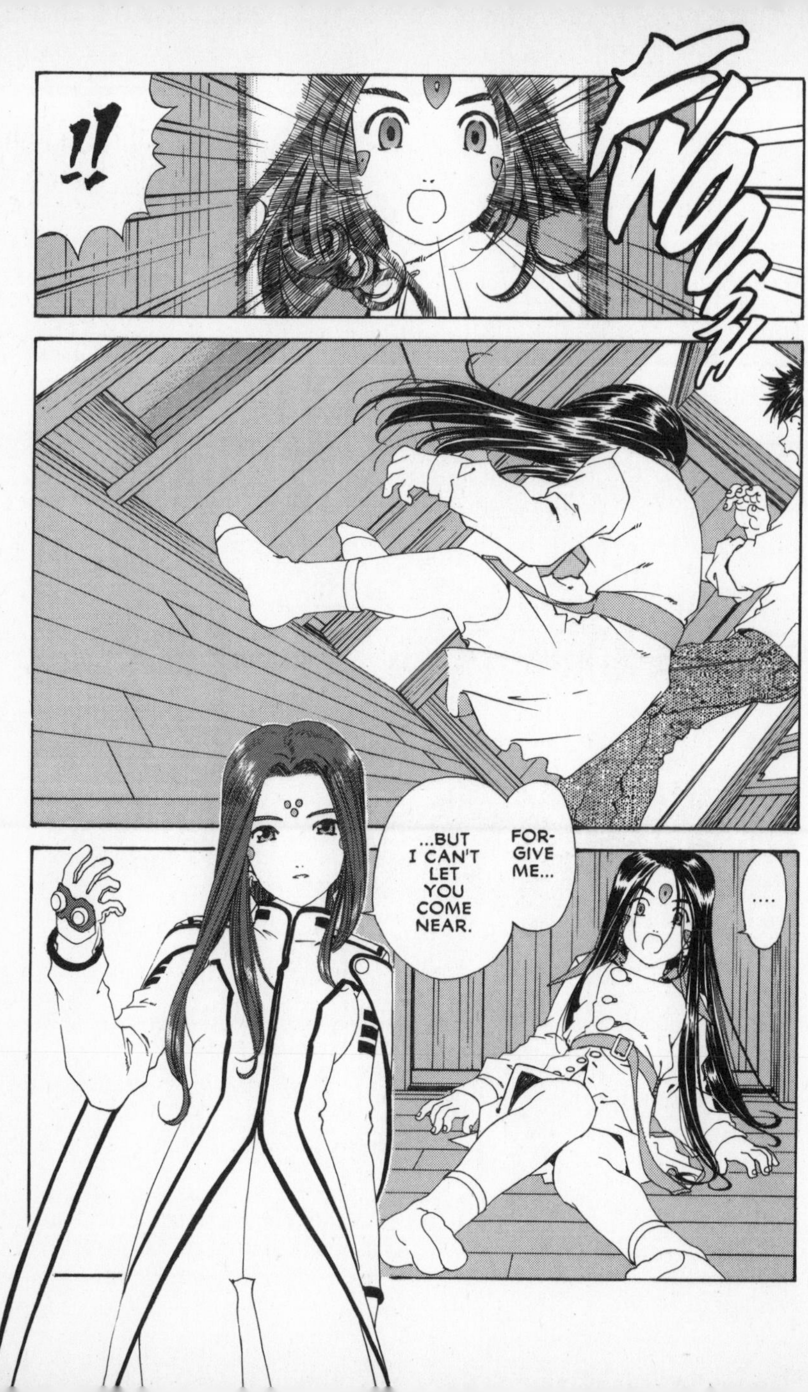

FWOOSH
!!
....
FORGIVE ME...
...BUT I CAN'T LET YOU COME NEAR.

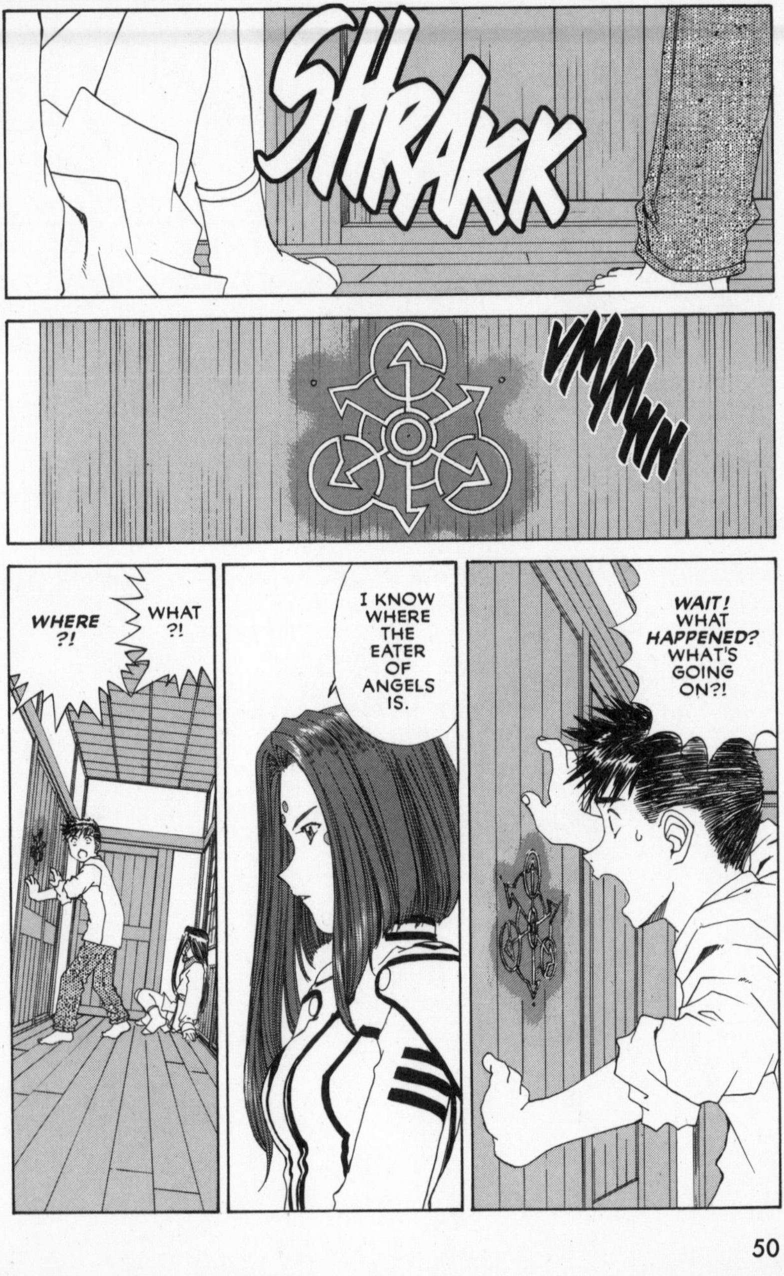
SHRAKK
VMMMNN
WAIT! WHAT HAPPENED? WHAT'S GOING ON?!
I KNOW WHERE THE EATER OF ANGELS IS.
WHAT ?!
WHERE ?!

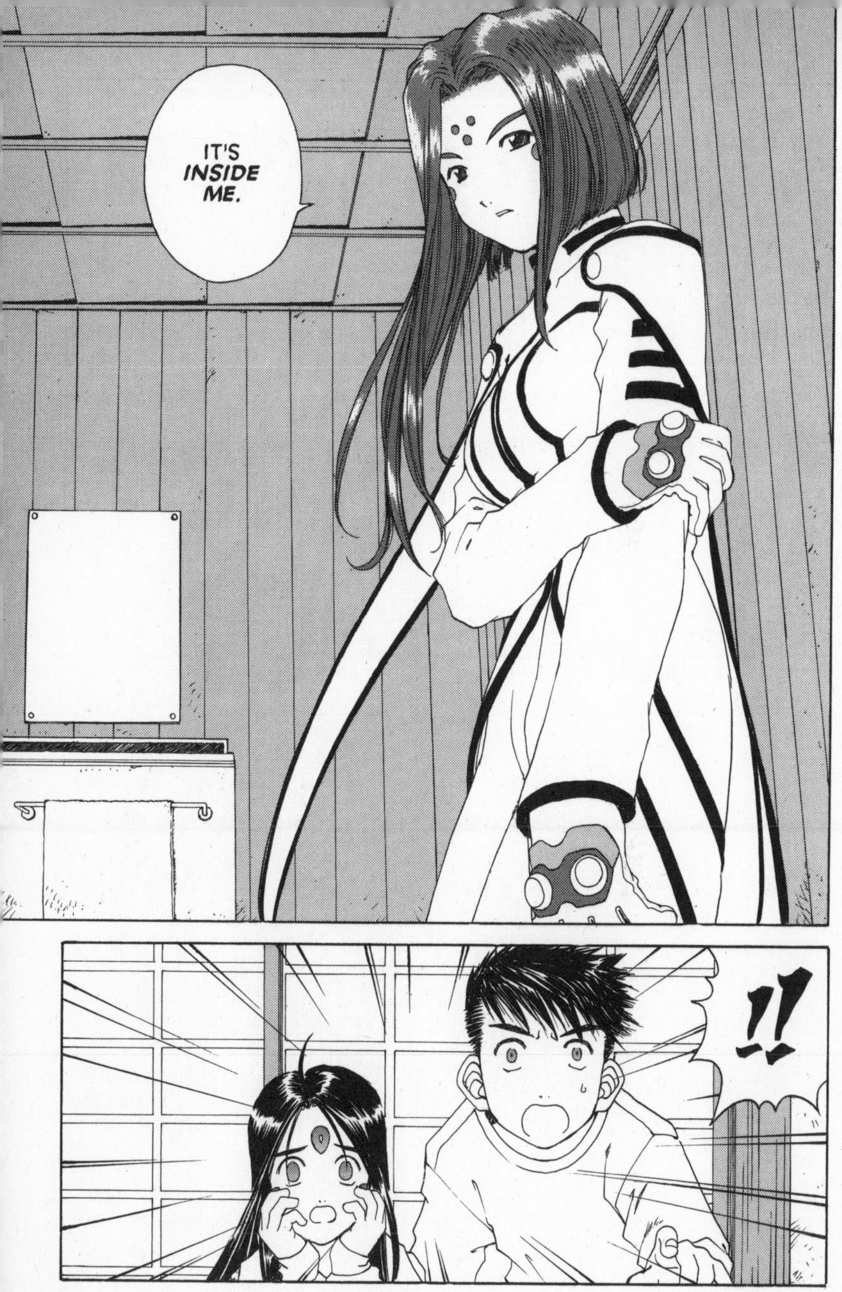
IT'S INSIDE ME.
!!

OH MY GODDESS!
HILD&MARA

CHAPTER 158

The One-Winged Angel

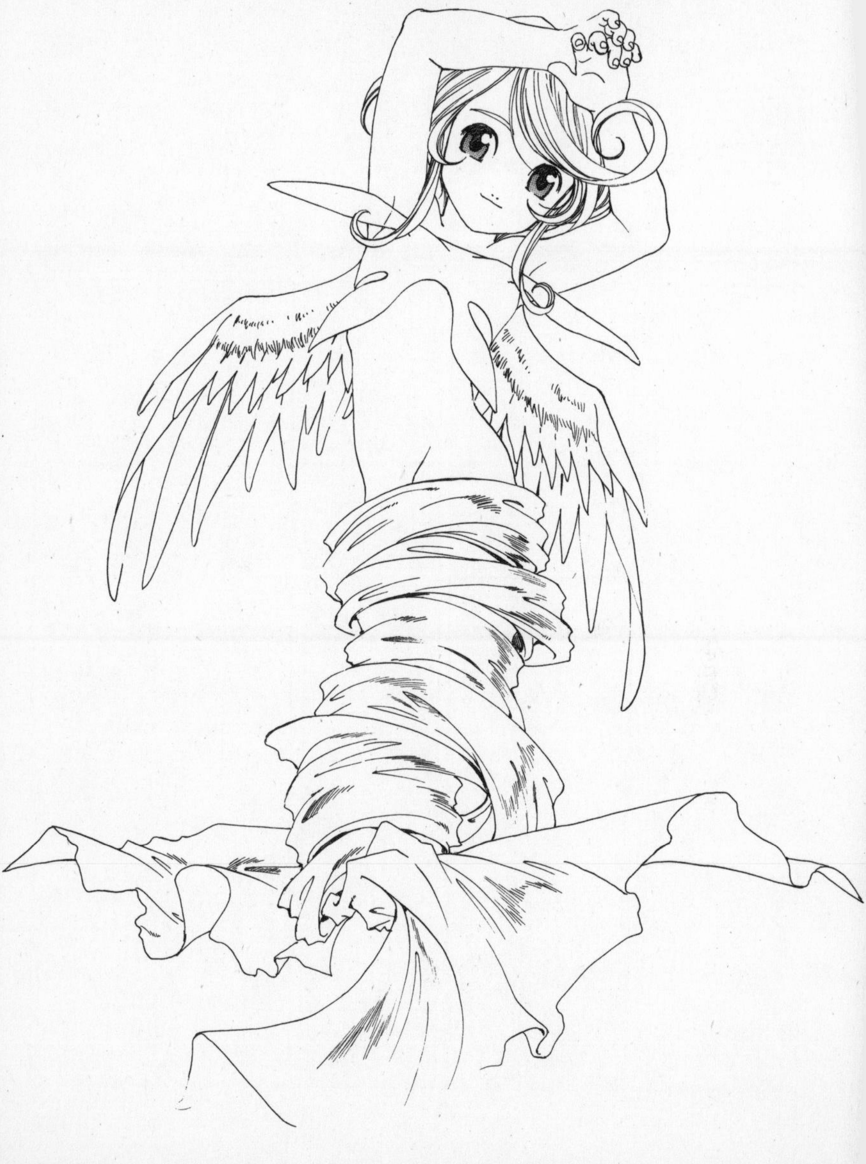

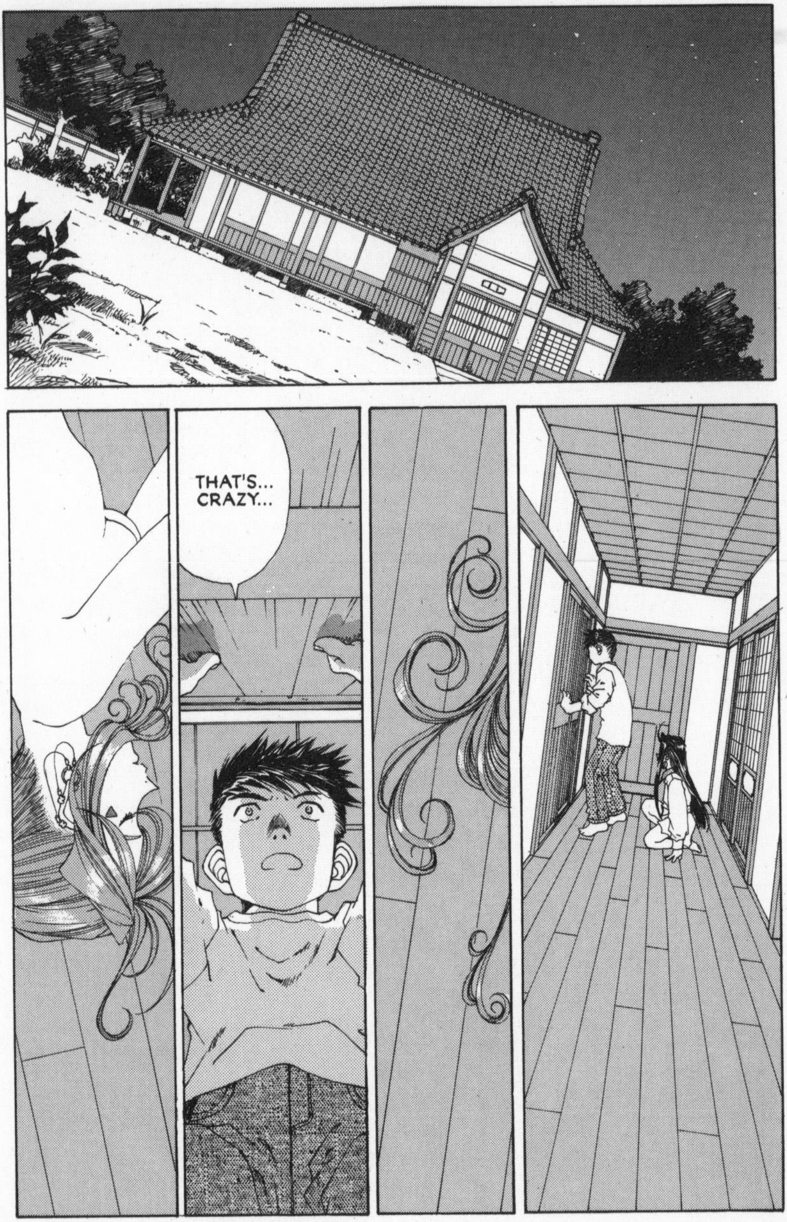
THAT'S... CRAZY...

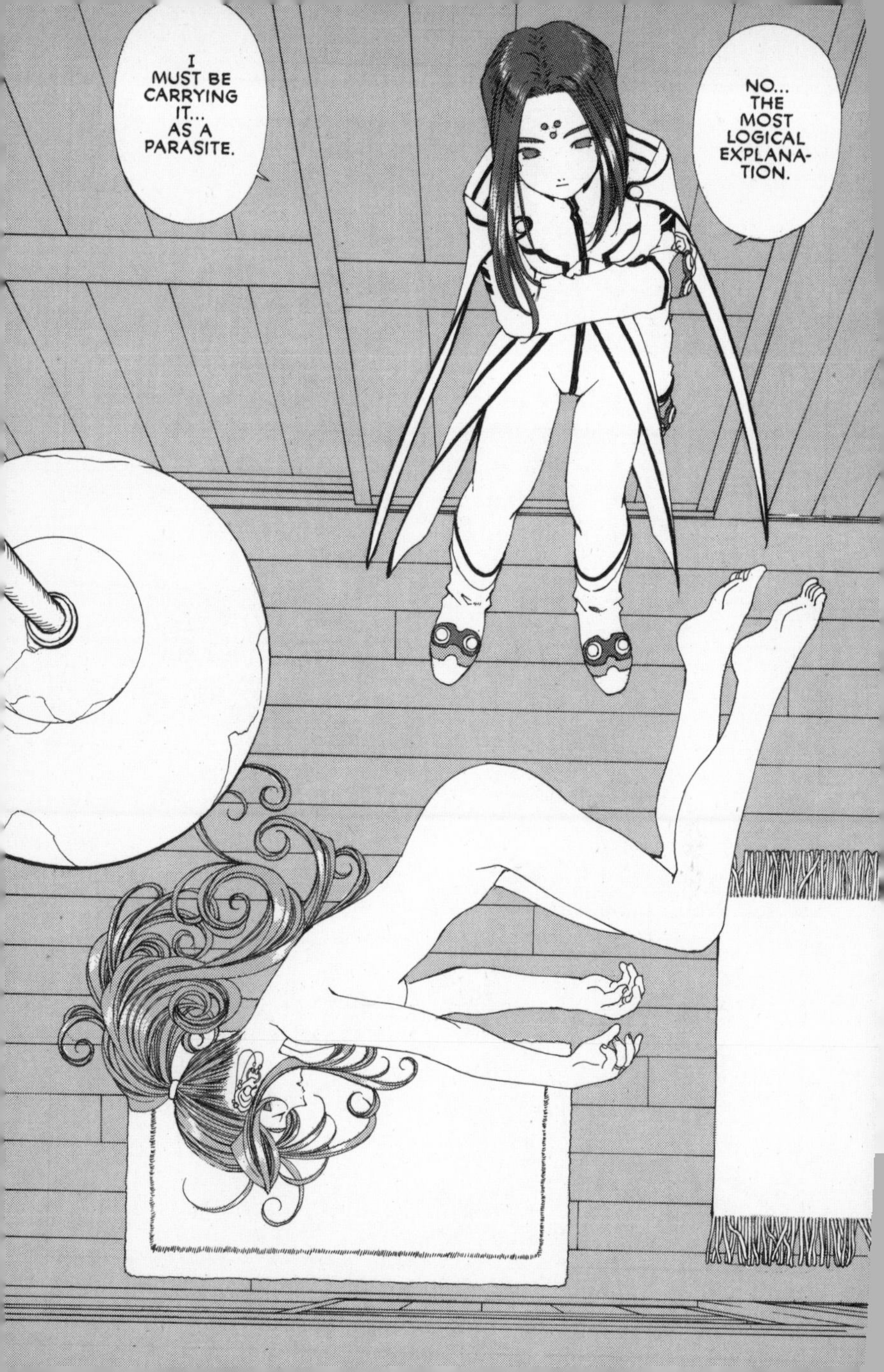
NO... THE MOST LOGICAL EXPLANATION.
I MUST BE CARRYING IT... AS A PARASITE.

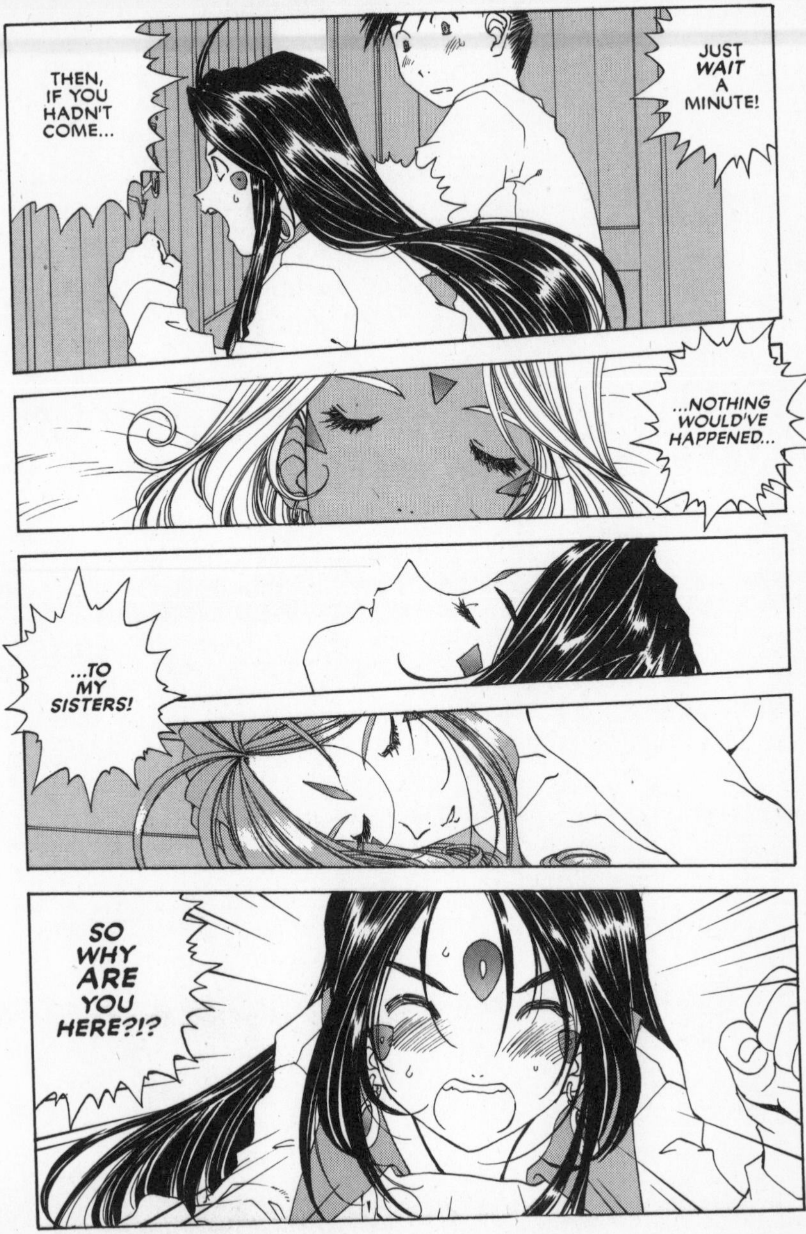
JUST WAIT A MINUTE!
THEN, IF YOU HADN'T COME...
...NOTHING WOULD'VE HAPPENED...
...TO MY SISTERS!
SO WHY ARE YOU HERE?!?

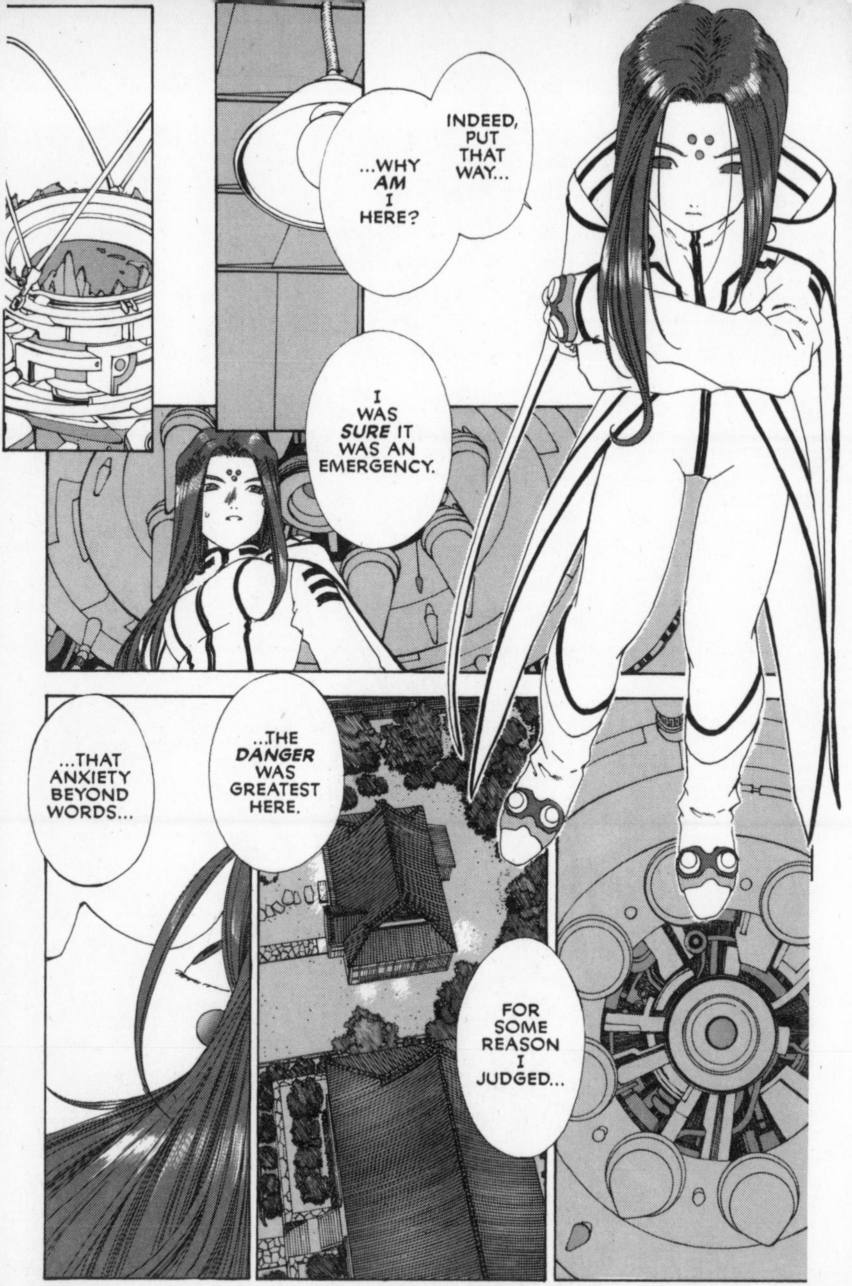
INDEED, PUT THAT WAY...
...WHY *AM* I HERE?
I WAS *SURE* IT WAS AN EMERGENCY.
FOR SOME REASON I JUDGED...
...THE *DANGER* WAS GREATEST HERE.
...THAT ANXIETY BEYOND WORDS...

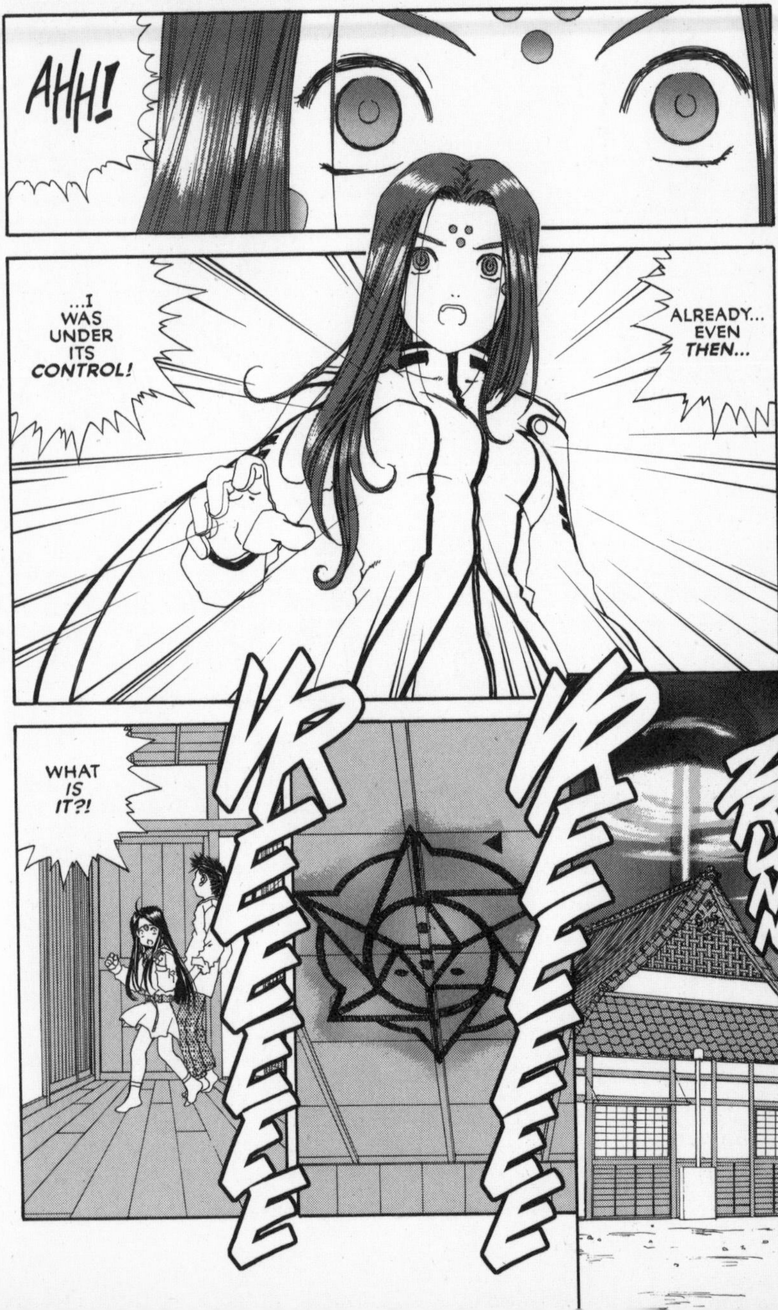
AHH!
ALREADY... EVEN *THEN*...
...I WAS UNDER ITS *CONTROL!*
NRUNN
VREEEEEEE
VREEEEEEE
WHAT *IS IT?!*

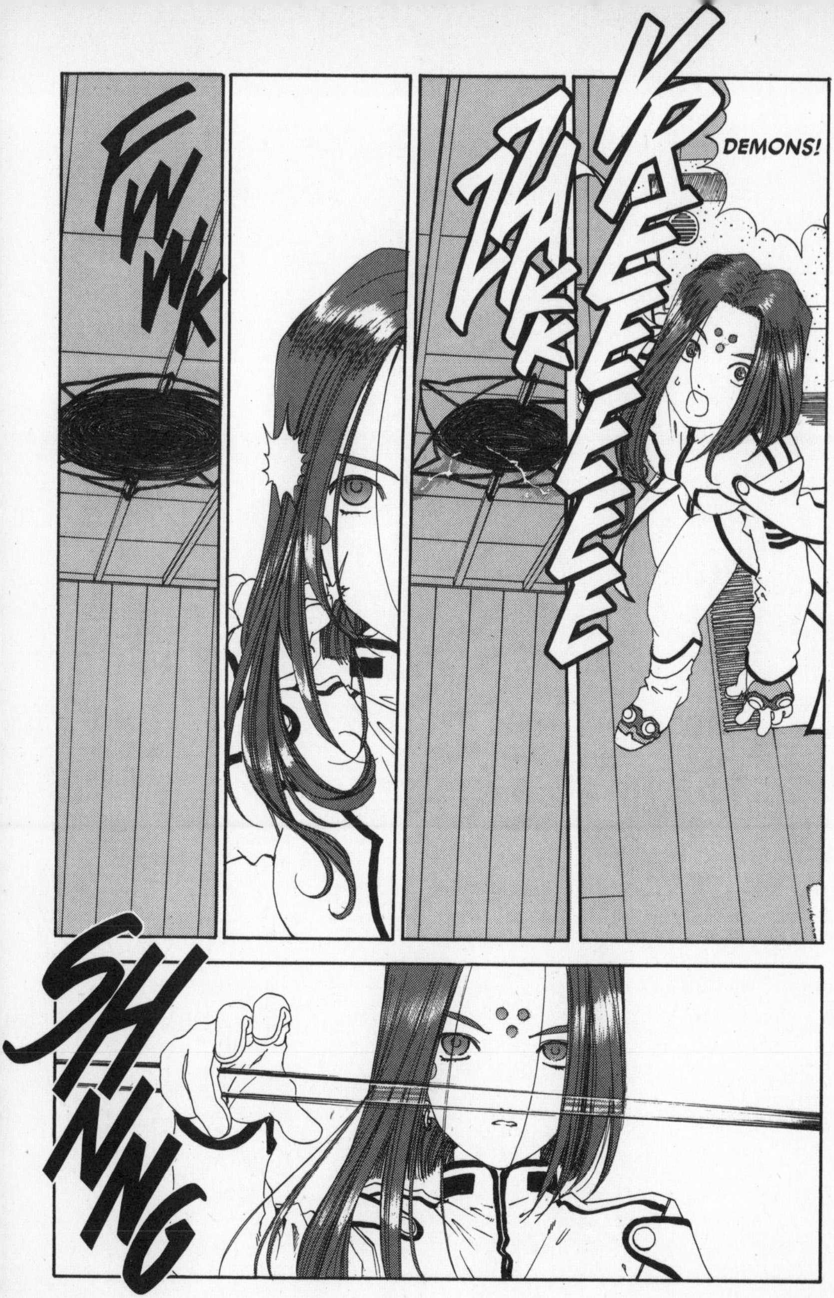
DEMONS!
VREEEEEEE
ZAKK
FWWK
SHNNG

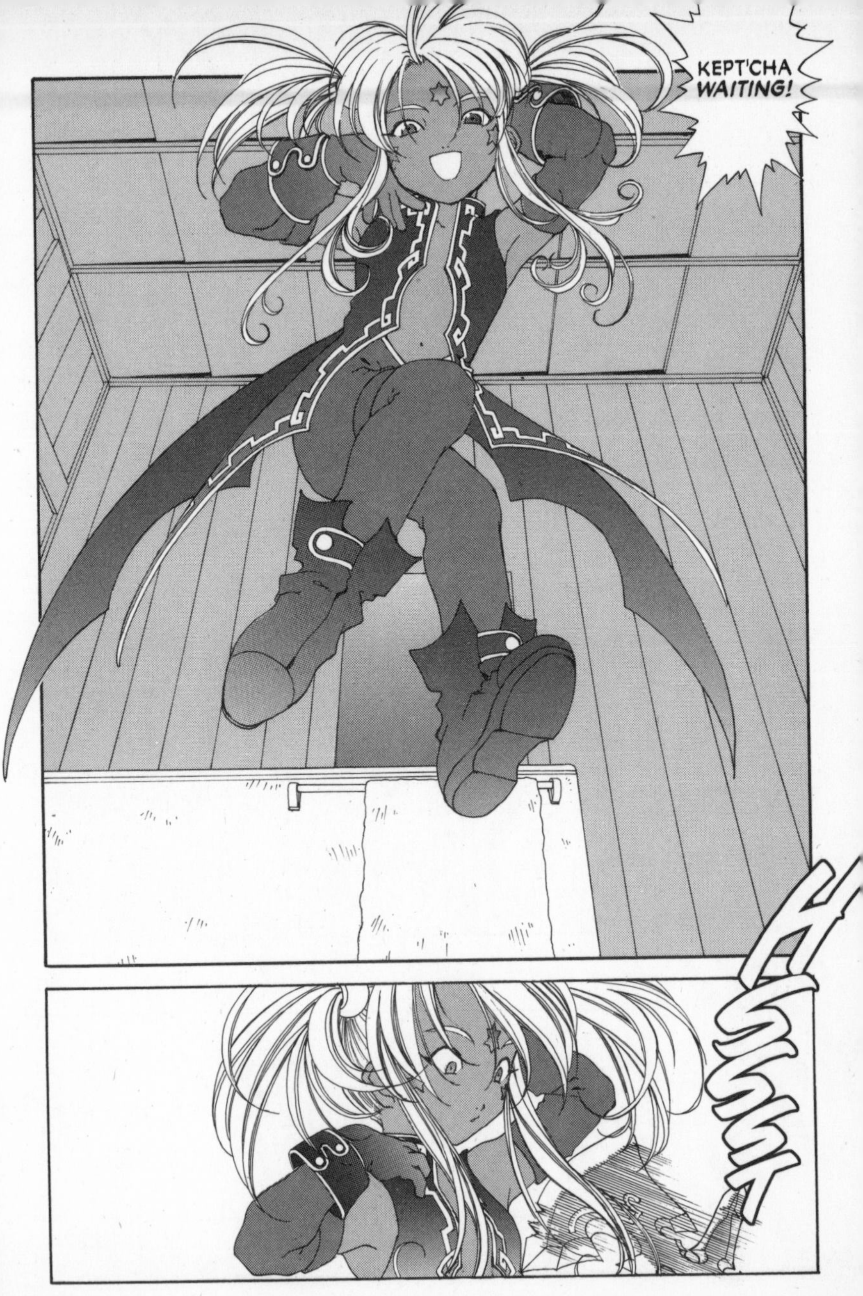
KEPT'CHA WAITING!

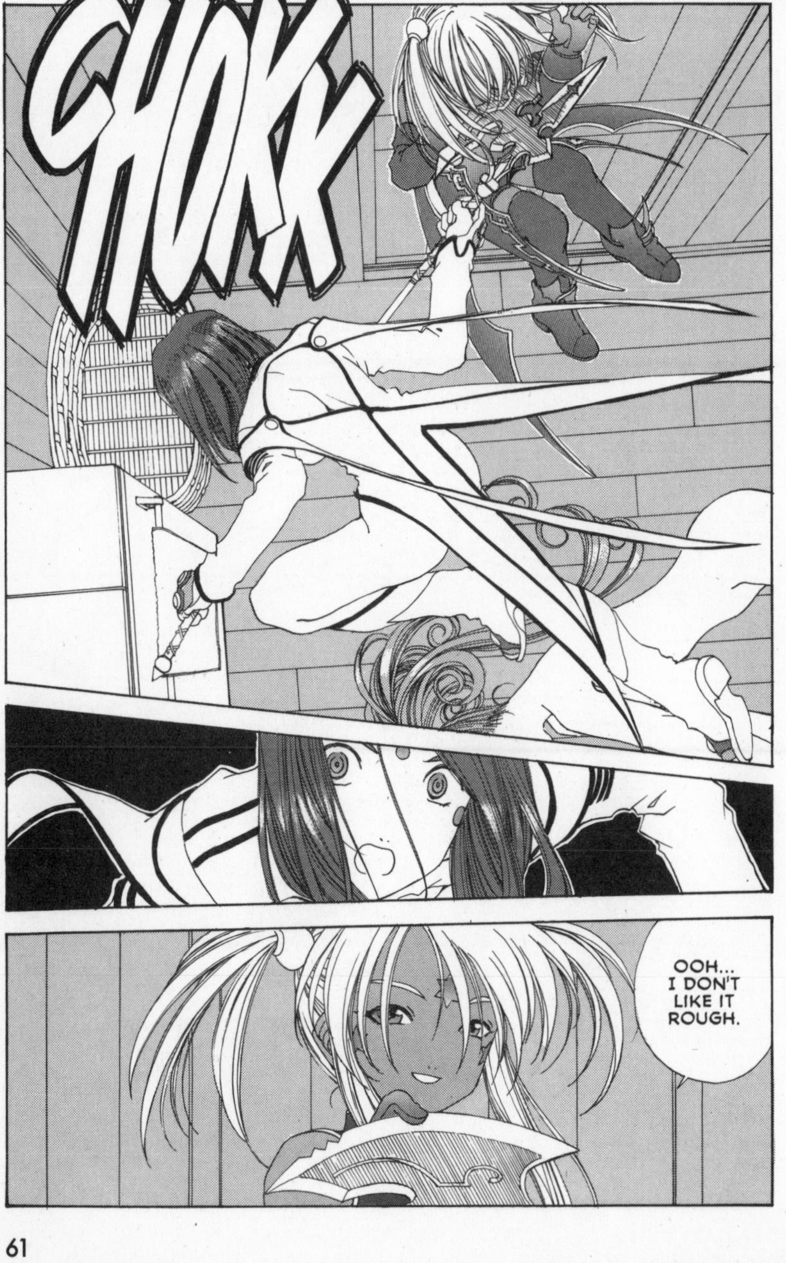
CHOKK
OOH... I DON'T LIKE IT ROUGH.

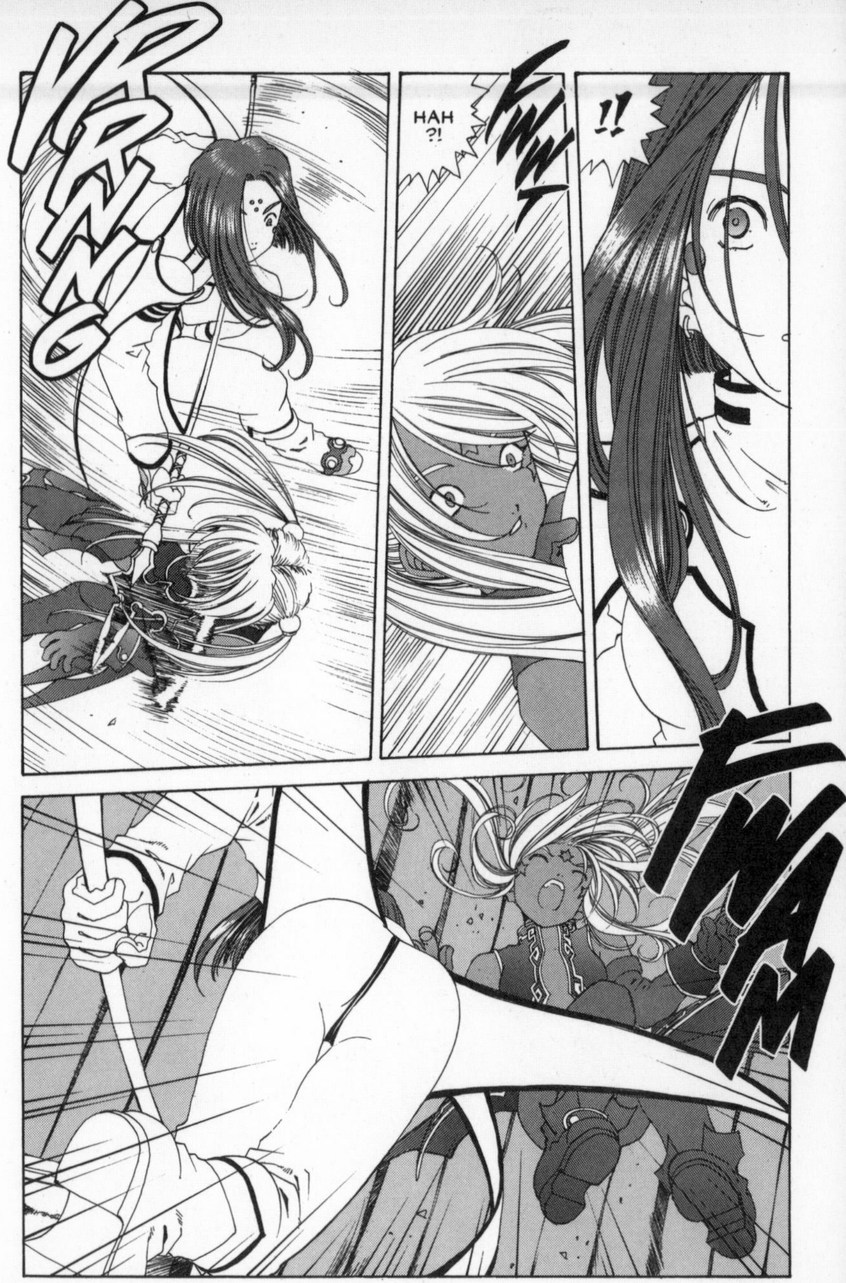
!!
HAH ?!
FWWWT
VRANNG
FWAM

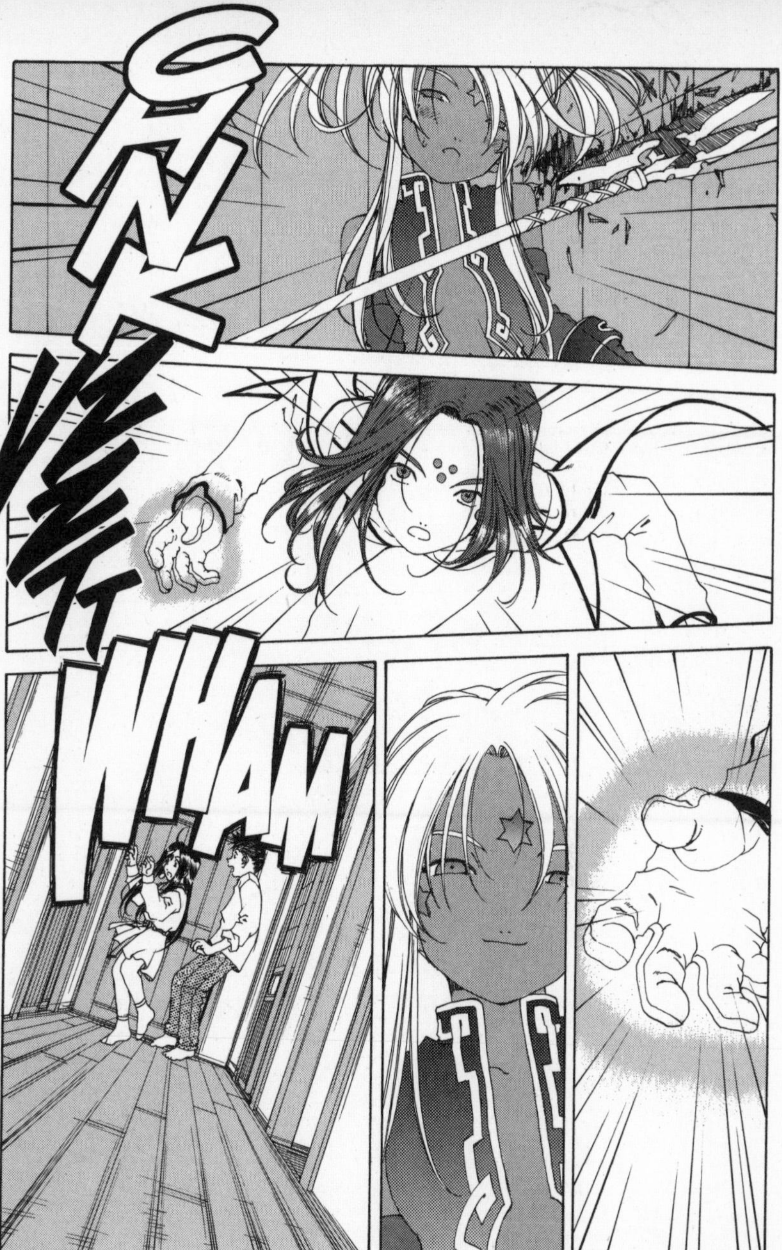
CHNK
WHAM

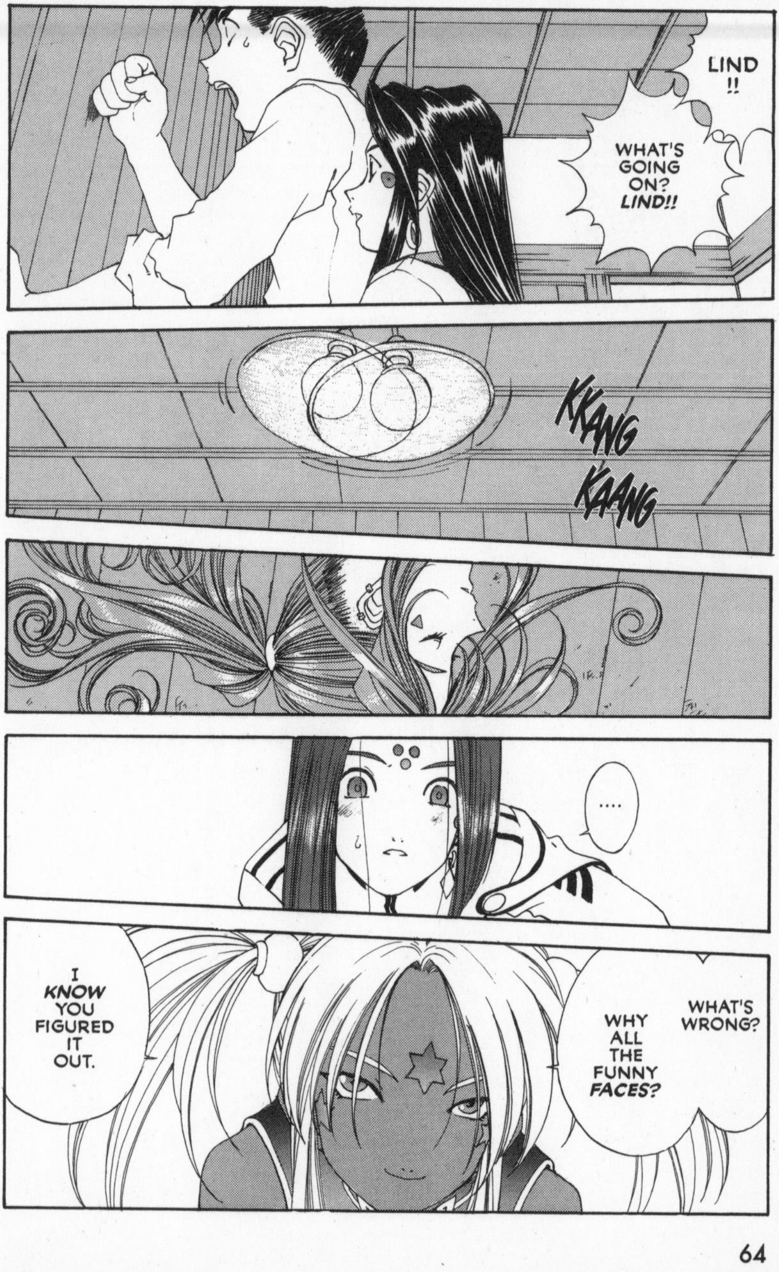
LIND !!
WHAT'S GOING ON? *LIND!!*
KKANG
KAANG
....
WHAT'S WRONG?
WHY ALL THE FUNNY *FACES?*
I *KNOW* YOU FIGURED IT OUT.

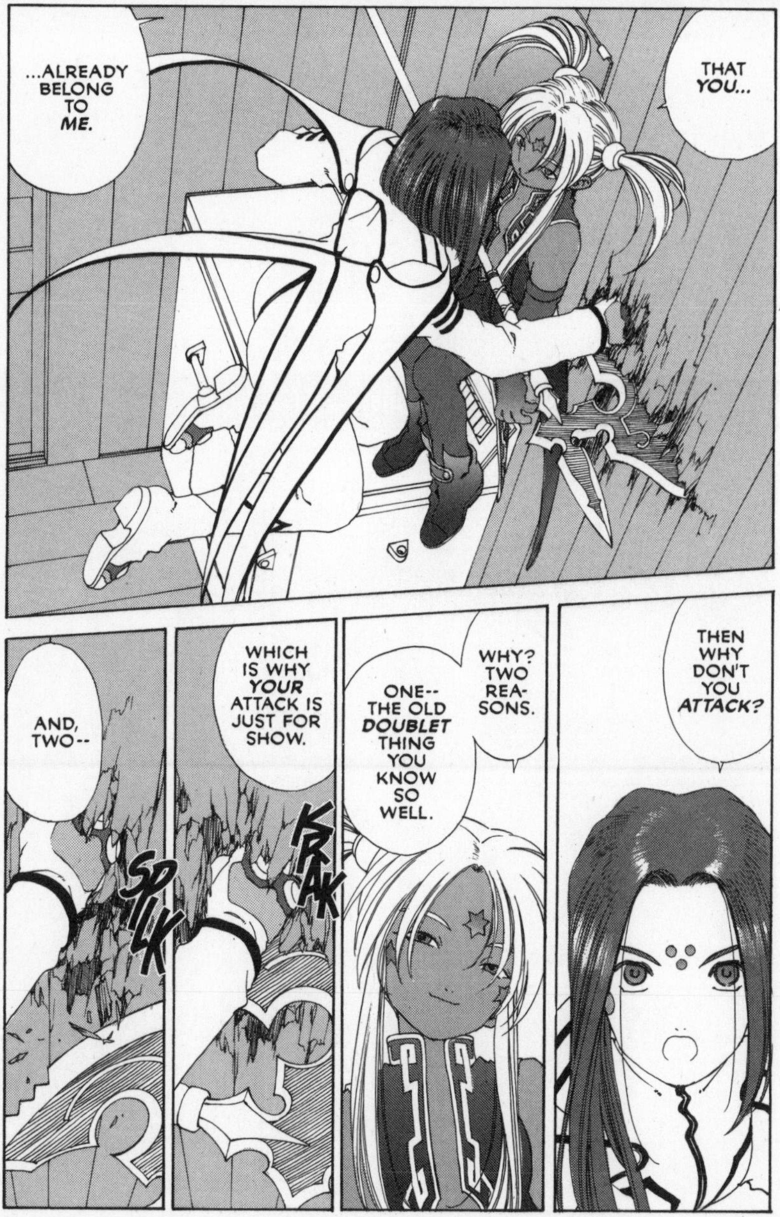
THAT *YOU...*
...ALREADY BELONG TO *ME.*
THEN WHY DON'T YOU *ATTACK?*
WHY? TWO REASONS.
ONE-- THE OLD *DOUBLET* THING YOU KNOW SO WELL.
WHICH IS WHY *YOUR* ATTACK IS JUST FOR SHOW.
KRAK
AND, TWO--
SPLIK

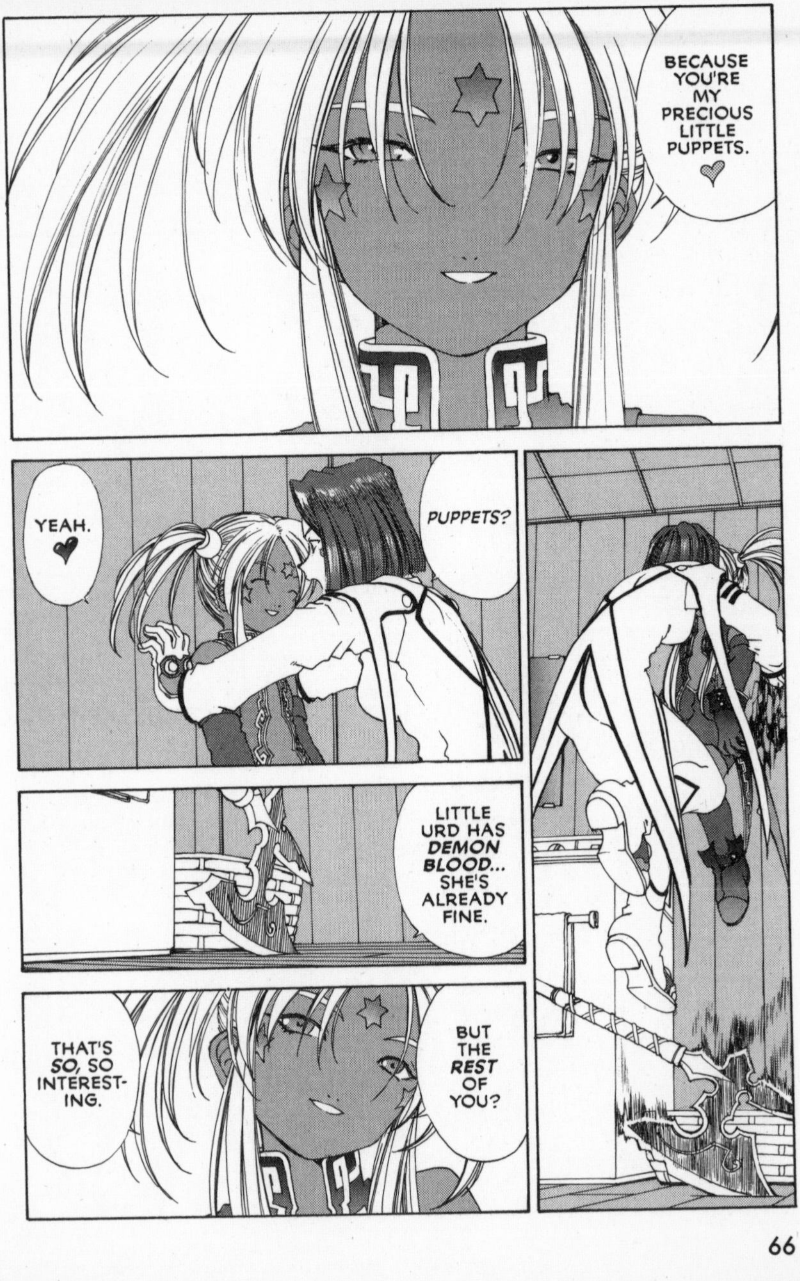
BECAUSE YOU'RE MY PRECIOUS LITTLE PUPPETS. ♥
PUPPETS?
YEAH. ♥
LITTLE URD HAS ***DEMON BLOOD...*** SHE'S ALREADY FINE.
BUT THE ***REST*** OF YOU?
THAT'S ***SO,*** SO INTEREST-ING.

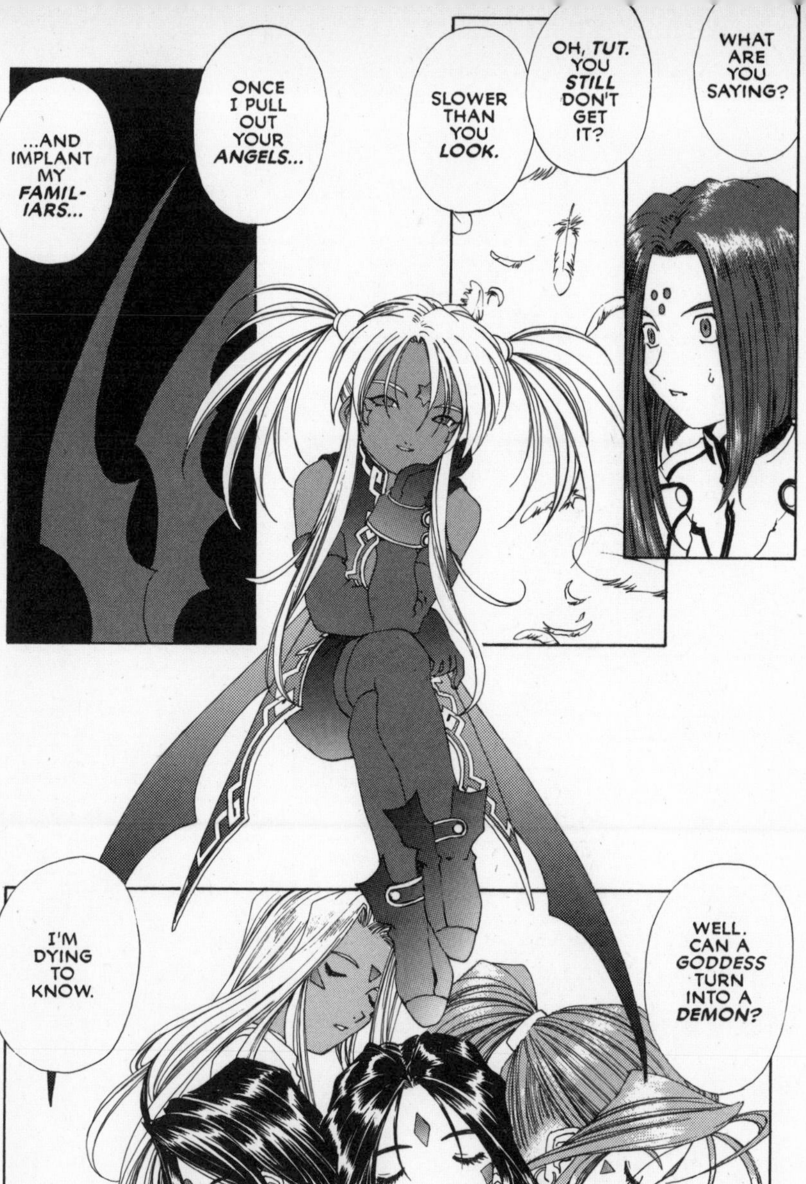
WHAT ARE YOU SAYING?
OH, *TUT.* YOU *STILL* DON'T GET IT?
SLOWER THAN YOU *LOOK.*
ONCE I PULL OUT YOUR *ANGELS...*
...AND IMPLANT MY *FAMILIARS...*
WELL. CAN A *GODDESS* TURN INTO A *DEMON?*
I'M DYING TO KNOW.

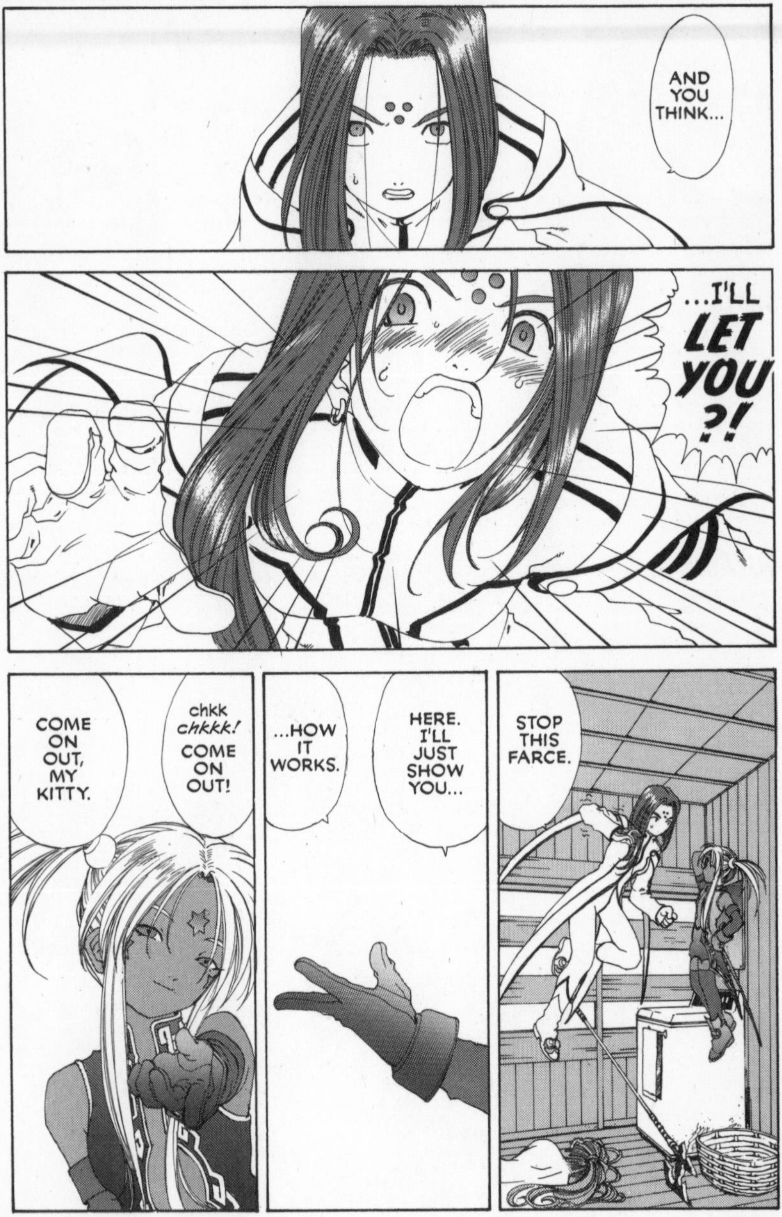
AND YOU THINK...
...I'LL LET YOU ?!
STOP THIS FARCE.
HERE. I'LL JUST SHOW YOU...
...HOW IT WORKS.
chkk chkkk! COME ON OUT!
COME ON OUT, MY KITTY.

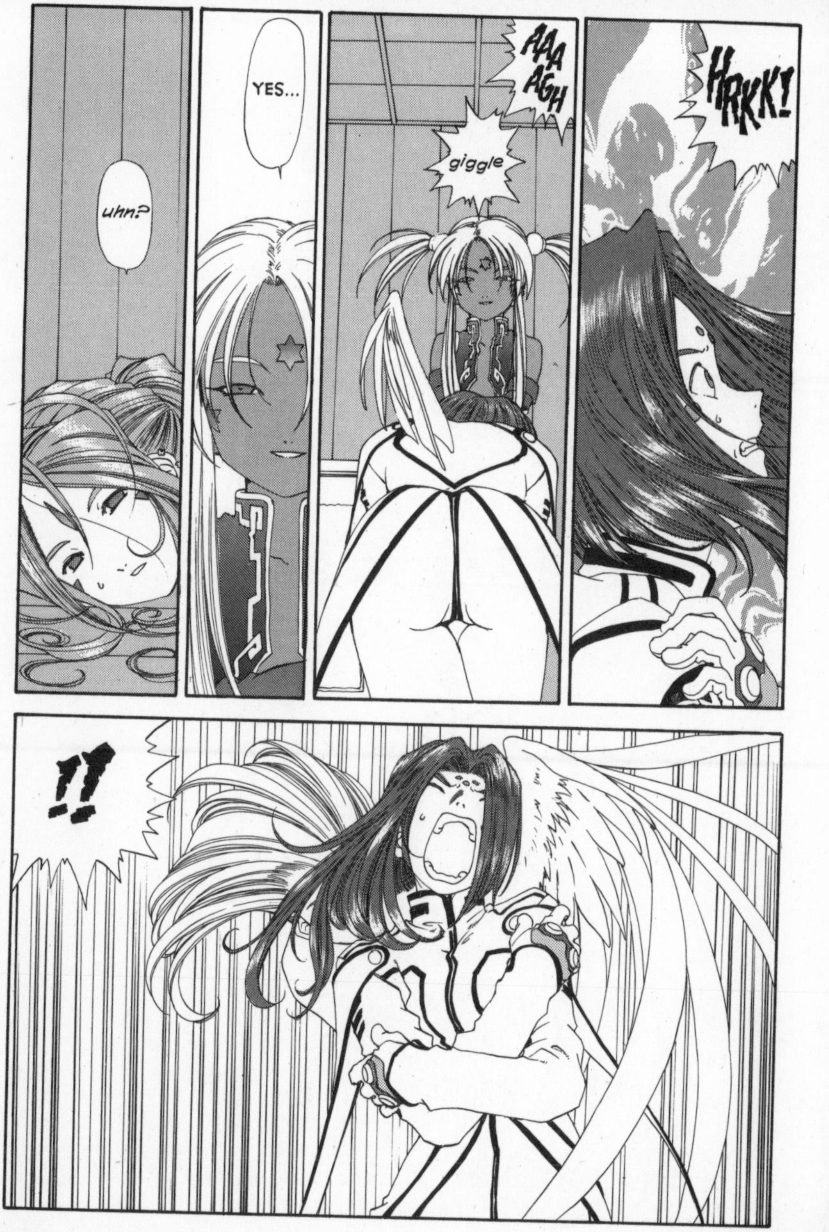
HRKK!
AAAAGH
giggle
YES...
uhn?
!!

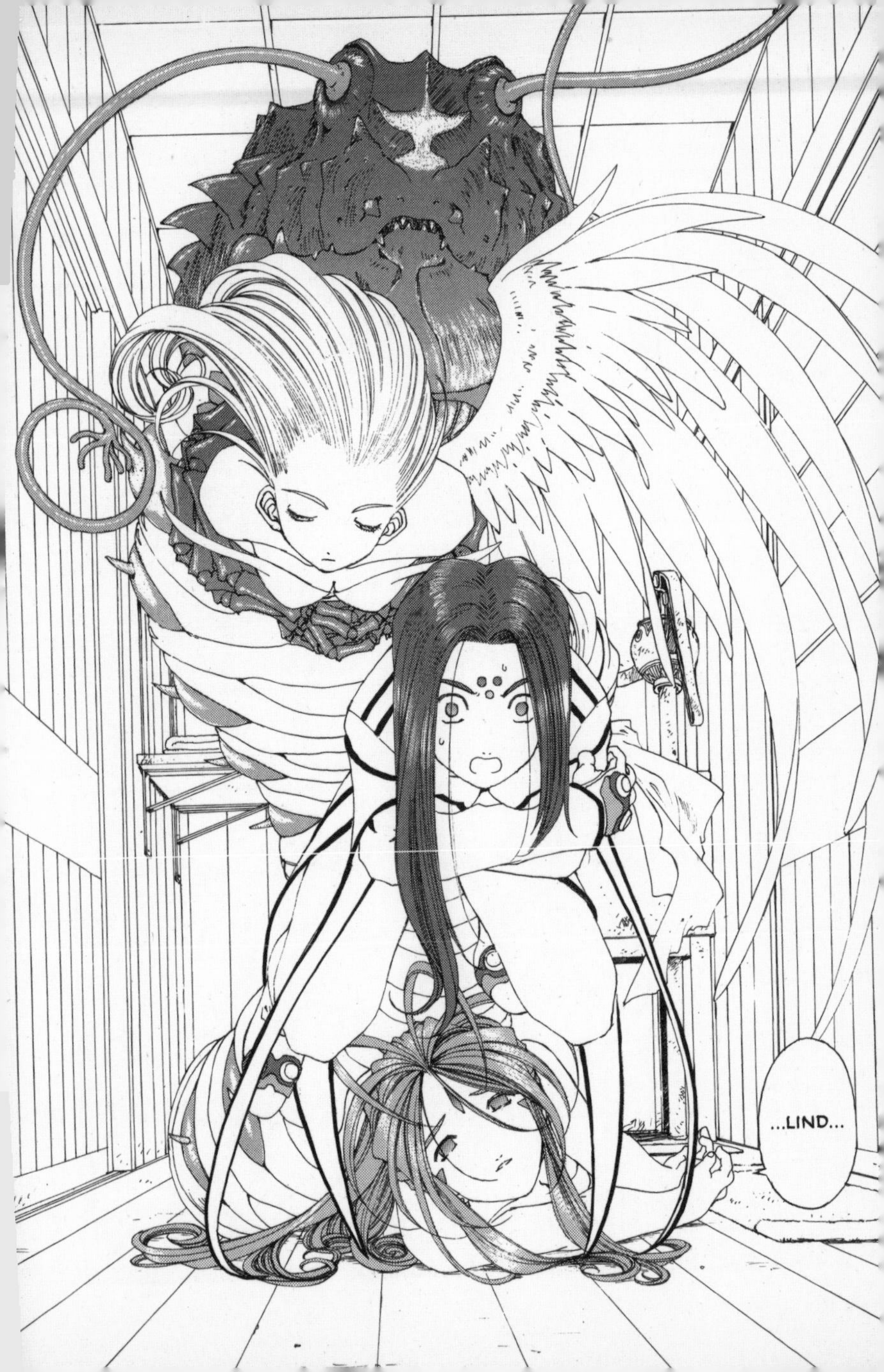
...LIND...

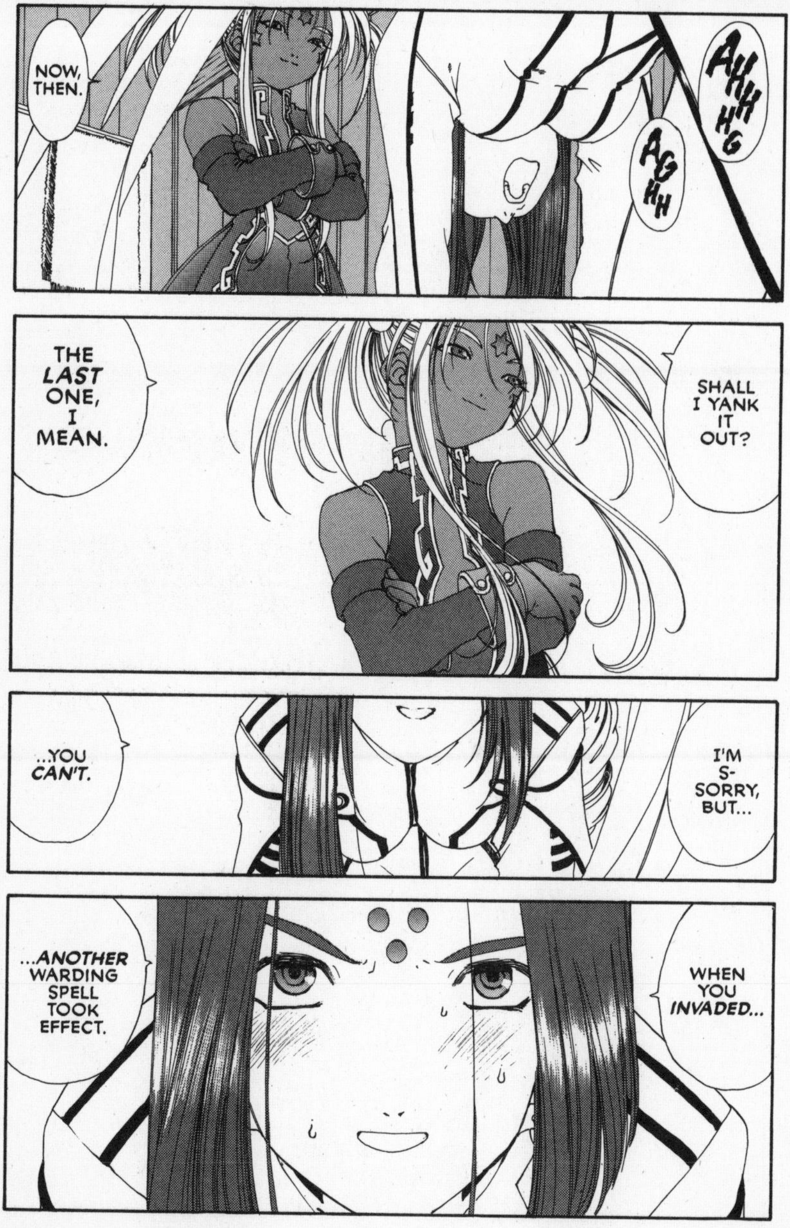
AHHHHG
AGHH
NOW, THEN.
SHALL I YANK IT OUT?
THE *LAST* ONE, I MEAN.
I'M S-SORRY, BUT...
...YOU *CAN'T.*
WHEN YOU *INVADED...*
...*ANOTHER* WARDING SPELL TOOK EFFECT.

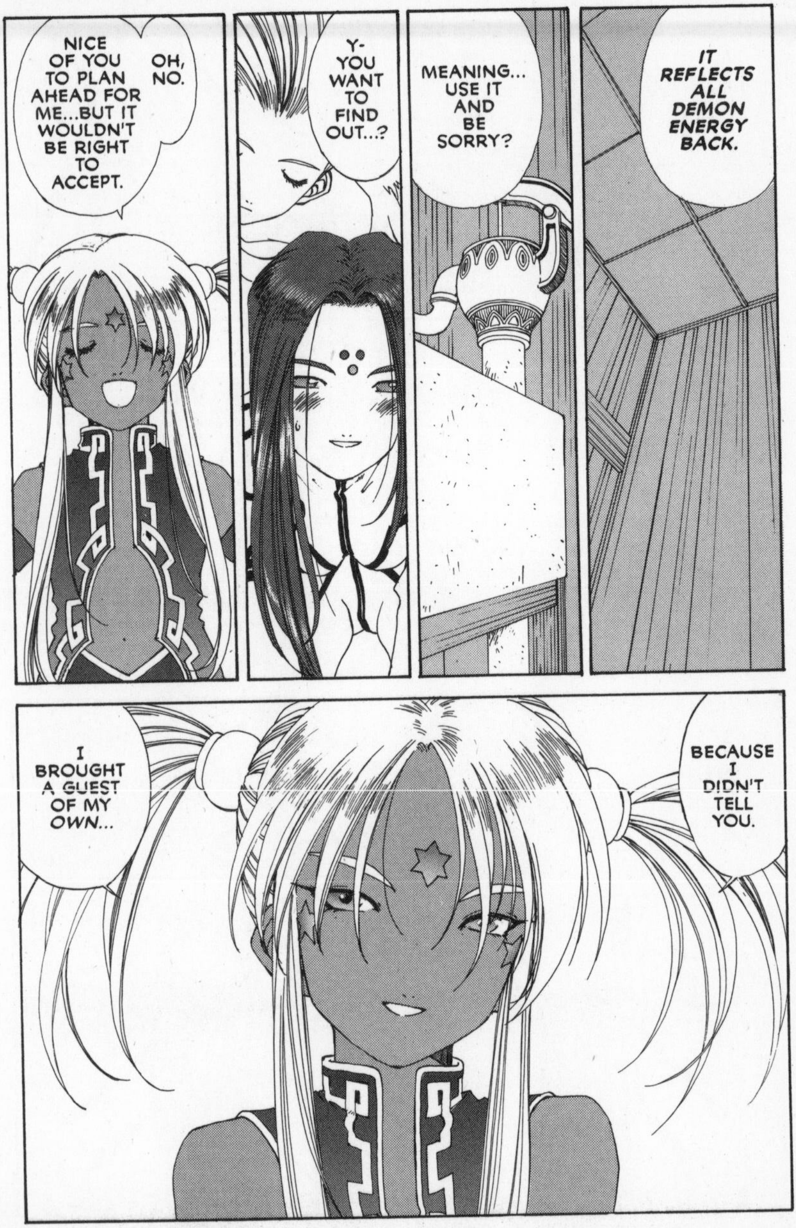
IT REFLECTS ALL DEMON ENERGY BACK.
MEANING... USE IT AND BE SORRY?
Y-YOU WANT TO FIND OUT...?
OH, NO.
NICE OF YOU TO PLAN AHEAD FOR ME...BUT IT WOULDN'T BE RIGHT TO ACCEPT.
BECAUSE I DIDN'T TELL YOU.
I BROUGHT A GUEST OF MY *OWN*...

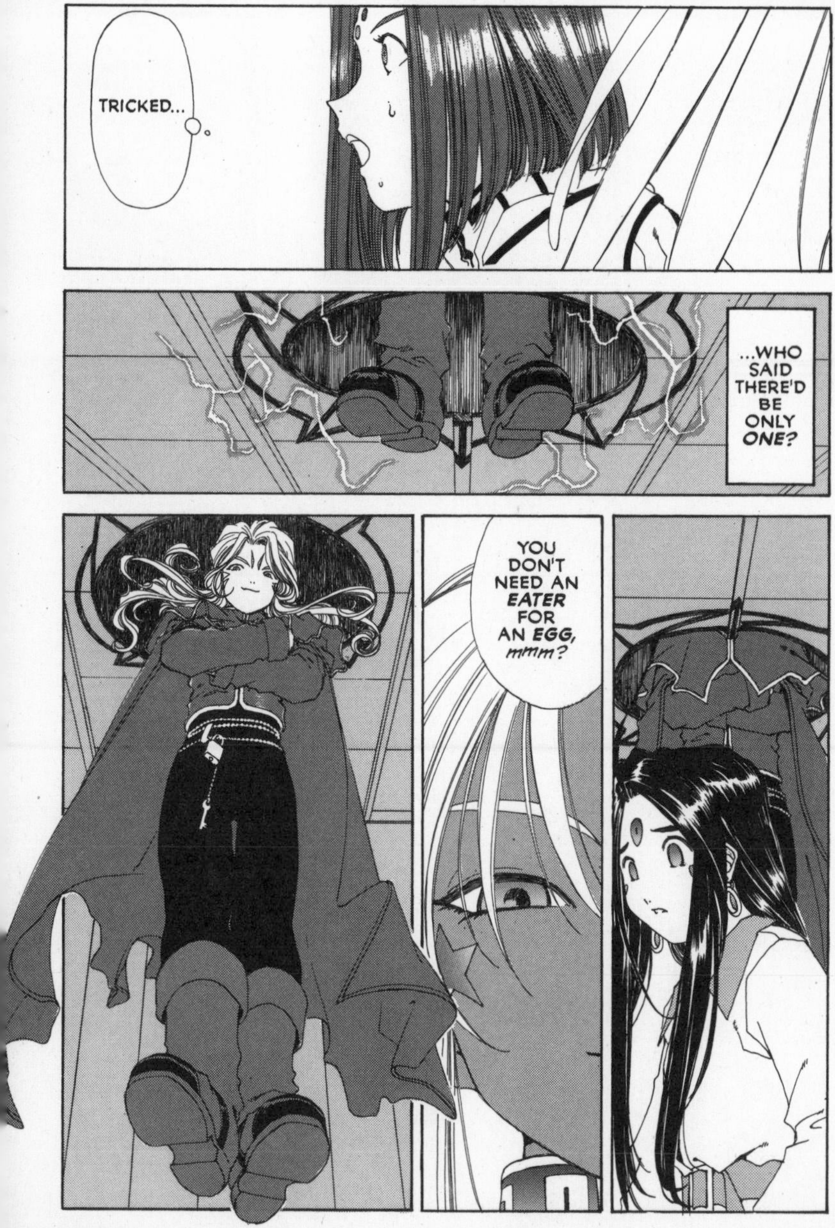
TRICKED...
...WHO SAID THERE'D BE ONLY *ONE?*
YOU DON'T NEED AN *EATER* FOR AN *EGG, mmm?*

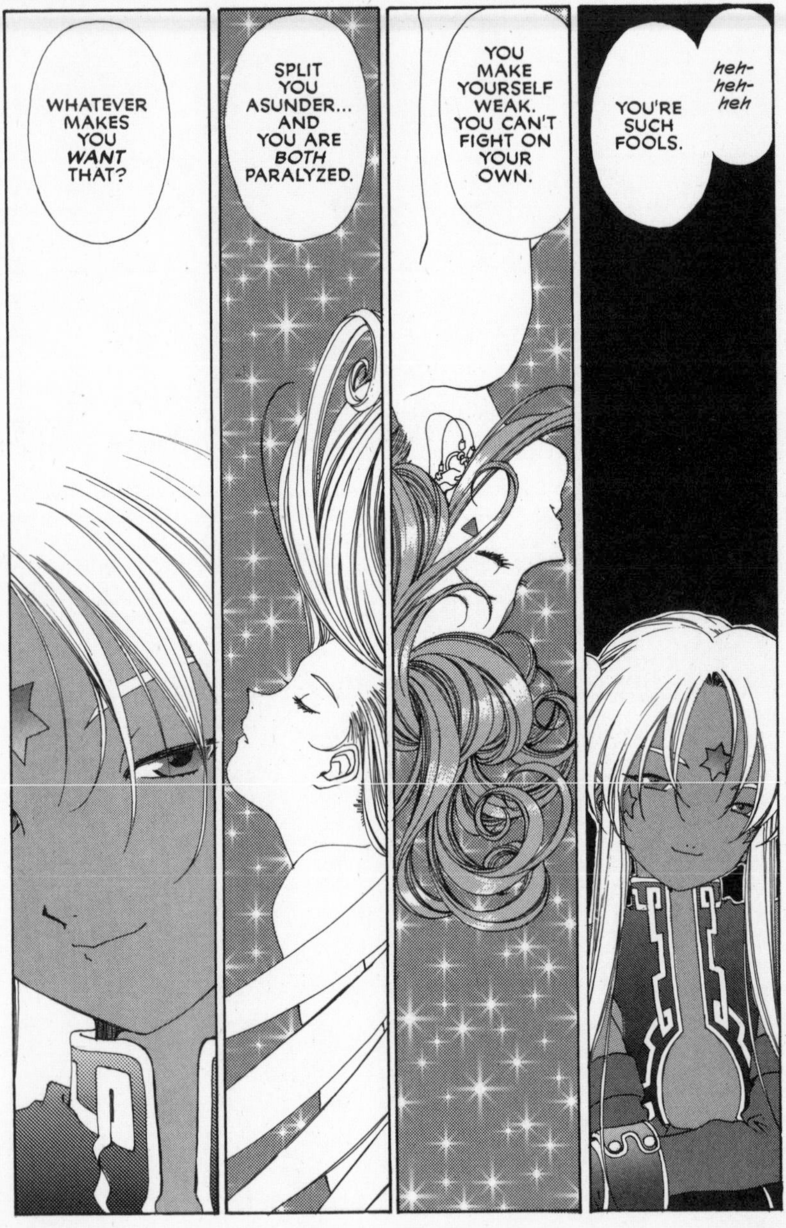

heh-heh-heh
YOU'RE SUCH FOOLS.
YOU MAKE YOURSELF WEAK. YOU CAN'T FIGHT ON YOUR OWN.
SPLIT YOU ASUNDER... AND YOU ARE *BOTH* PARALYZED.
WHATEVER MAKES YOU *WANT* THAT?

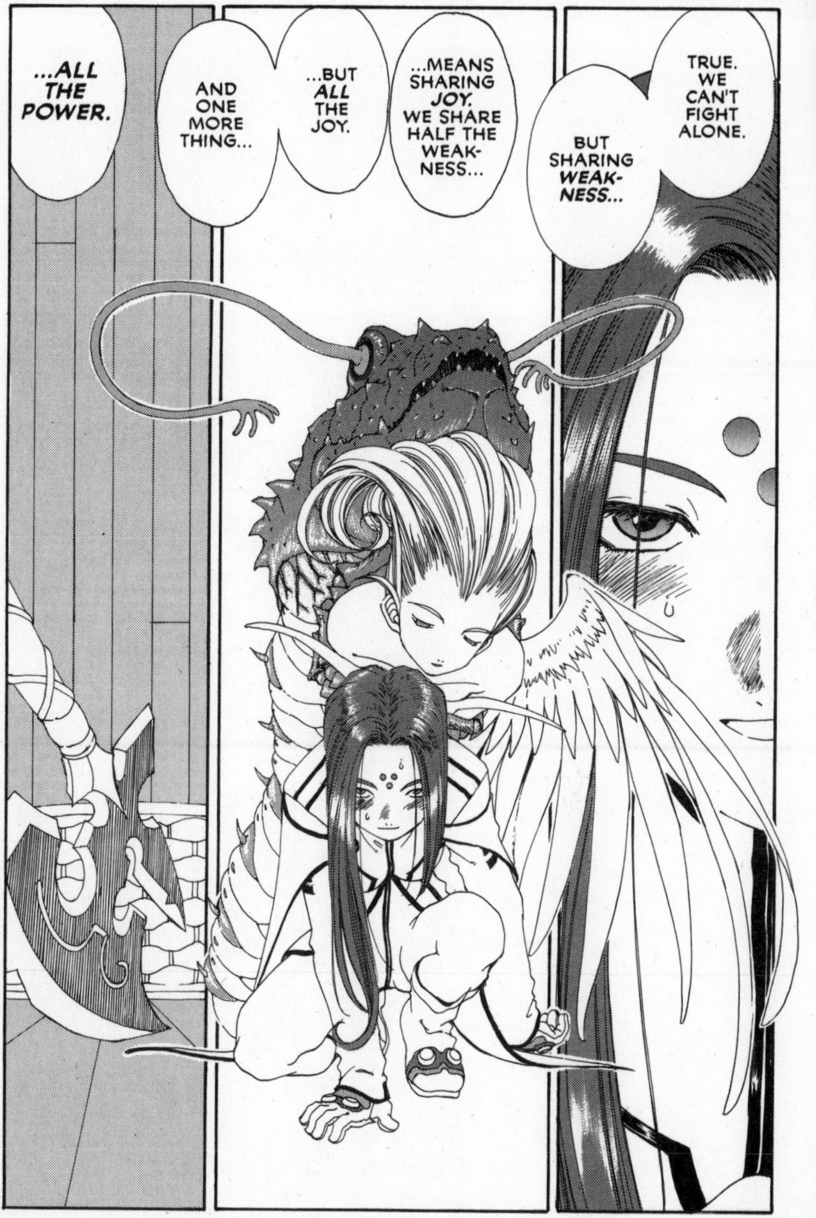
TRUE. WE CAN'T FIGHT ALONE.
BUT SHARING *WEAK-NESS...*
...MEANS SHARING *JOY.* WE SHARE HALF THE WEAK-NESS...
...BUT *ALL* THE JOY.
AND ONE MORE THING...
...ALL THE POWER.

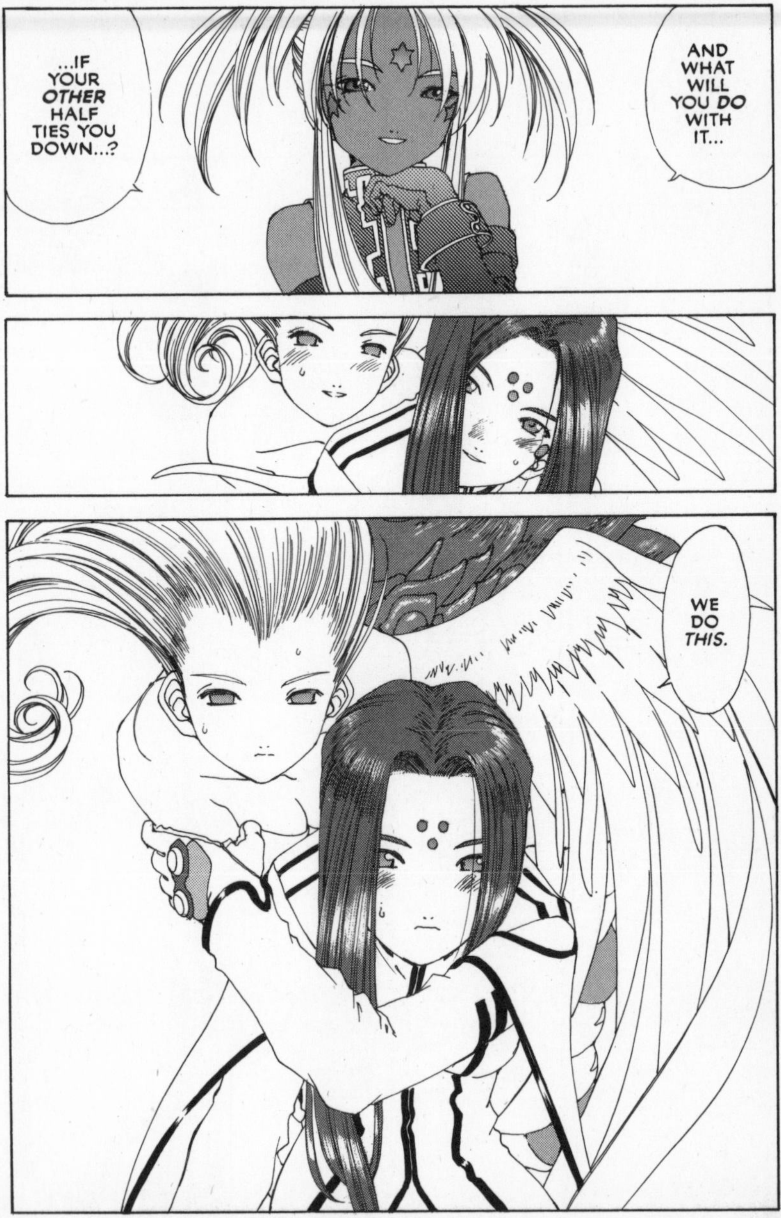
AND WHAT WILL YOU *DO* WITH IT...
...IF YOUR *OTHER* HALF TIES YOU DOWN...?
WE DO *THIS.*

CHAPTER 159

Devil of a Plot

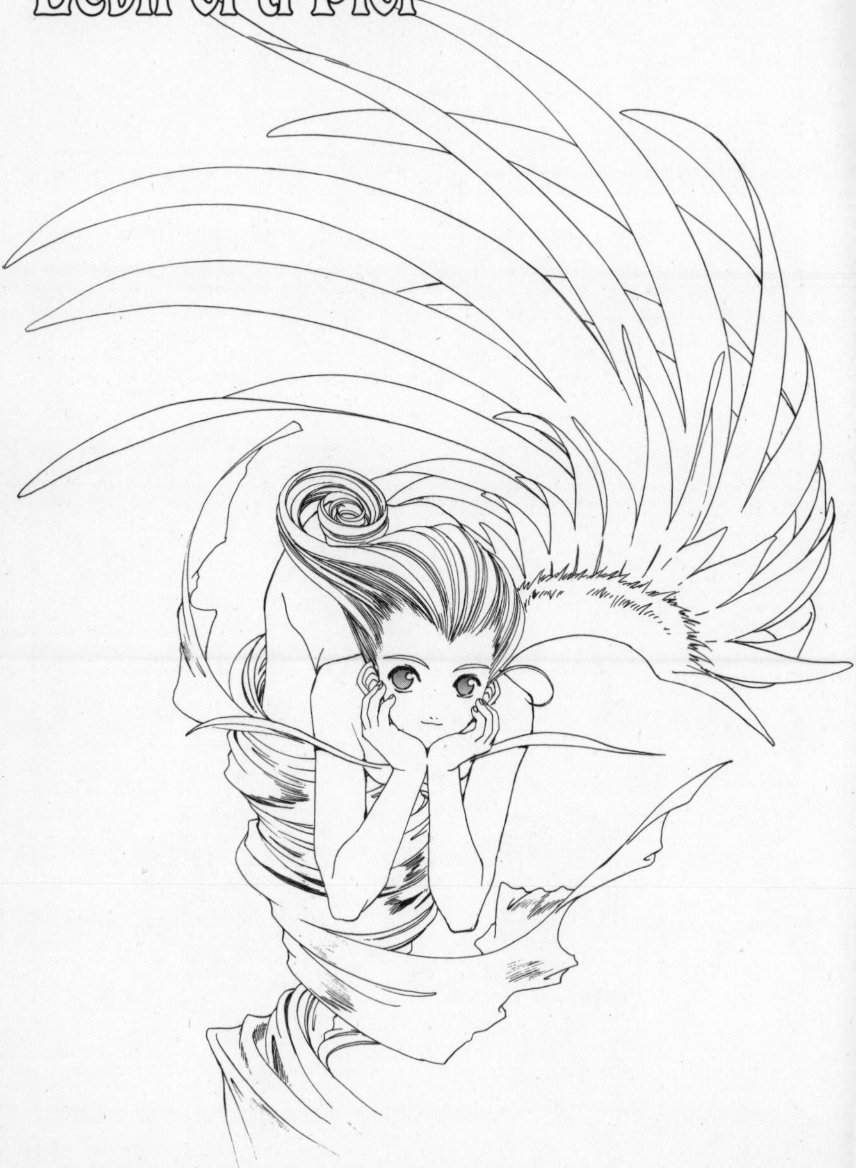

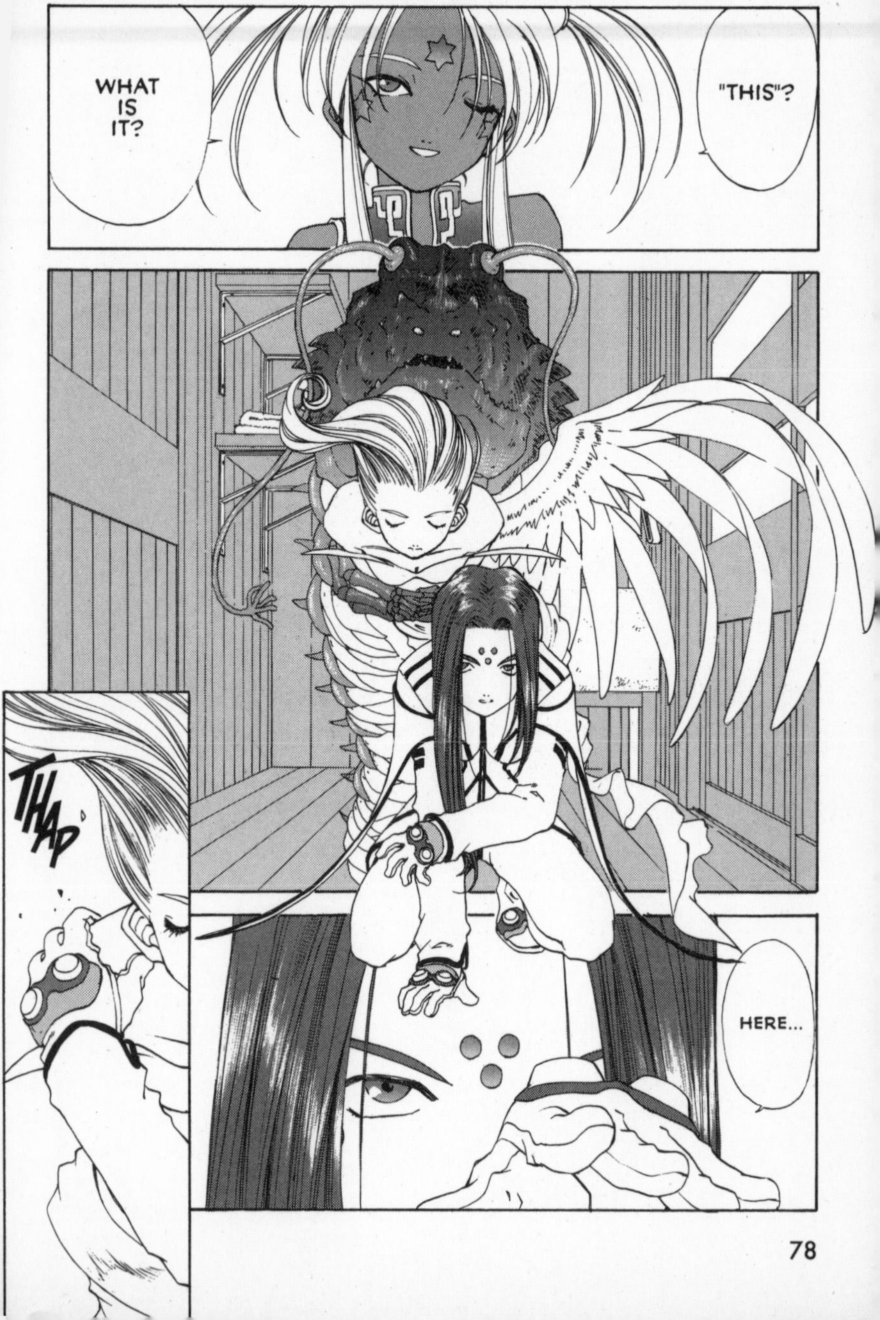
"THIS"?
WHAT IS IT?
HERE...
THAP

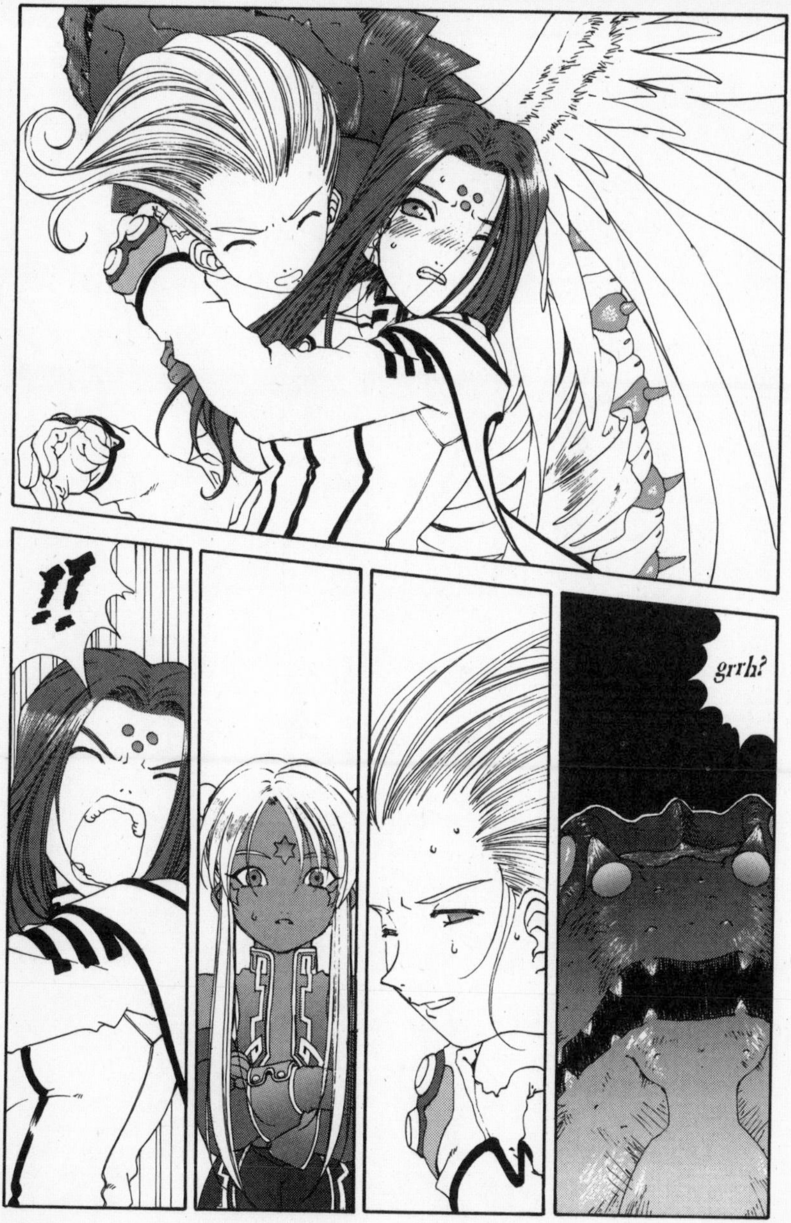
grrh?
!!

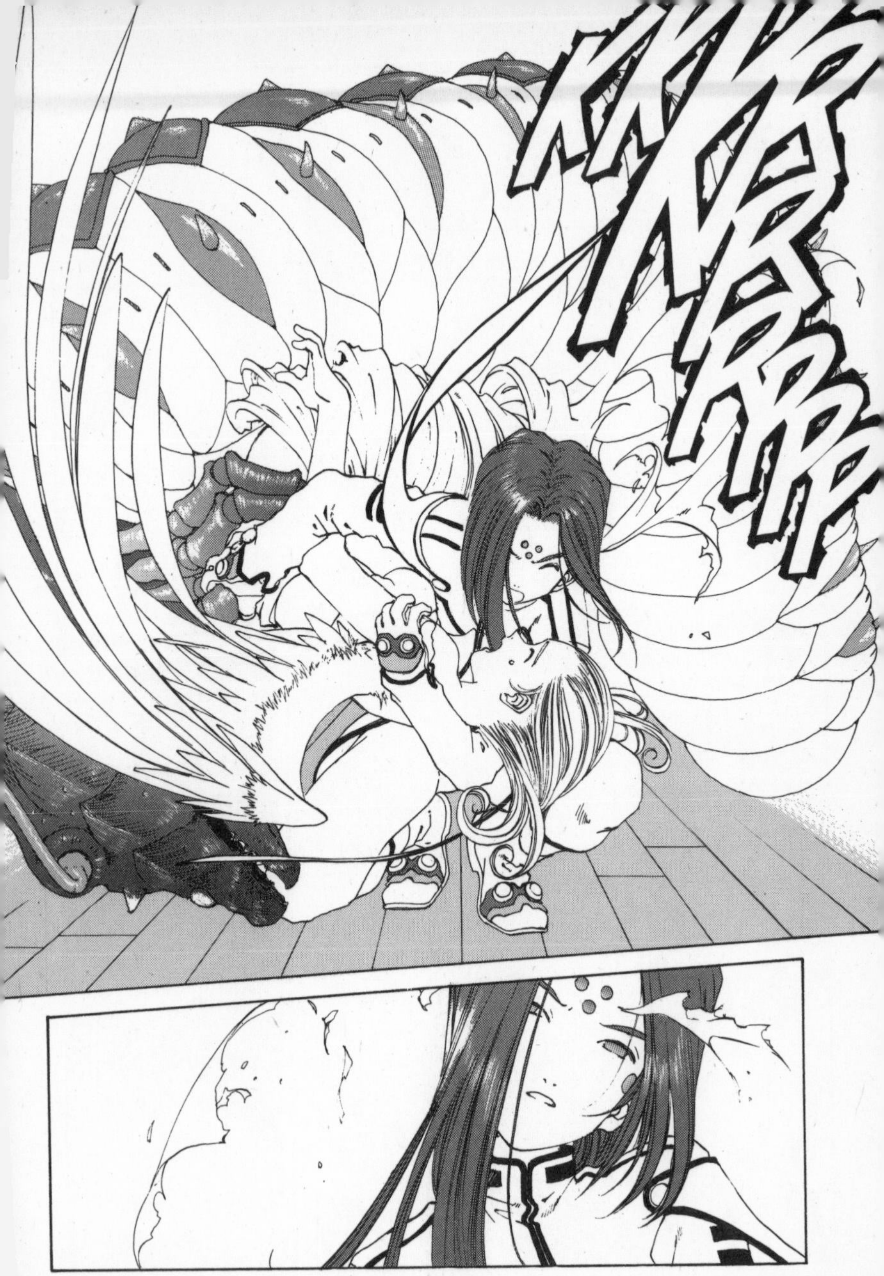

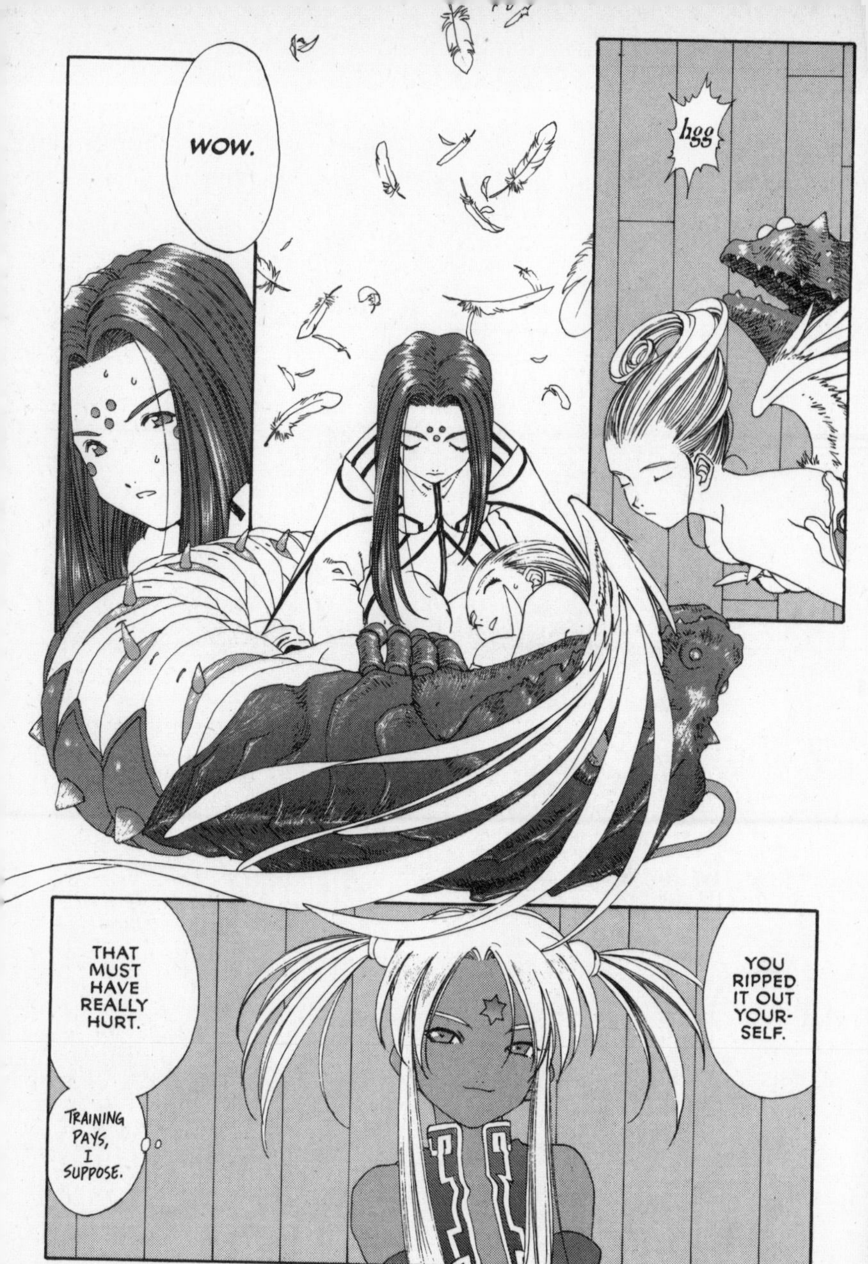
hgg
WOW.
YOU RIPPED IT OUT YOURSELF.
THAT MUST HAVE REALLY HURT.
TRAINING PAYS, I SUPPOSE.

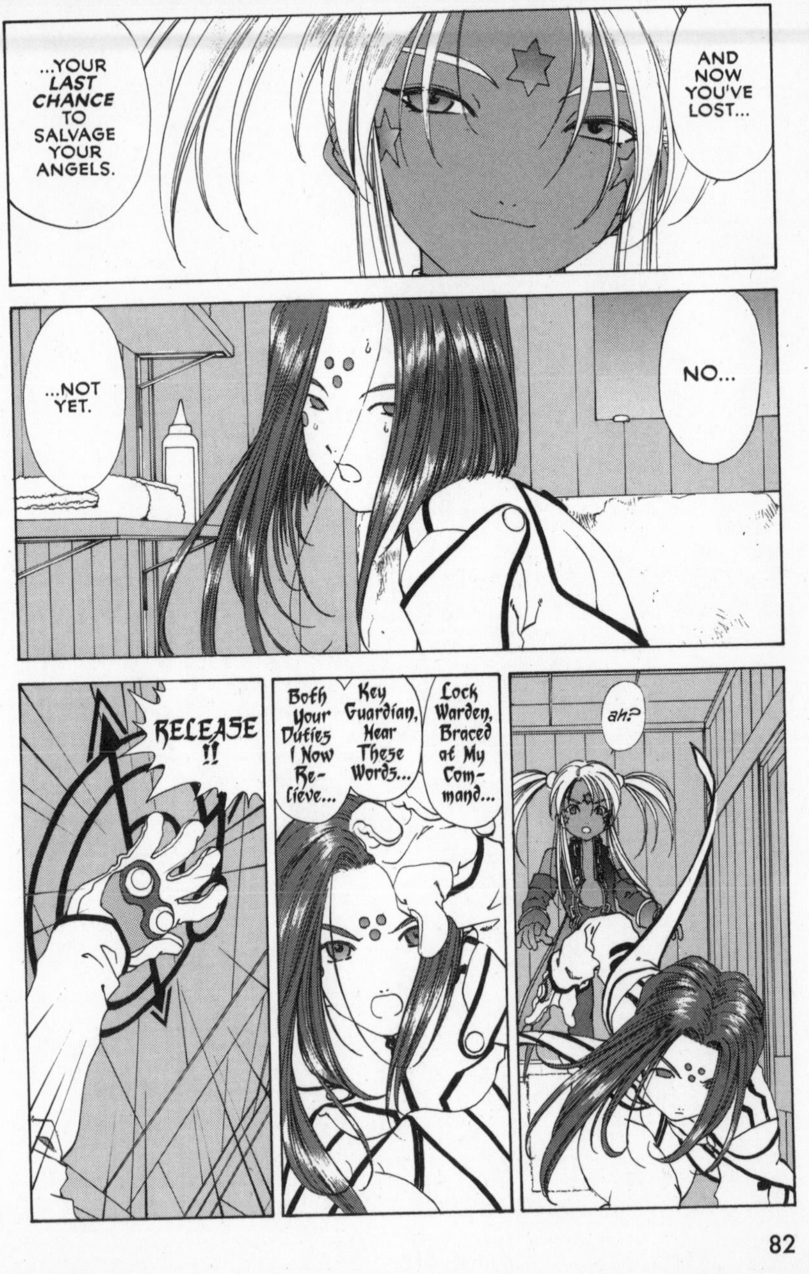
AND NOW YOU'VE LOST...
...YOUR *LAST CHANCE* TO SALVAGE YOUR ANGELS.
NO...
...NOT YET.
ah?
Lock Warden, Braced at My Command...
Key Guardian, Hear These Words...
Both Your Duties I Now Re-lieve...
RELEASE !!

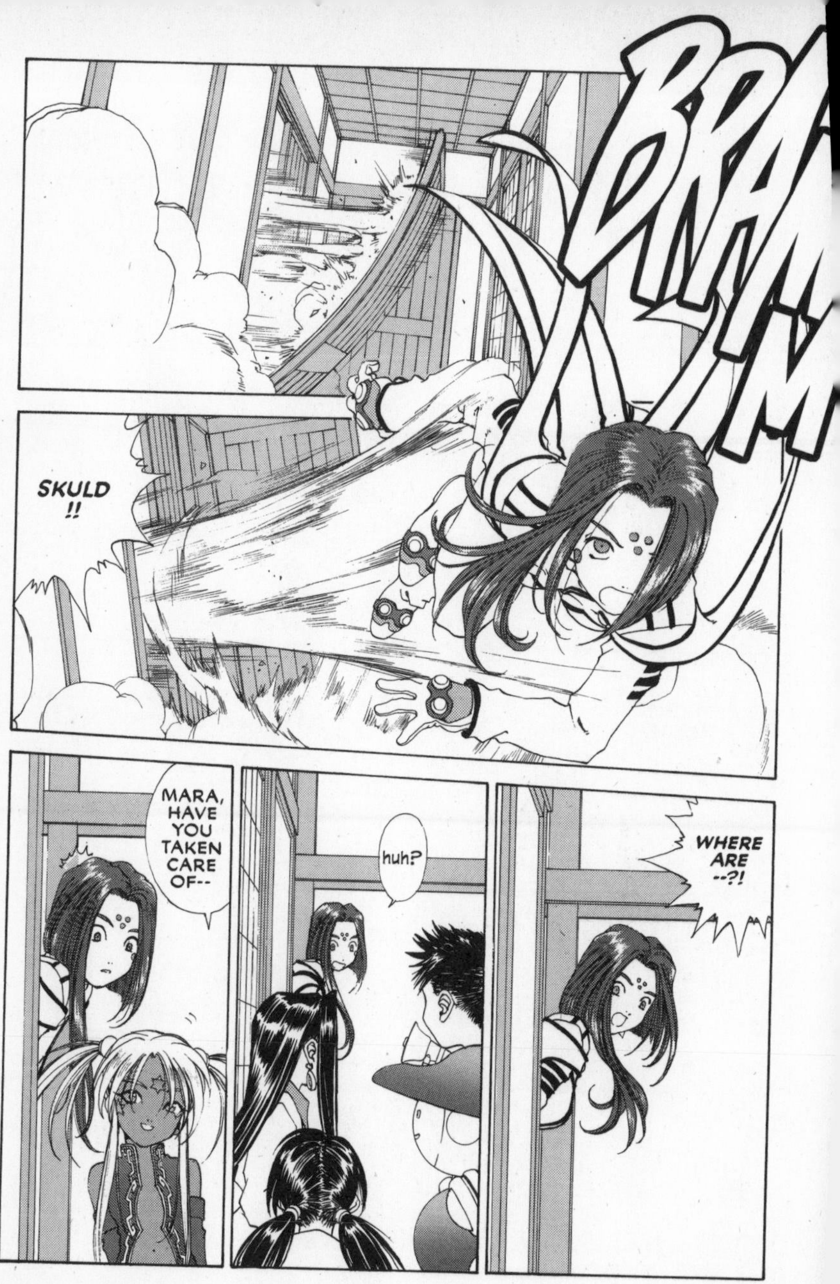
BRAM
SKULD !!
WHERE ARE --?!
huh?
MARA, HAVE YOU TAKEN CARE OF--

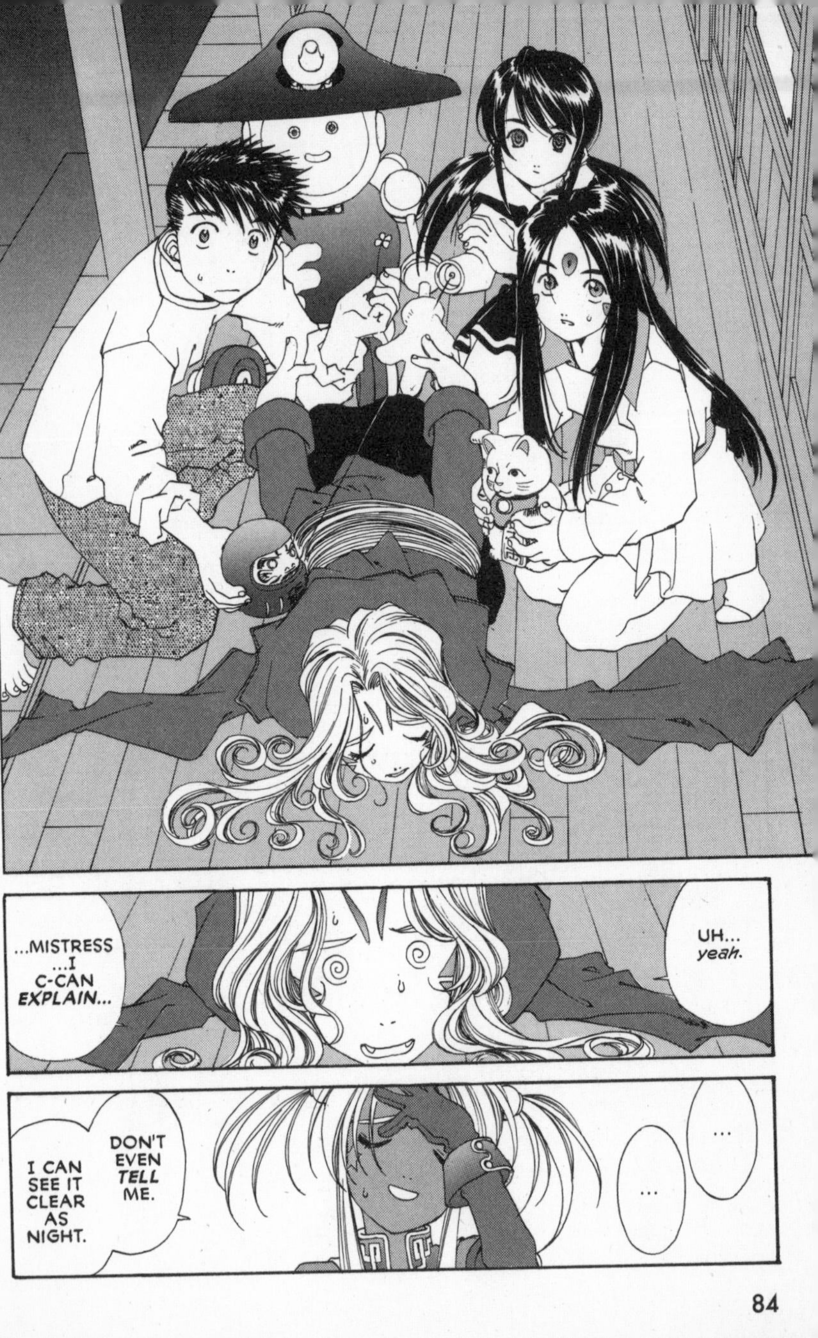
UH... *yeah.*
...MISTRESS ...I C-CAN **EXPLAIN...**
...
...
DON'T EVEN **TELL** ME.
I CAN SEE IT CLEAR AS NIGHT.

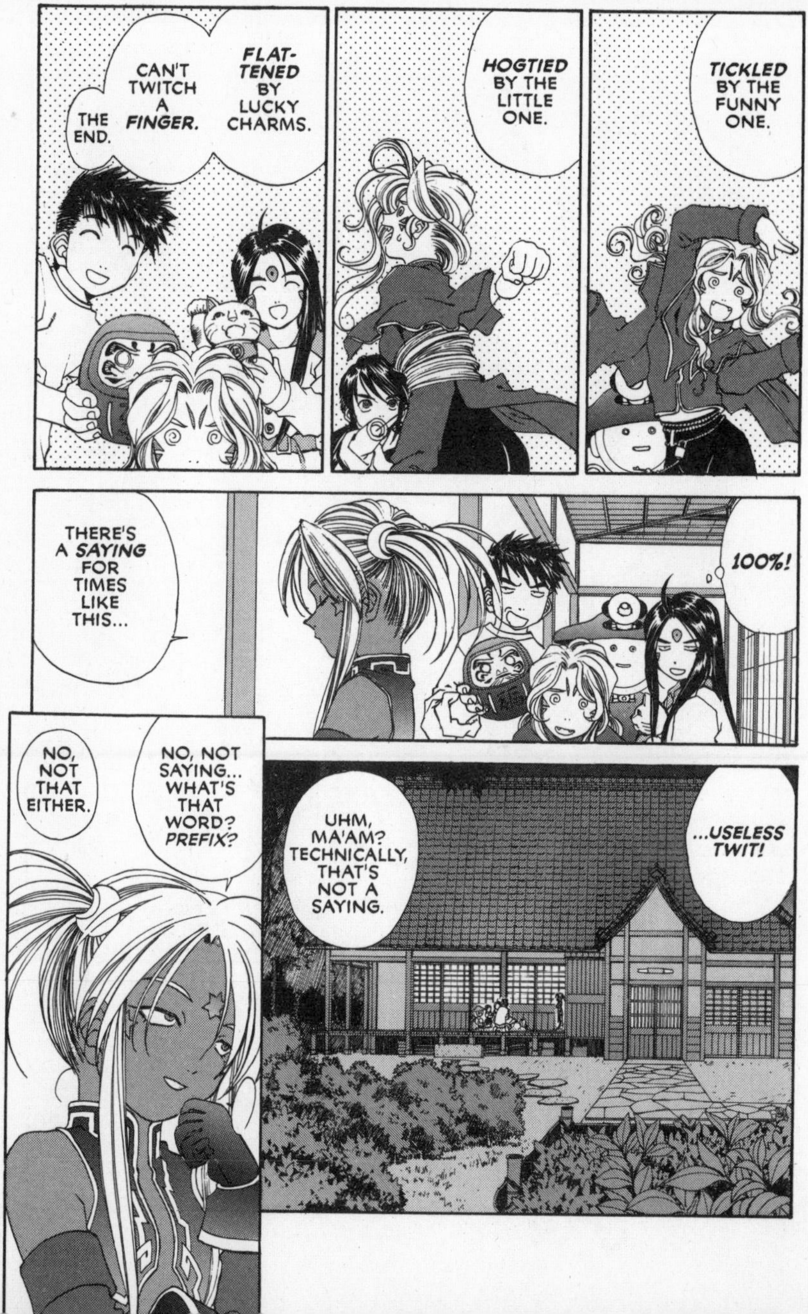
TICKLED BY THE FUNNY ONE.
HOGTIED BY THE LITTLE ONE.
FLAT-TENED BY LUCKY CHARMS.
CAN'T TWITCH A FINGER.
THE END.
100%!
THERE'S A SAYING FOR TIMES LIKE THIS...
...USELESS TWIT!
UHM, MA'AM? TECHNICALLY, THAT'S NOT A SAYING.
NO, NOT SAYING... WHAT'S THAT WORD? PREFIX?
NO, NOT THAT EITHER.

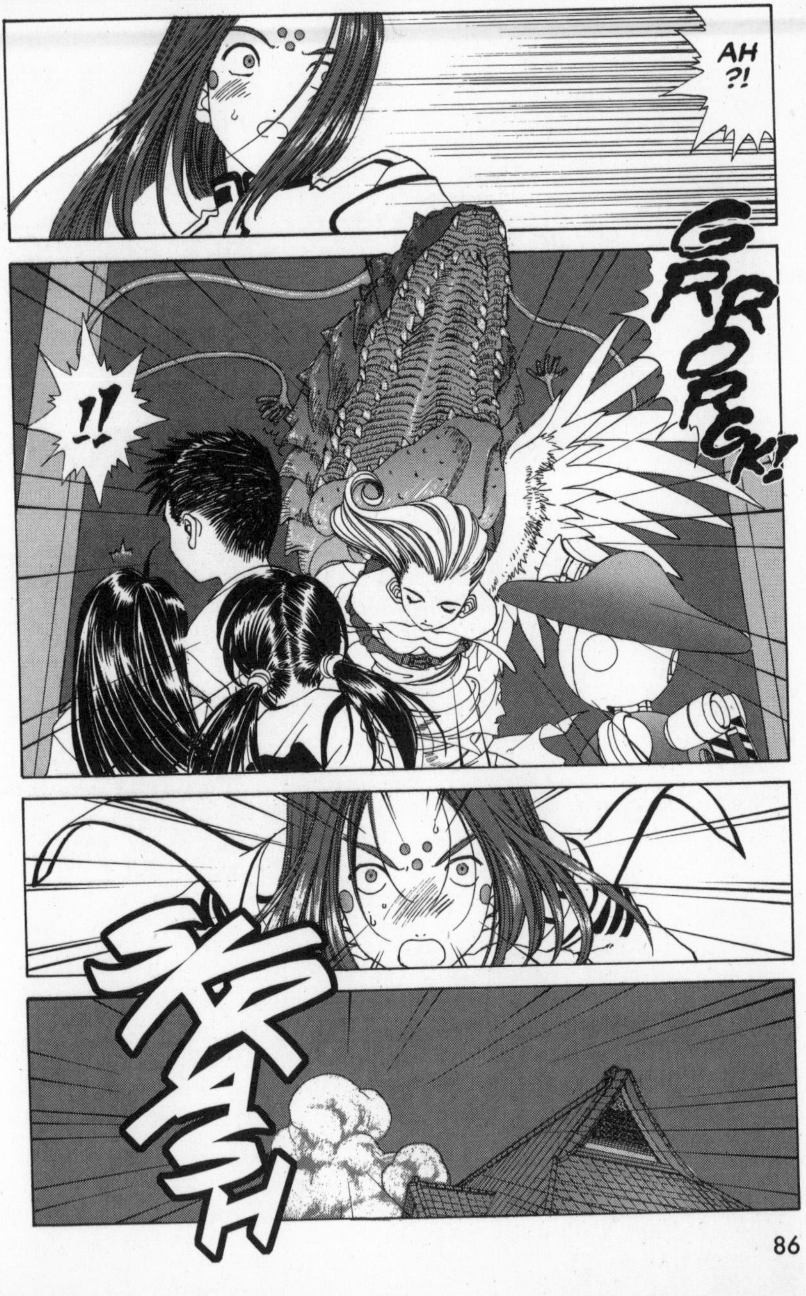
AH ?!
GRRORGK!
!!

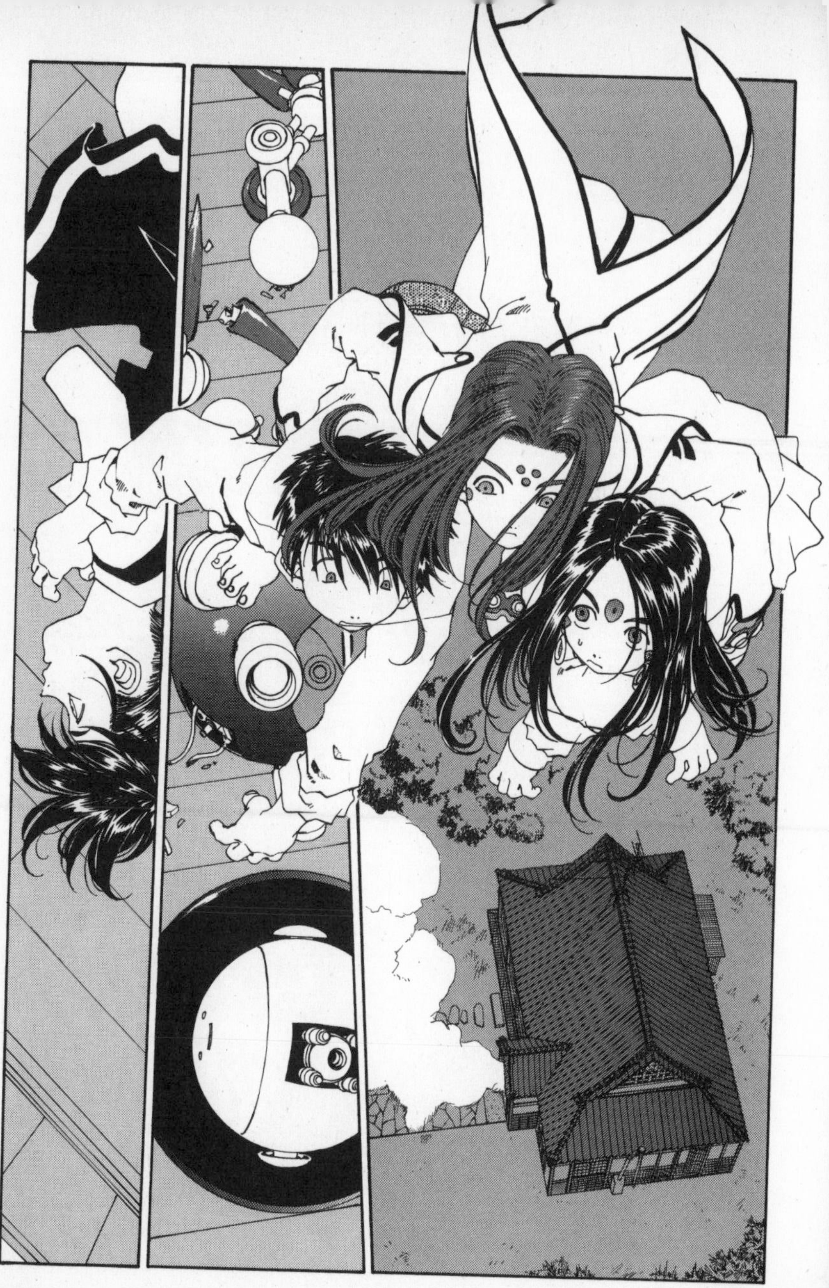

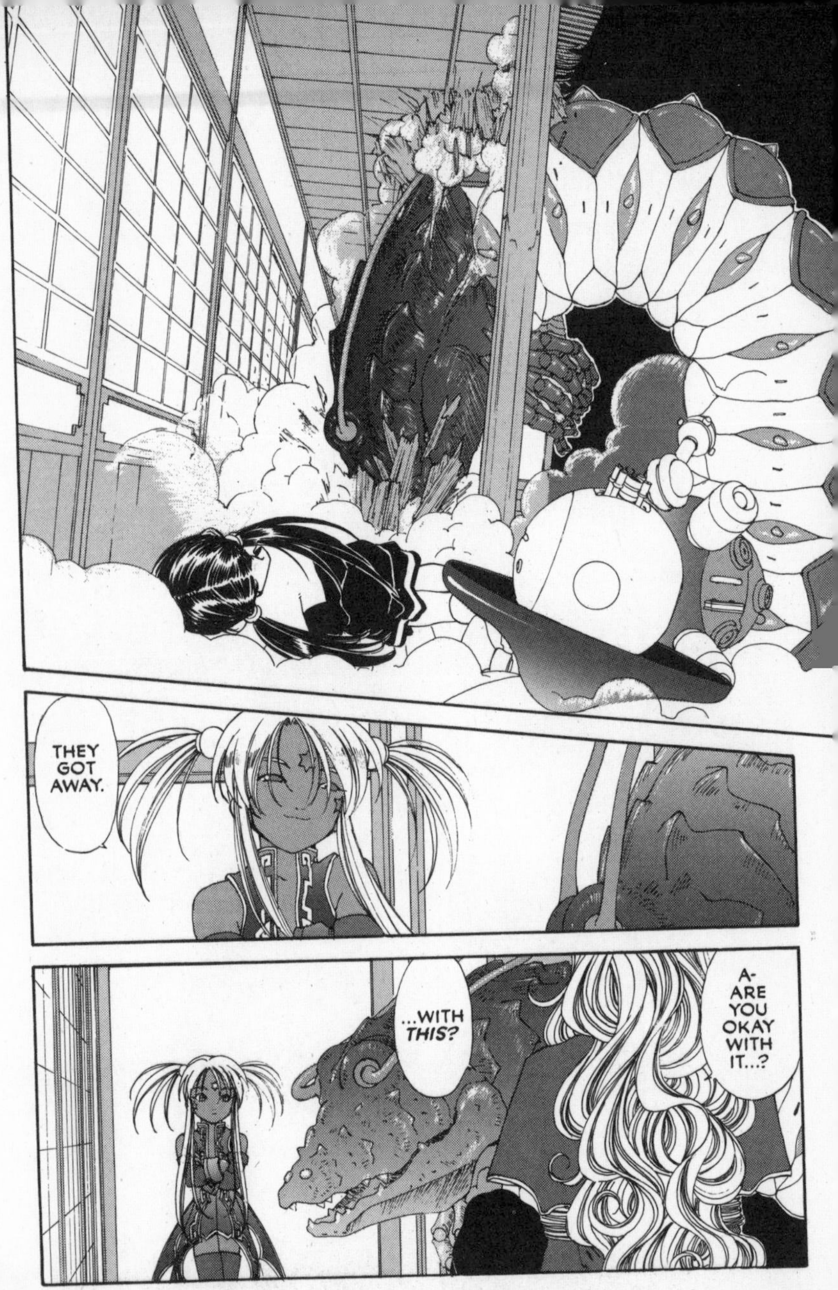
THEY GOT AWAY.
A-ARE YOU OKAY WITH IT...?
...WITH THIS?

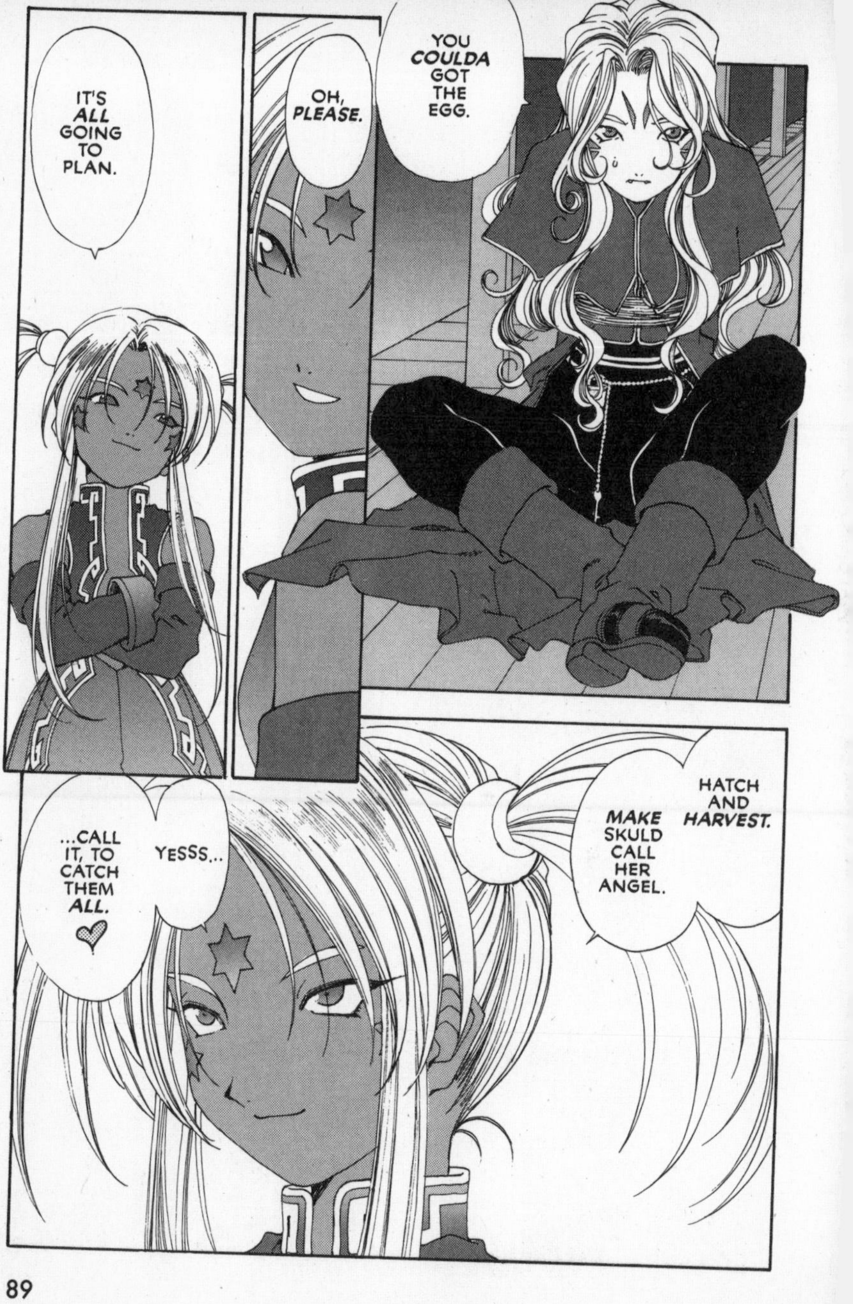
YOU COULDA GOT THE EGG.
OH, PLEASE.
IT'S ALL GOING TO PLAN.
HATCH AND HARVEST. MAKE SKULD CALL HER ANGEL.
YESSS...
...CALL IT, TO CATCH THEM ALL. ♥

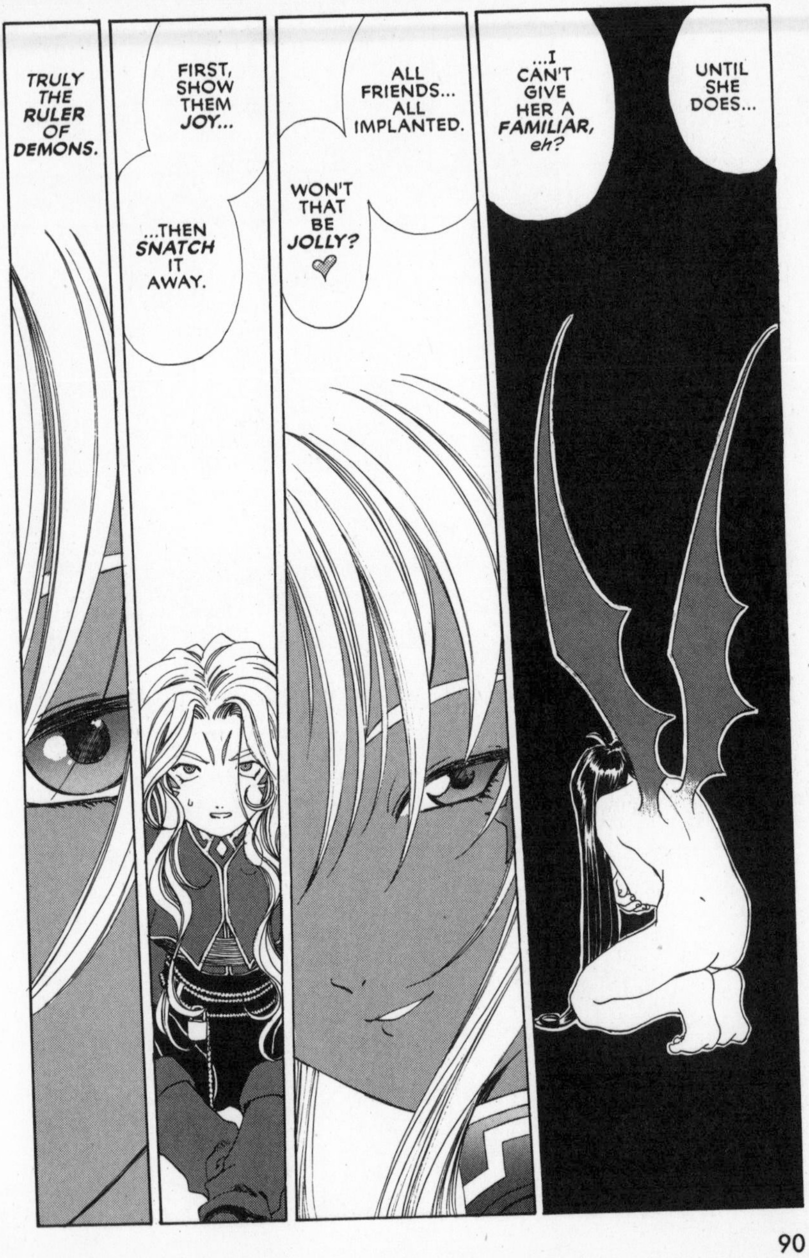
UNTIL SHE DOES...
...I CAN'T GIVE HER A *FAMILIAR*, *eh?*
ALL FRIENDS... ALL IMPLANTED.
WON'T THAT BE *JOLLY?* ♡
FIRST, SHOW THEM *JOY...*
...THEN *SNATCH* IT AWAY.
TRULY THE RULER OF DEMONS.

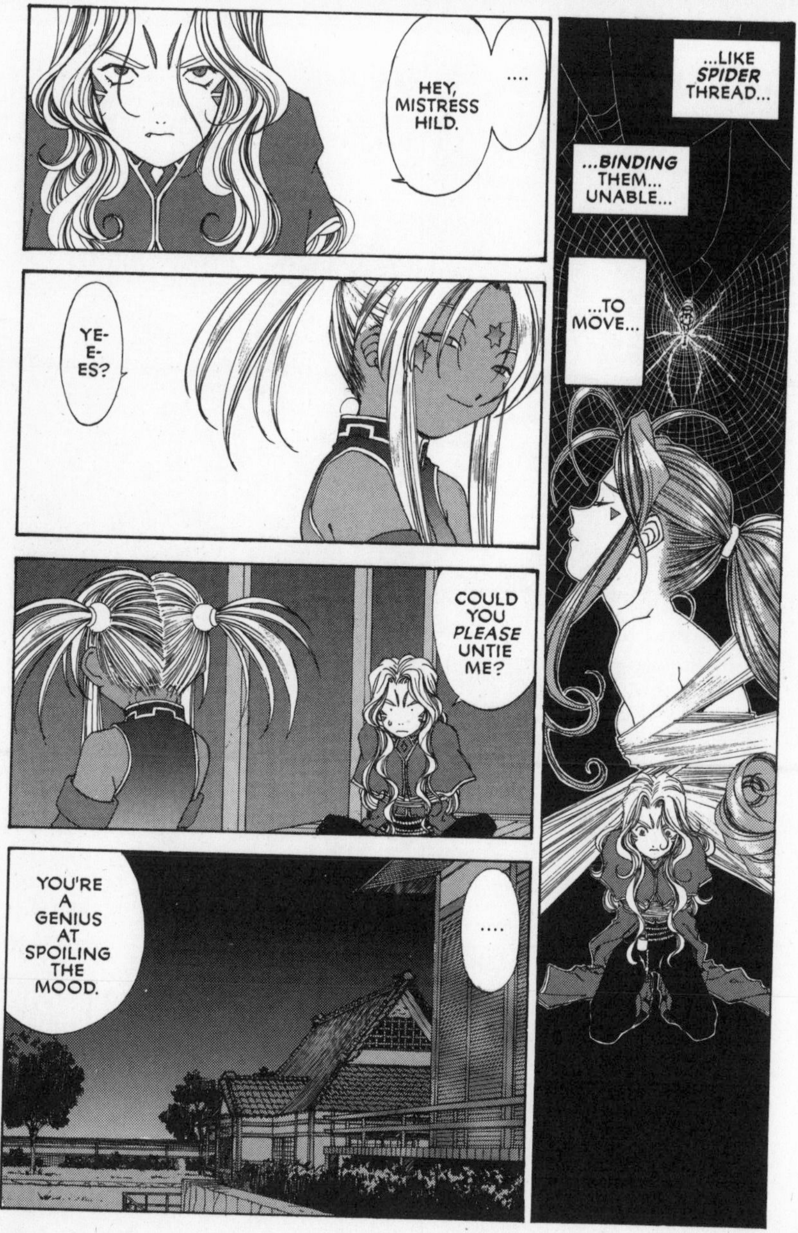
...LIKE *SPIDER* THREAD...
...*BINDING* THEM... UNABLE...
...TO MOVE...
....
HEY, MISTRESS HILD.
YE- E- ES?
COULD YOU *PLEASE* UNTIE ME?
....
YOU'RE A GENIUS AT SPOILING THE MOOD.

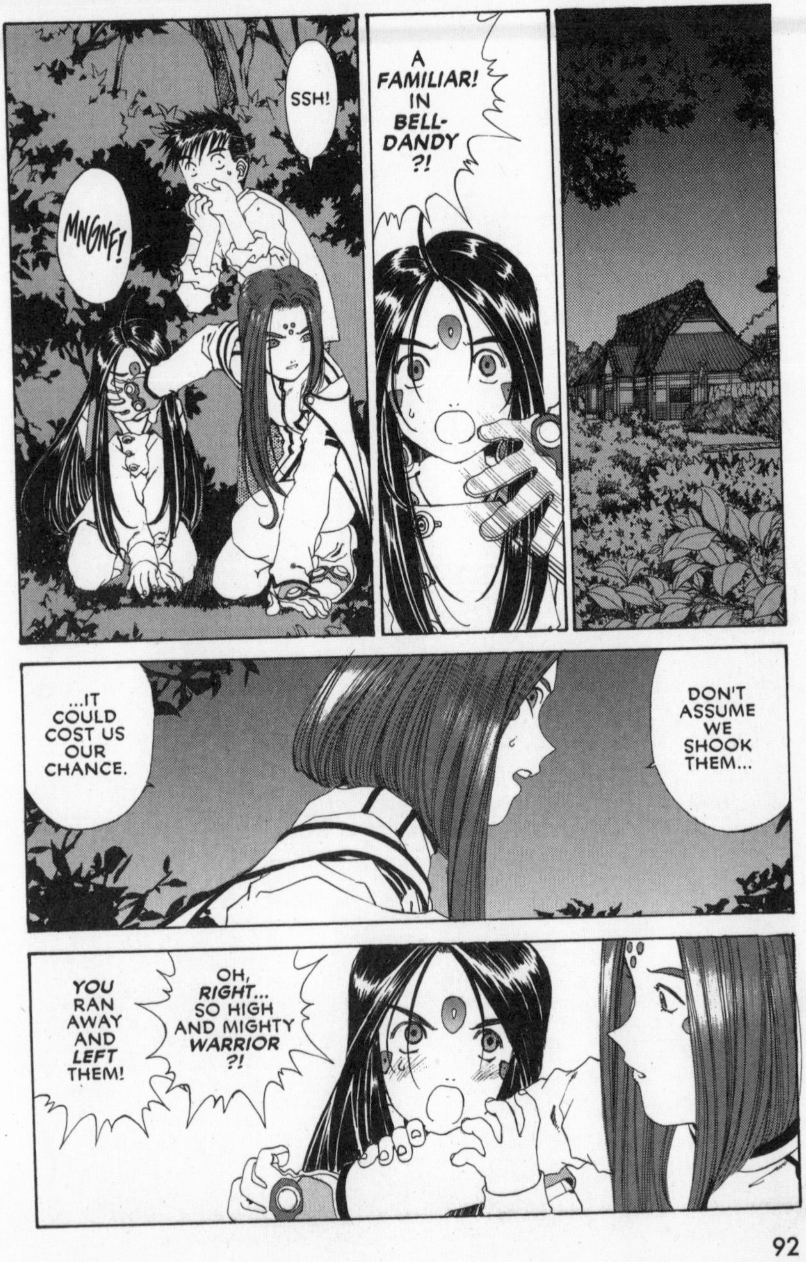
A FAMILIAR! IN BELL-DANDY ?!
SSH!
MNGNF!
DON'T ASSUME WE SHOOK THEM...
...IT COULD COST US OUR CHANCE.
OH, *RIGHT*... SO HIGH AND MIGHTY *WARRIOR* ?!
YOU RAN AWAY AND *LEFT* THEM!

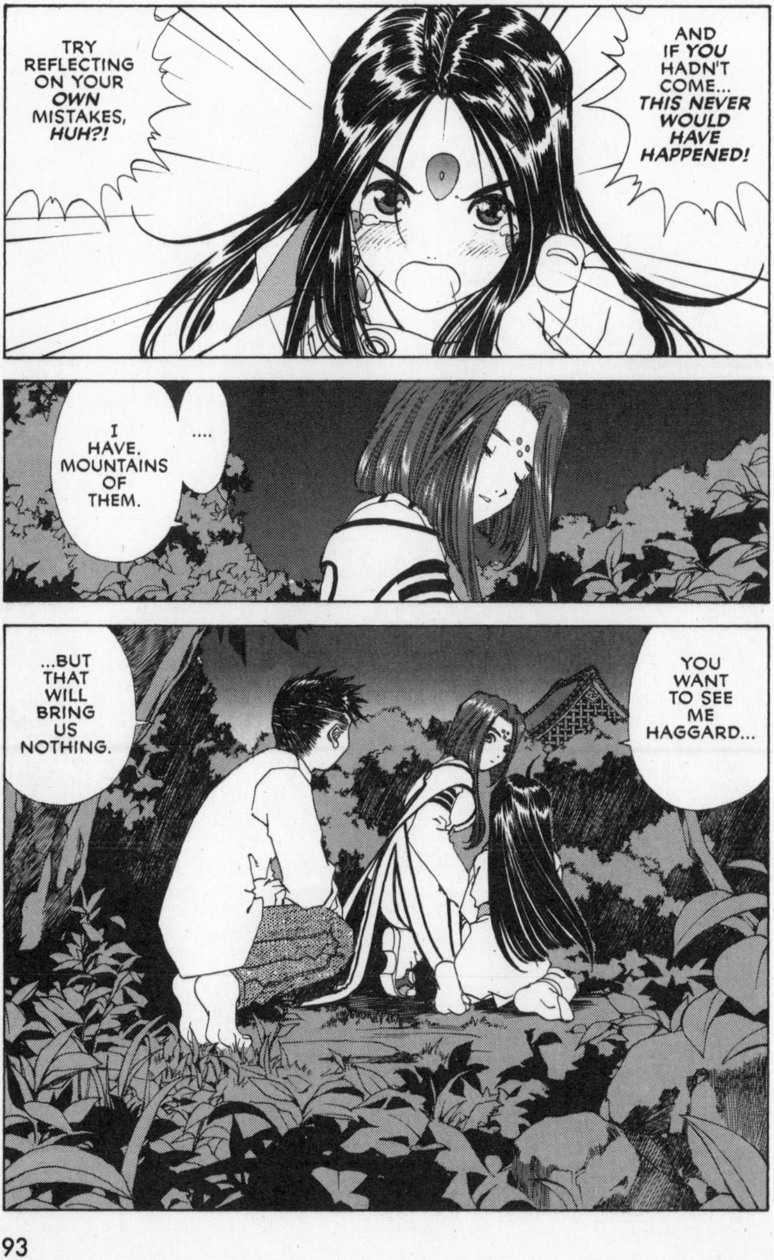
AND IF YOU HADN'T COME... THIS NEVER WOULD HAVE HAPPENED!
TRY REFLECTING ON YOUR OWN MISTAKES, HUH?!
....
I HAVE. MOUNTAINS OF THEM.
YOU WANT TO SEE ME HAGGARD...
...BUT THAT WILL BRING US NOTHING.

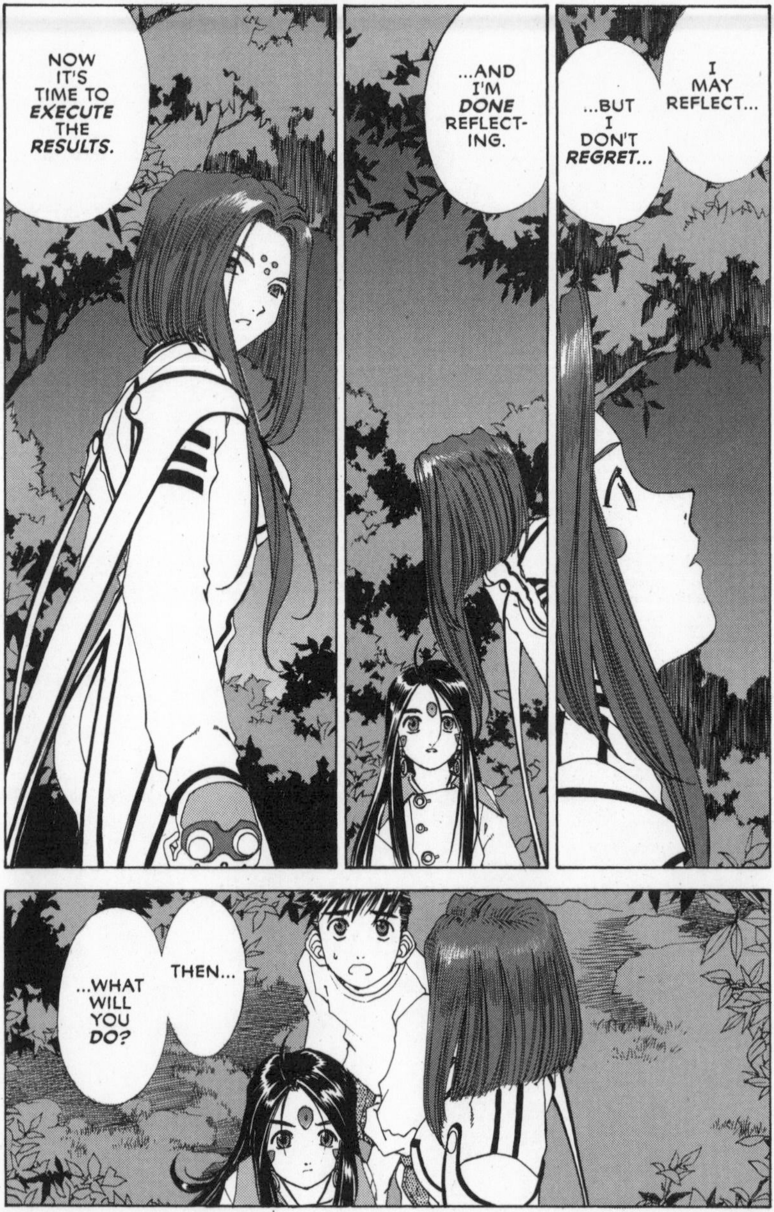
I MAY REFLECT...
...BUT I DON'T *REGRET*...
...AND I'M *DONE* REFLECTING.
NOW IT'S TIME TO *EXECUTE* THE *RESULTS*.
THEN...
...WHAT WILL YOU *DO*?

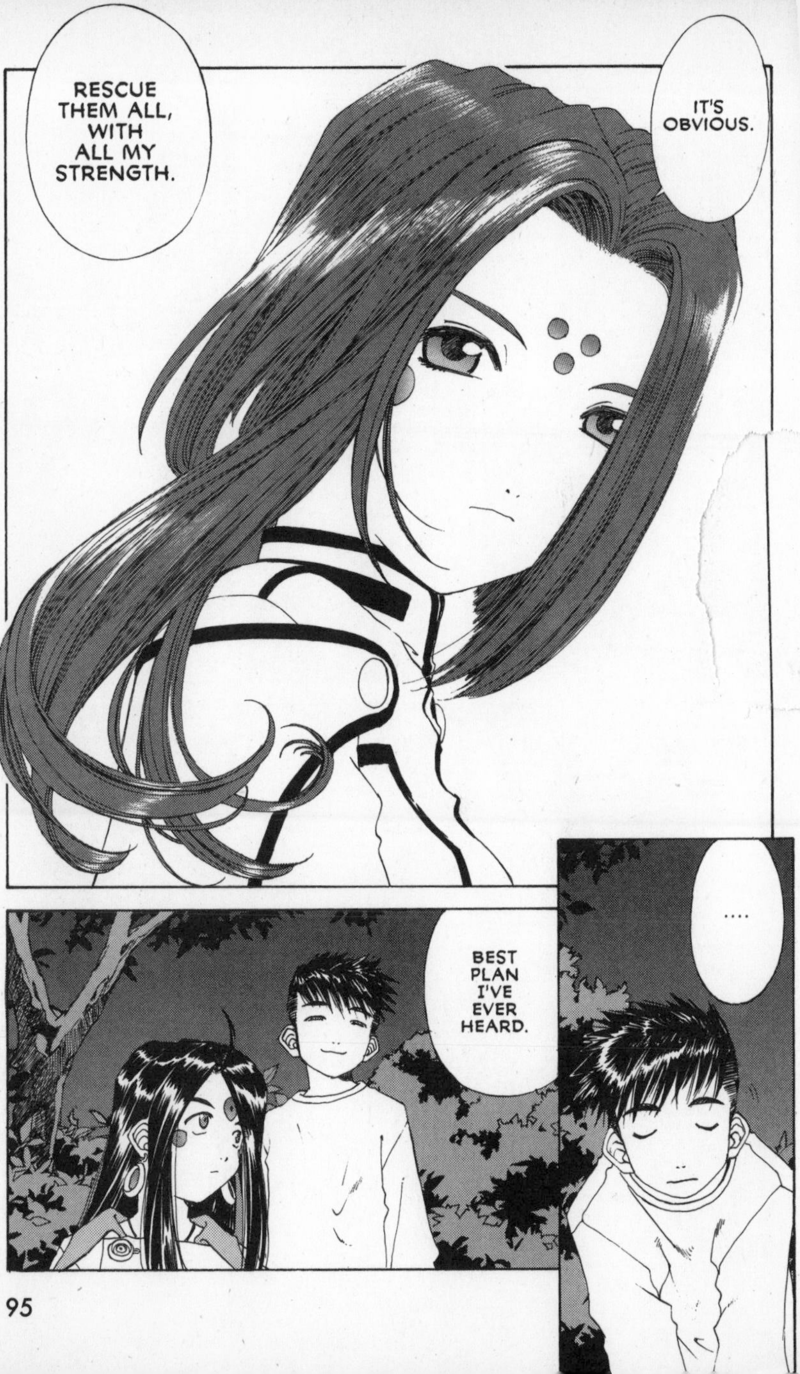
IT'S OBVIOUS.
RESCUE THEM ALL, WITH ALL MY STRENGTH.
....
BEST PLAN I'VE EVER HEARD.

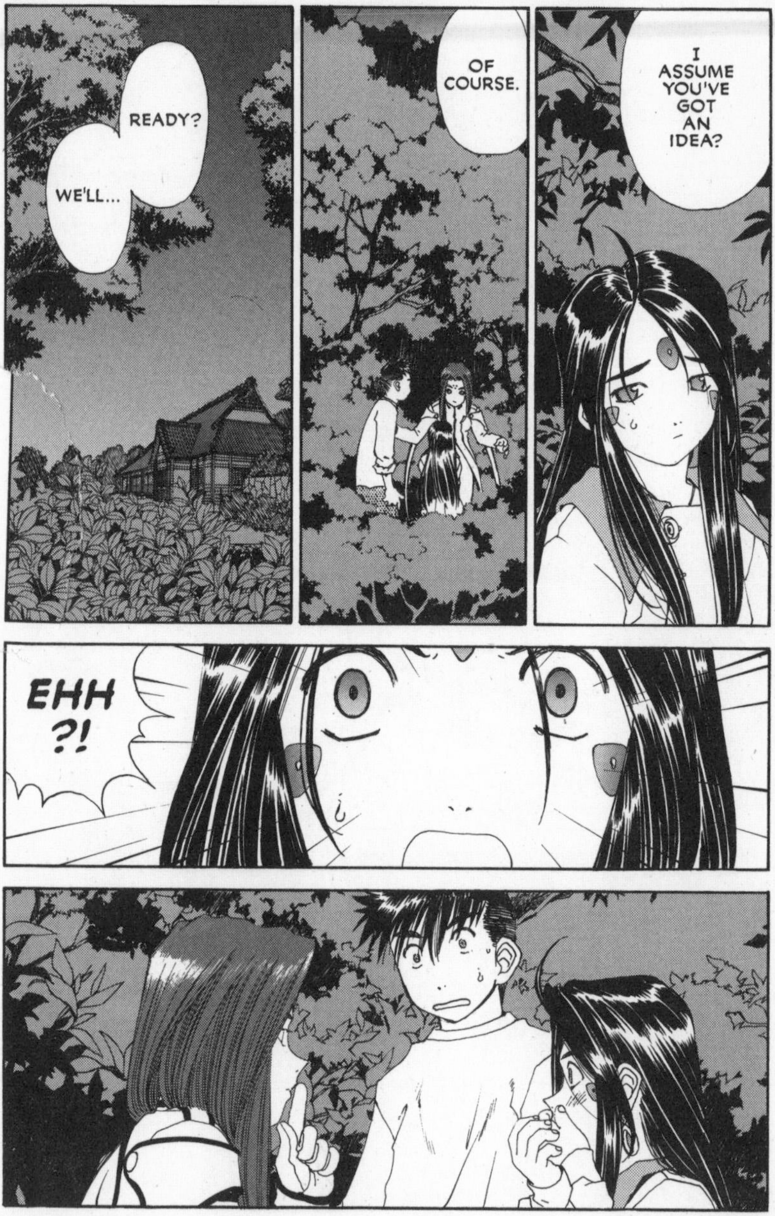
I ASSUME YOU'VE GOT AN IDEA?
OF COURSE.
READY?
WE'LL...
EHH ?!

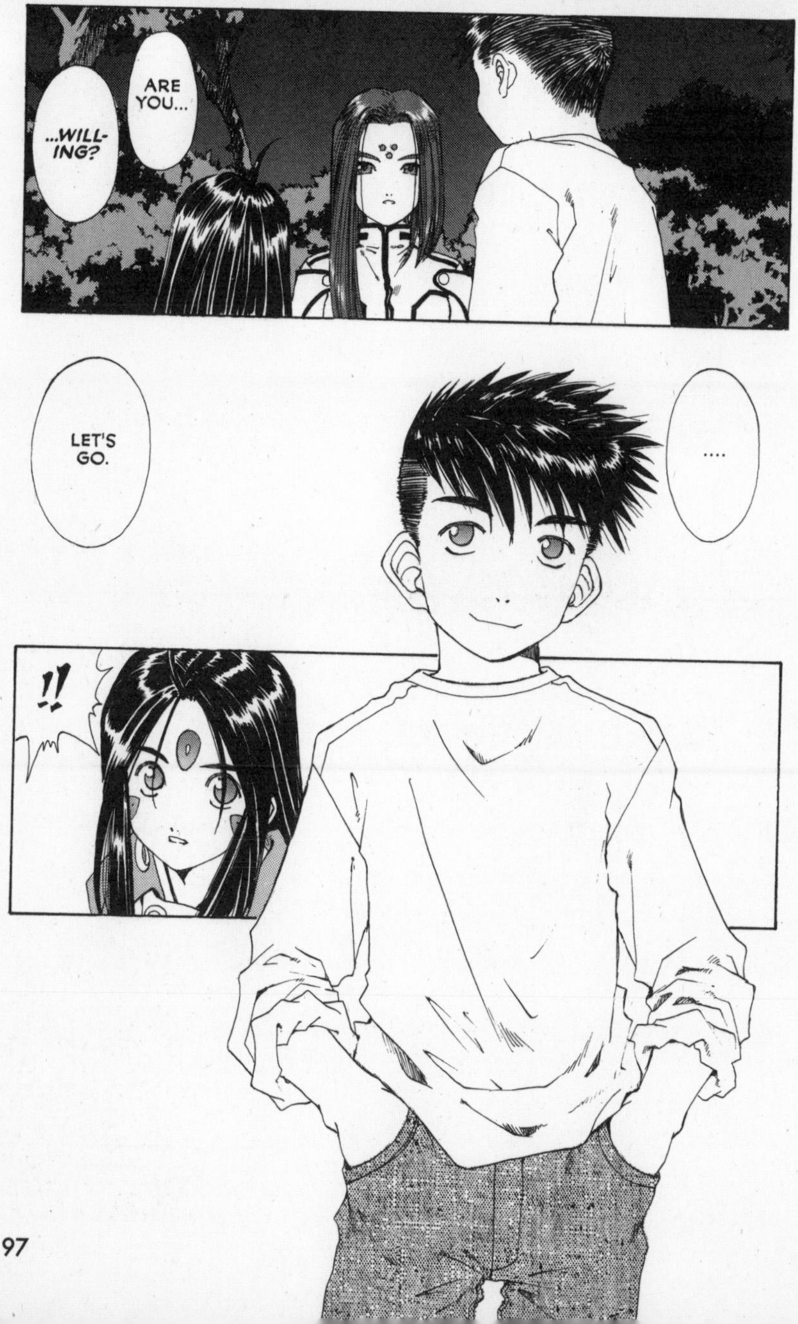
ARE YOU...
...WILL-ING?
....
LET'S GO.
!!

OH MY GODDESS!

DUMMY ANGEL

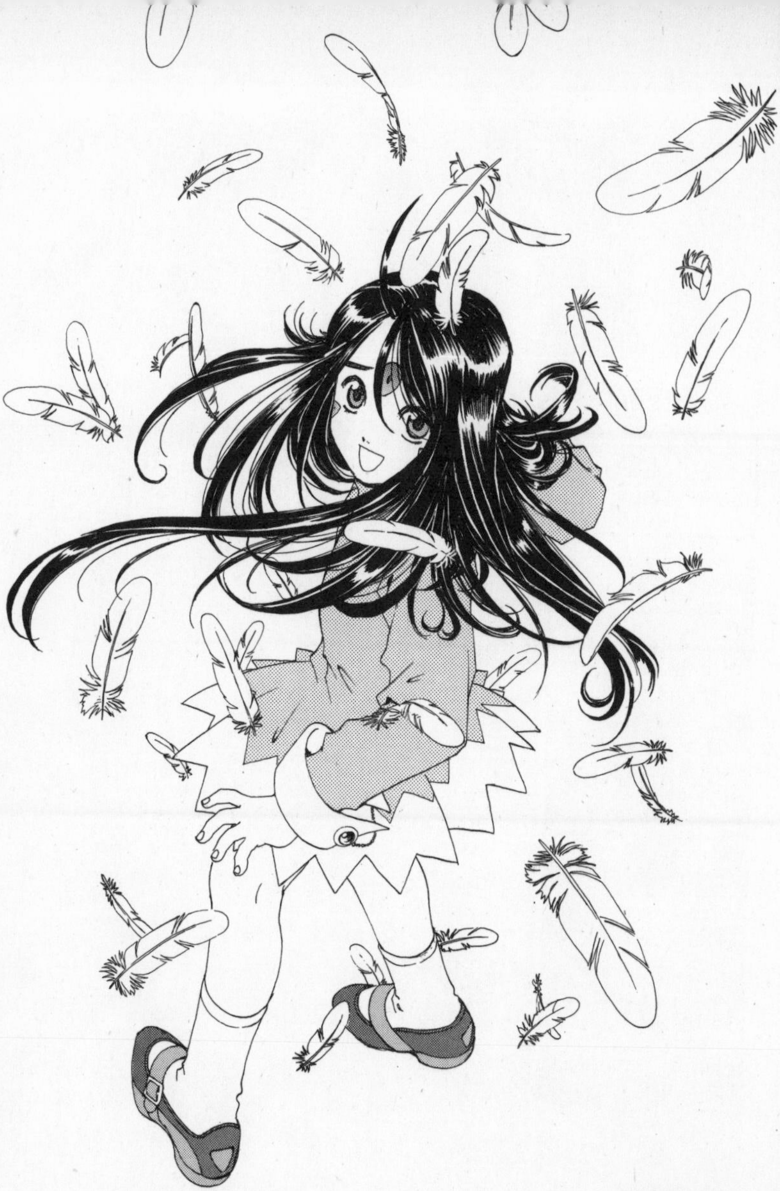

CHAPTER 160

What Times Demand

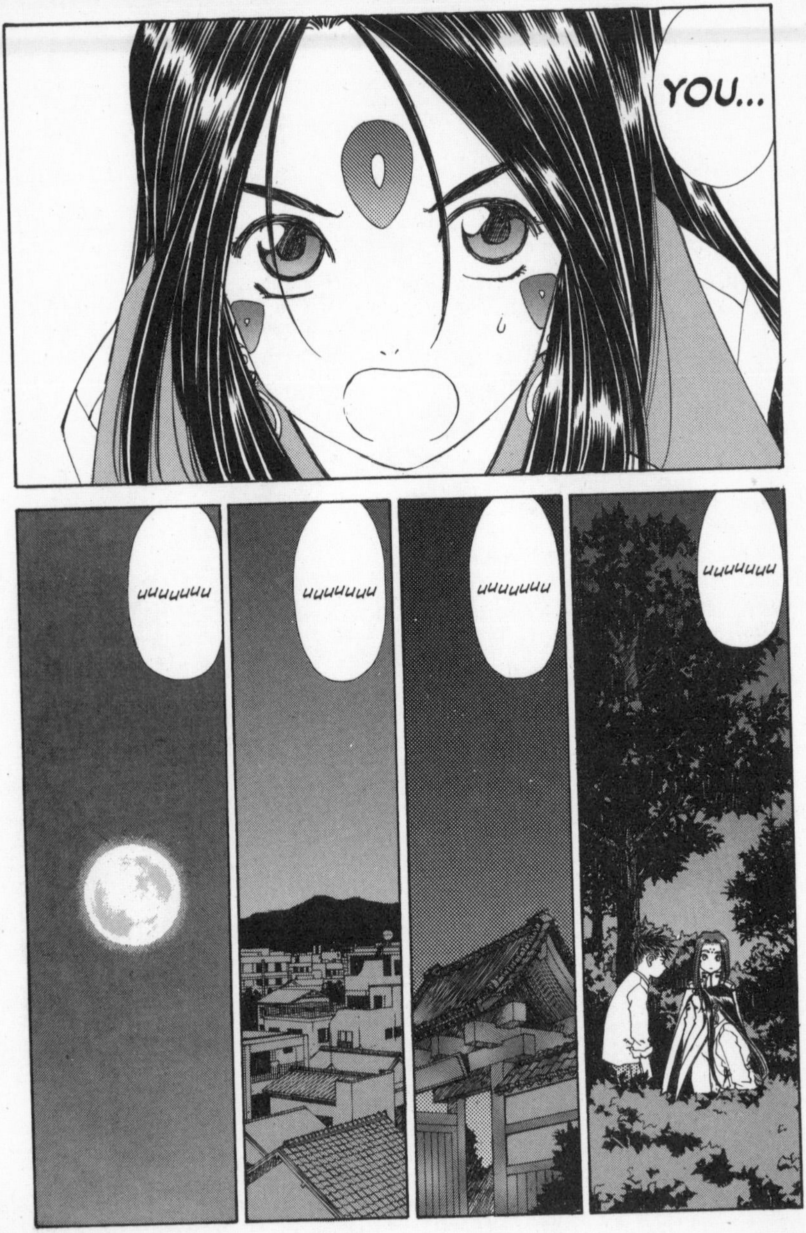
YOU...
uuuuuuu
uuuuuuu
uuuuuuu
uuuuuuu

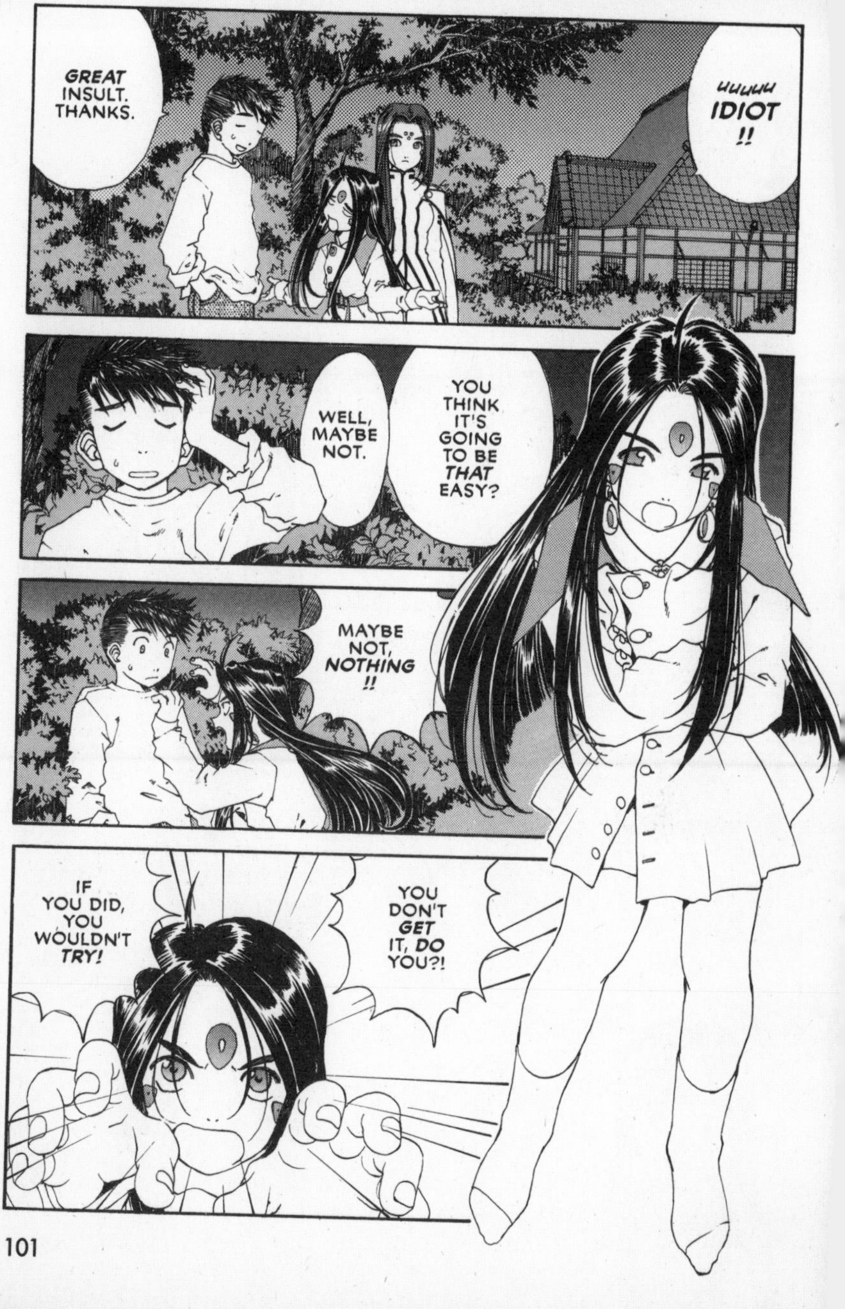
uuuuu IDIOT !!
GREAT INSULT. THANKS.
YOU THINK IT'S GOING TO BE *THAT* EASY?
WELL, MAYBE NOT.
MAYBE NOT, *NOTHING* !!
YOU DON'T *GET* IT, *DO* YOU?!
IF YOU DID, YOU WOULDN'T *TRY!*

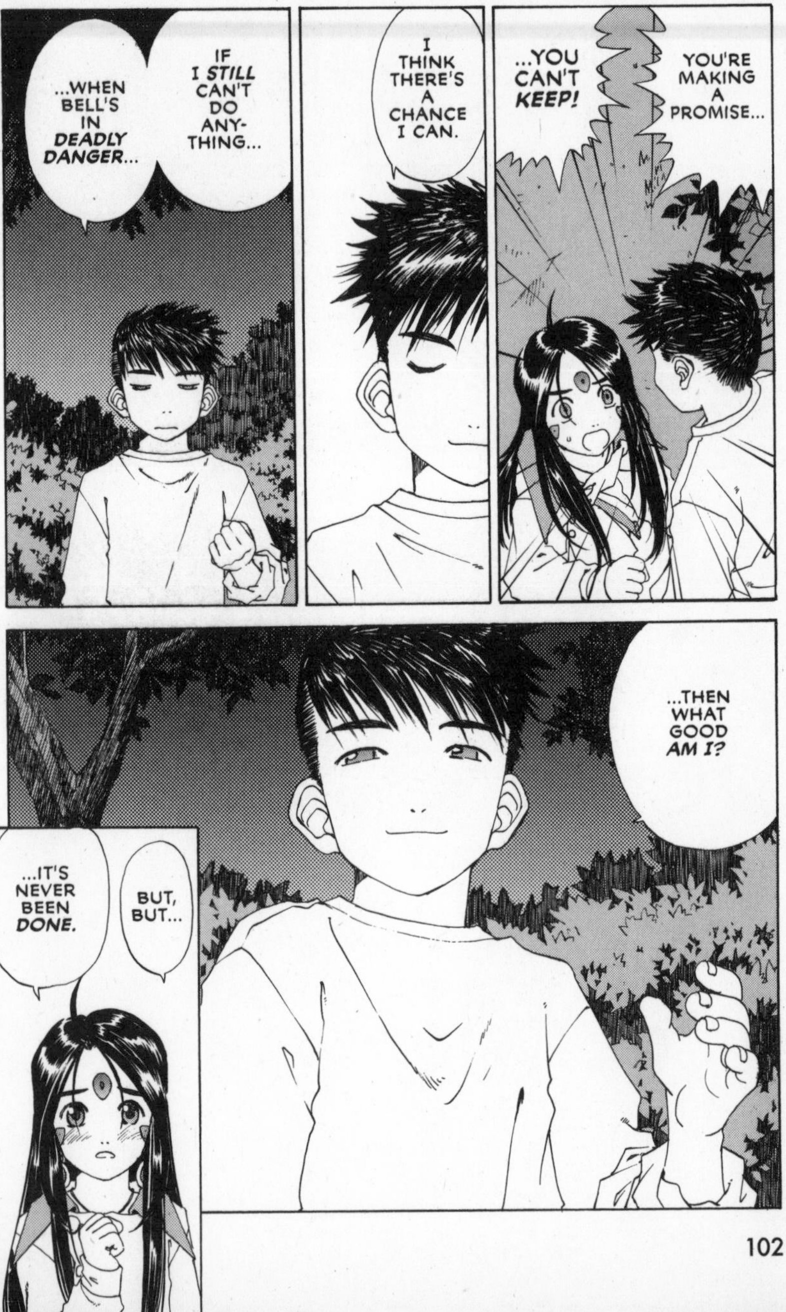
YOU'RE MAKING A PROMISE...
...YOU CAN'T KEEP!
I THINK THERE'S A CHANCE I CAN.
IF I STILL CAN'T DO ANYTHING...
...WHEN BELL'S IN DEADLY DANGER...
...THEN WHAT GOOD AM I?
BUT, BUT...
...IT'S NEVER BEEN DONE.

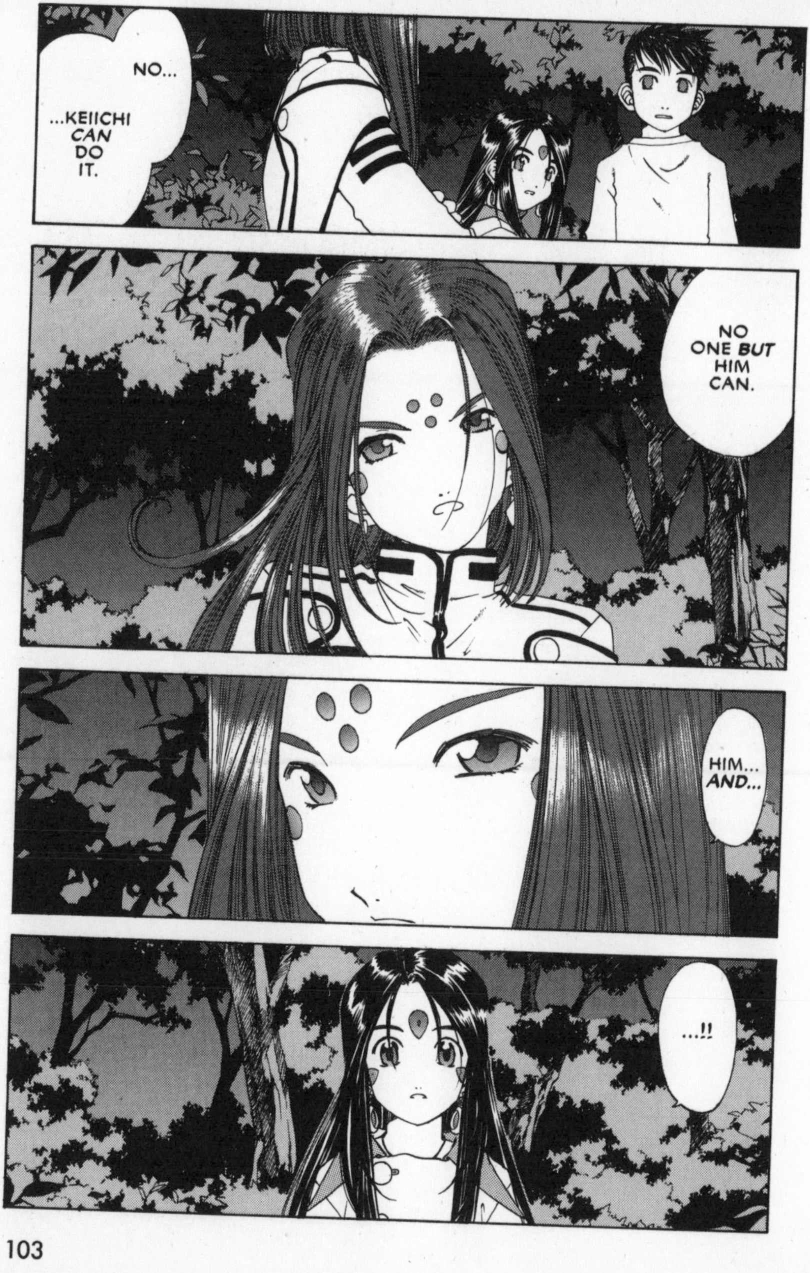
NO...
...KEIICHI CAN DO IT.
NO ONE BUT HIM CAN.
HIM... AND...
...!!

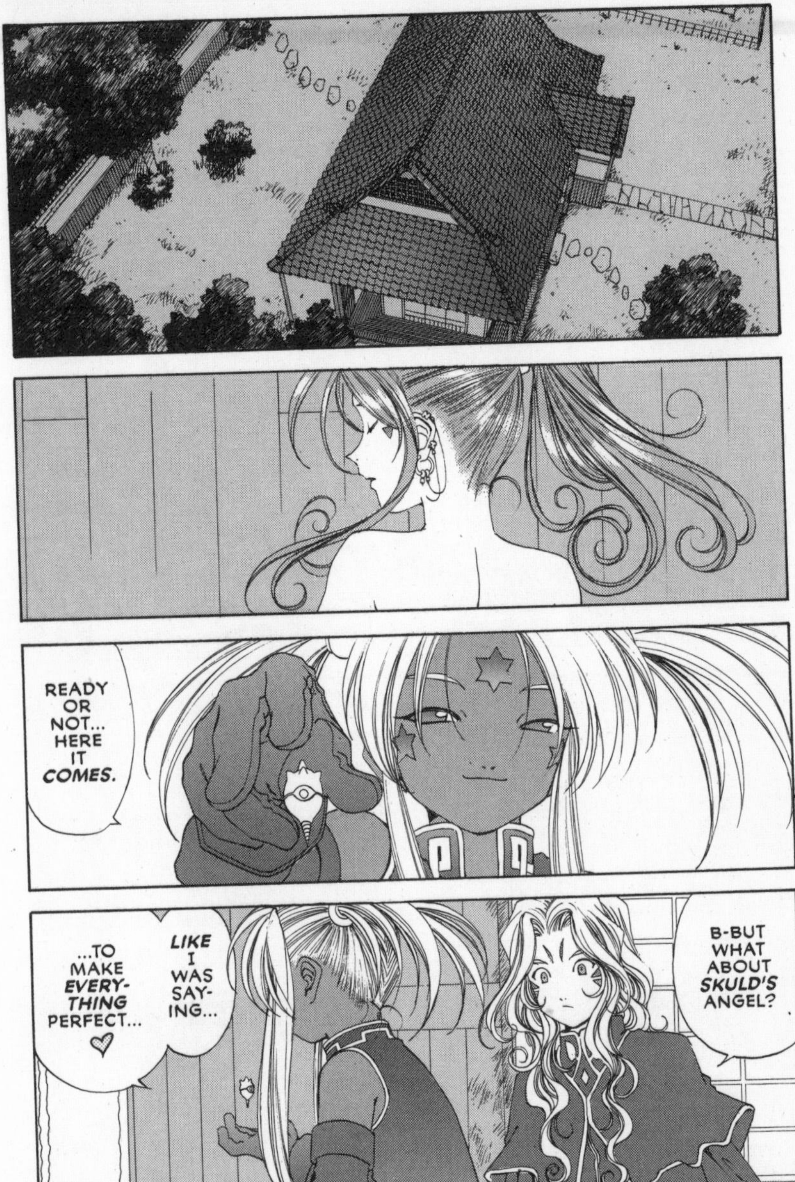
READY OR NOT... HERE IT COMES.
B-BUT WHAT ABOUT SKULD'S ANGEL?
LIKE I WAS SAYING...
...TO MAKE EVERYTHING PERFECT... ♡

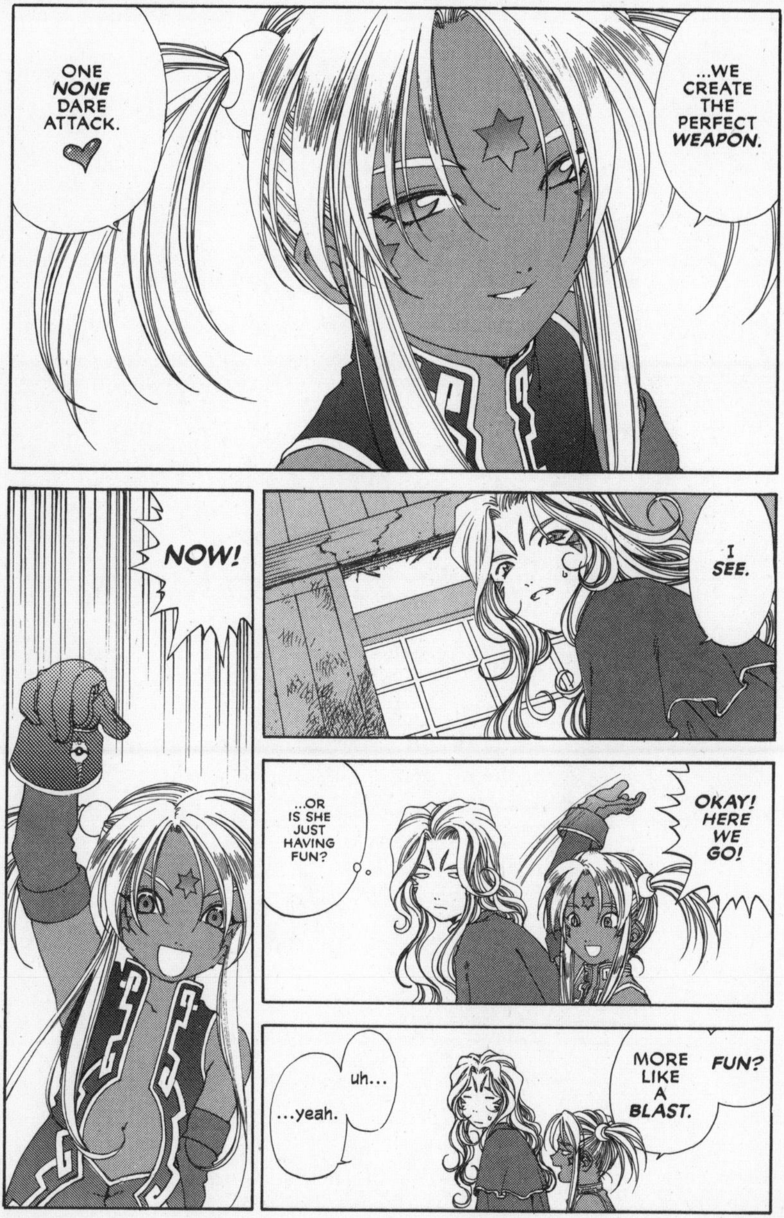
...WE CREATE THE PERFECT WEAPON.
ONE NONE DARE ATTACK. ♥
I SEE.
OKAY! HERE WE GO!
...OR IS SHE JUST HAVING FUN?
FUN?
MORE LIKE A BLAST.
uh...
...yeah.
NOW!

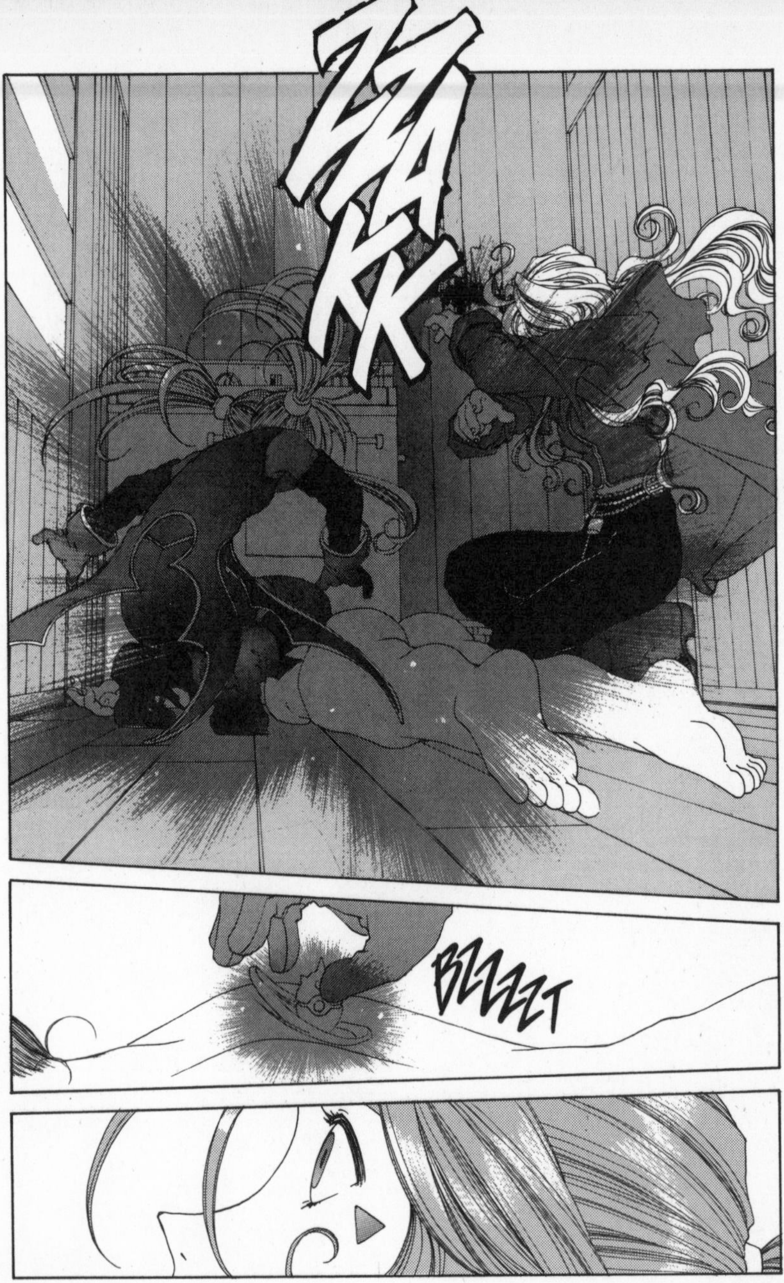
ZAKK
BZZZZT

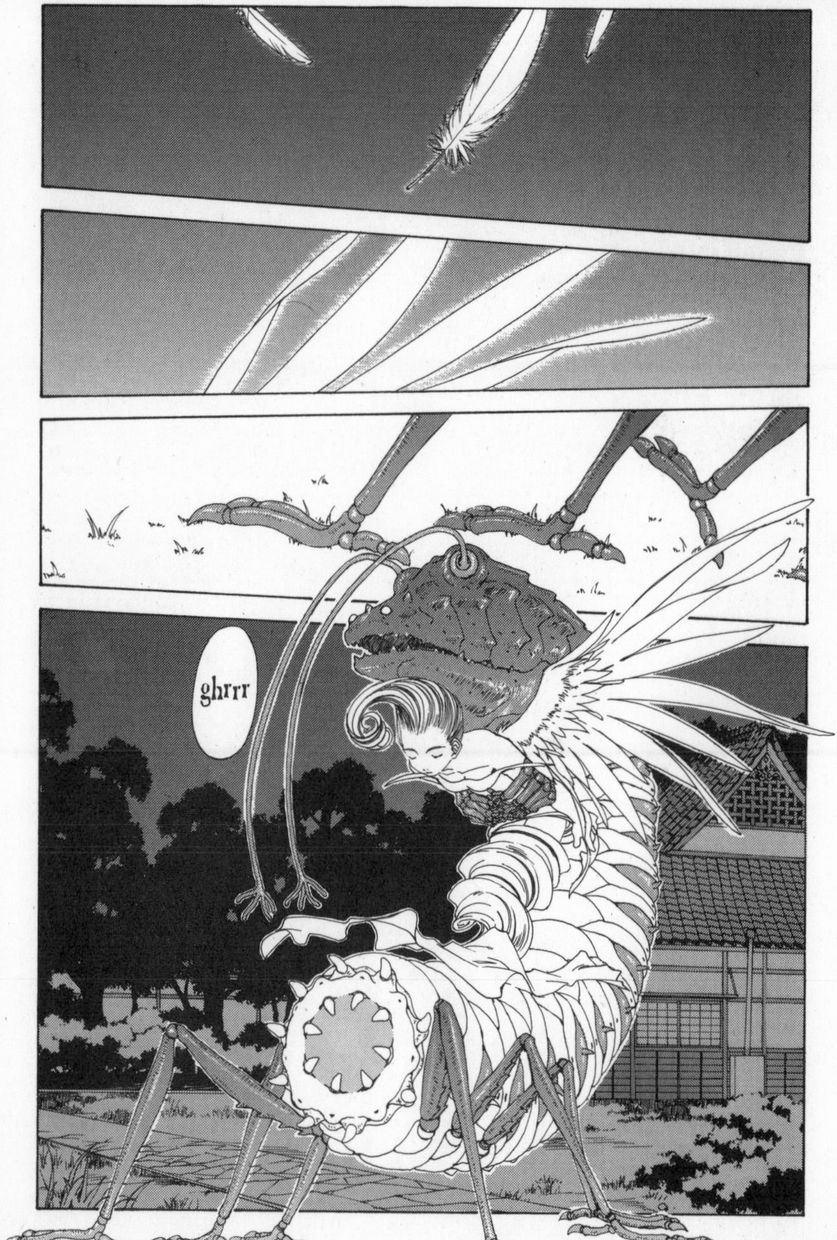
ghrrr

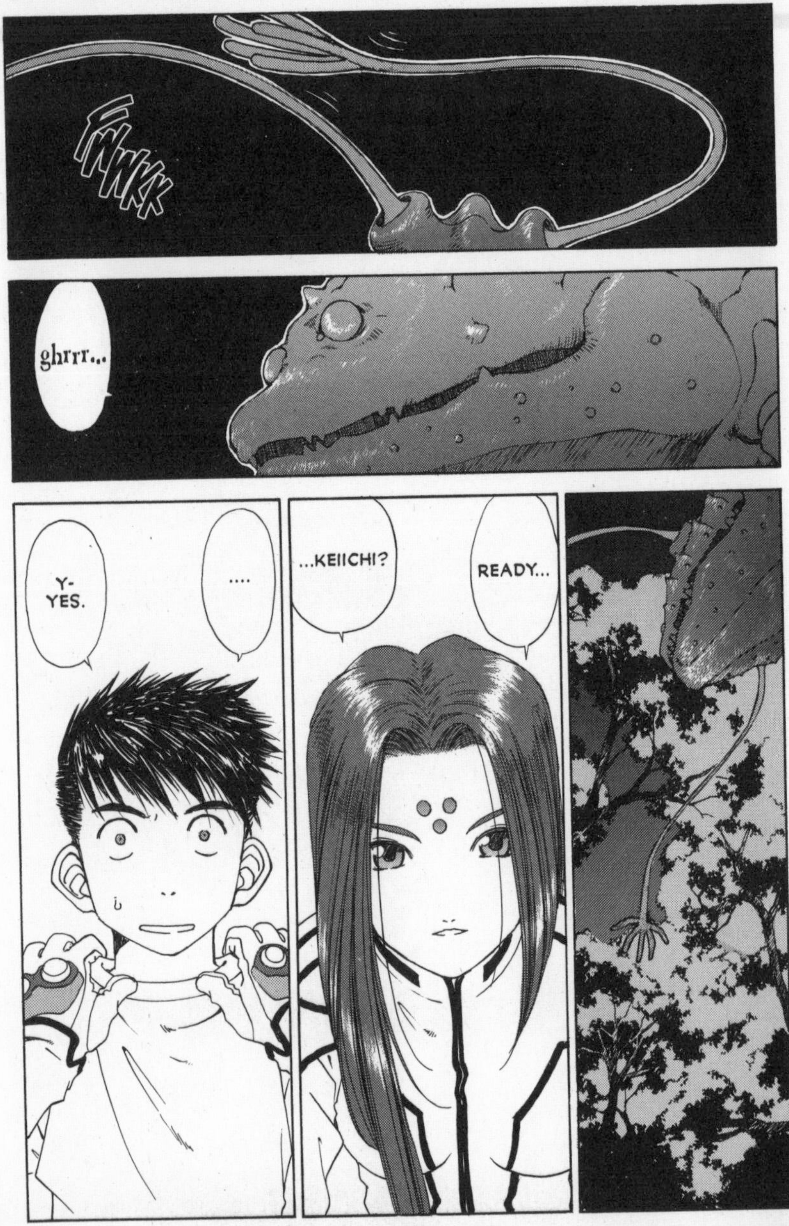
FWWKK
ghrrr...
READY...
...KEIICHI?
....
Y- YES.

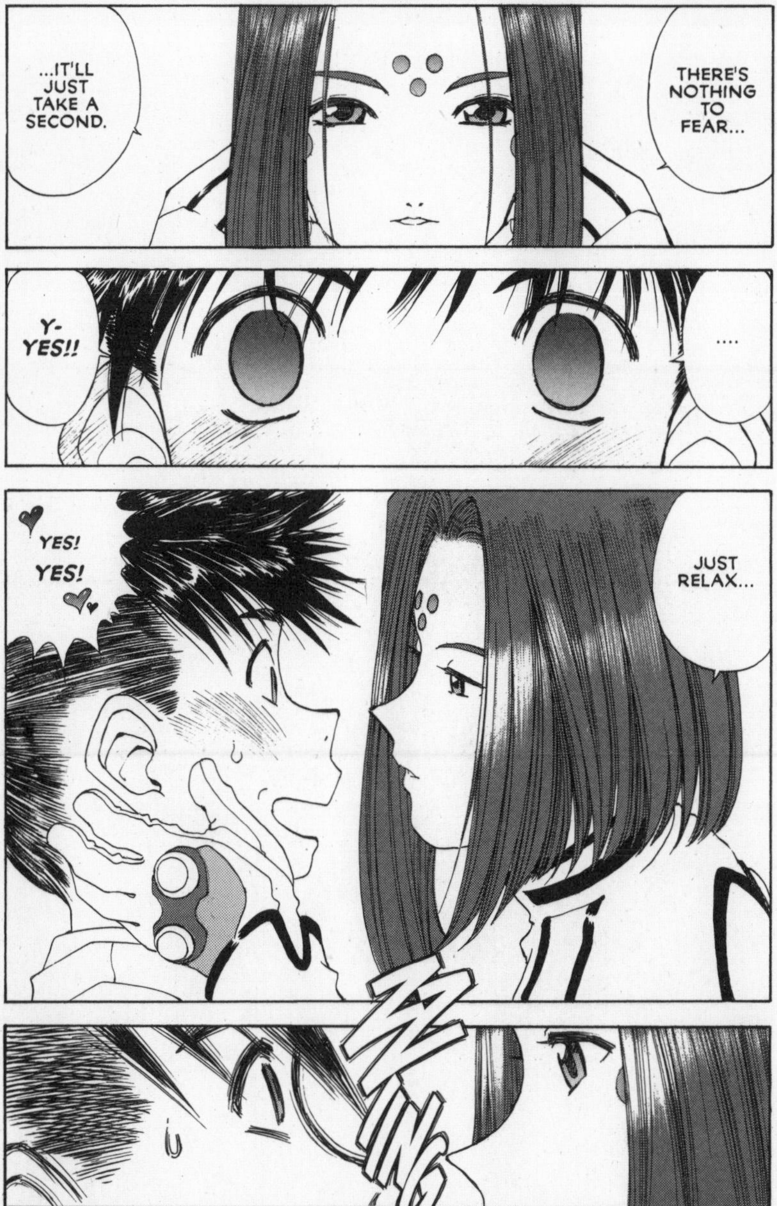
THERE'S NOTHING TO FEAR...
...IT'LL JUST TAKE A SECOND.
....
Y-YES!!
JUST RELAX...
YES! YES!

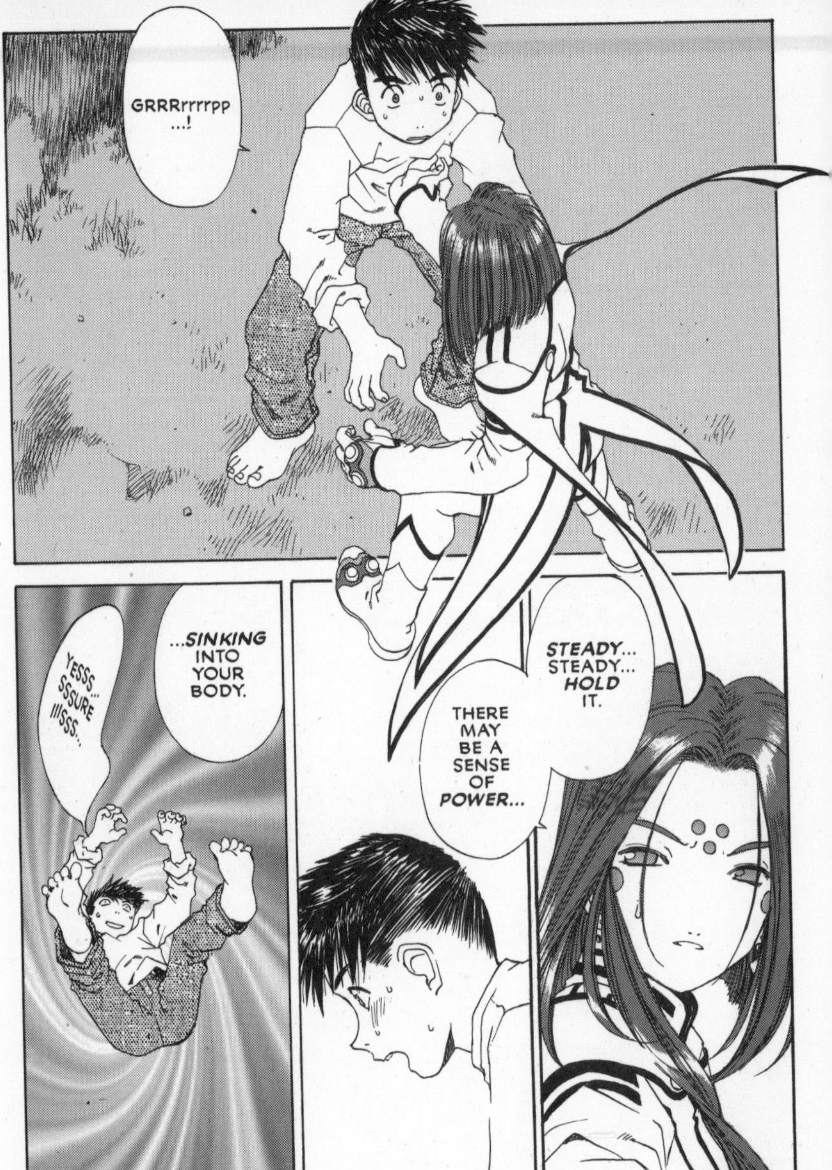
GRRRrrrrpp ...!
STEADY... STEADY... HOLD IT.
THERE MAY BE A SENSE OF POWER...
...SINKING INTO YOUR BODY.
YESSS... SSSURE !!!SSS...

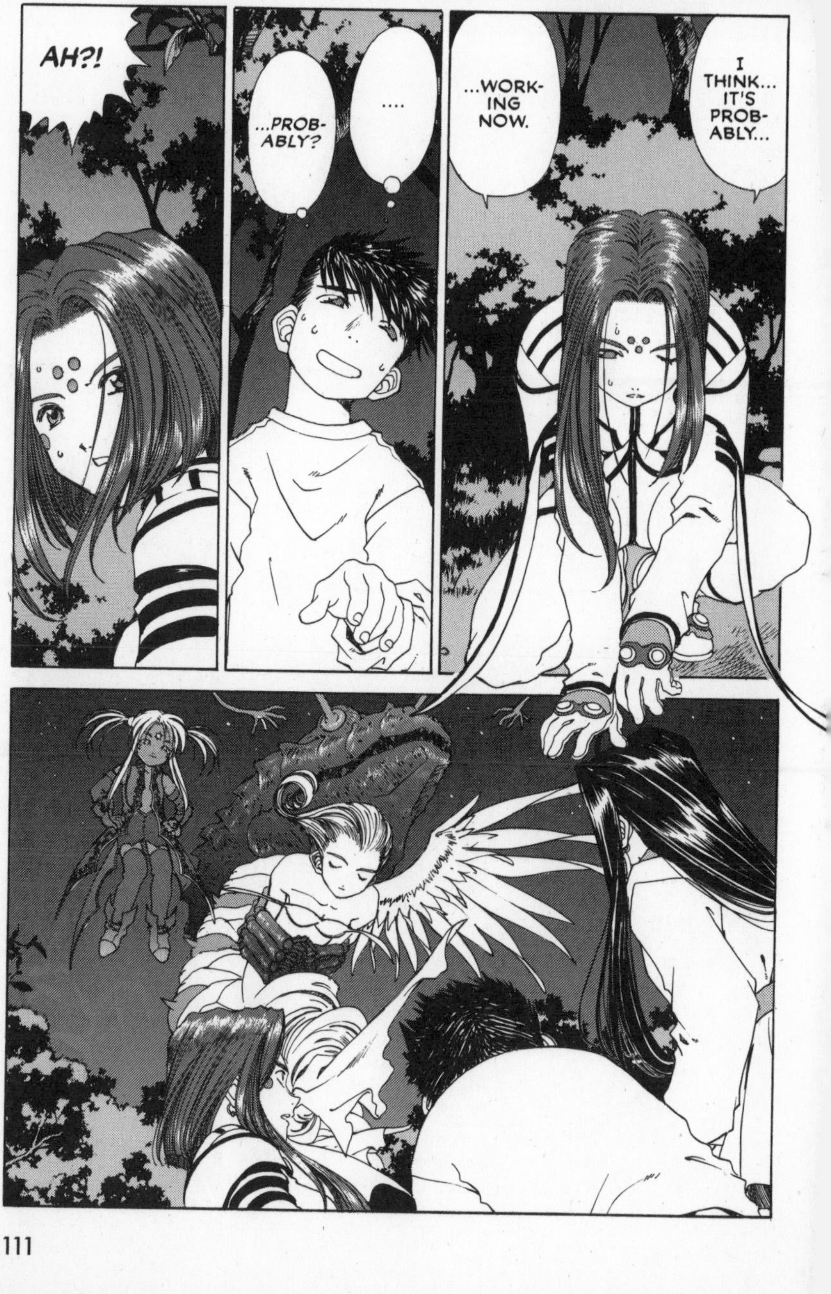
I THINK... IT'S PROBABLY...
...WORKING NOW.
....
...PROBABLY?
AH?!

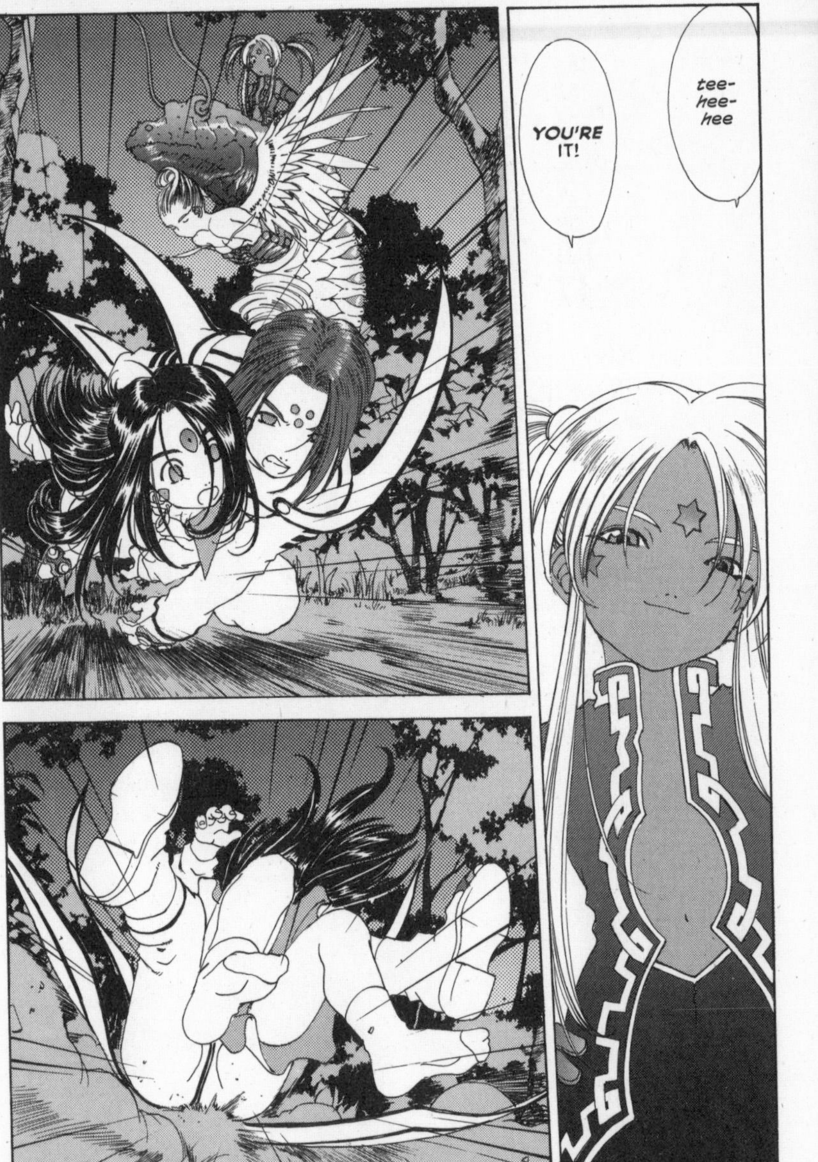
tee-hee-hee
YOU'RE IT!

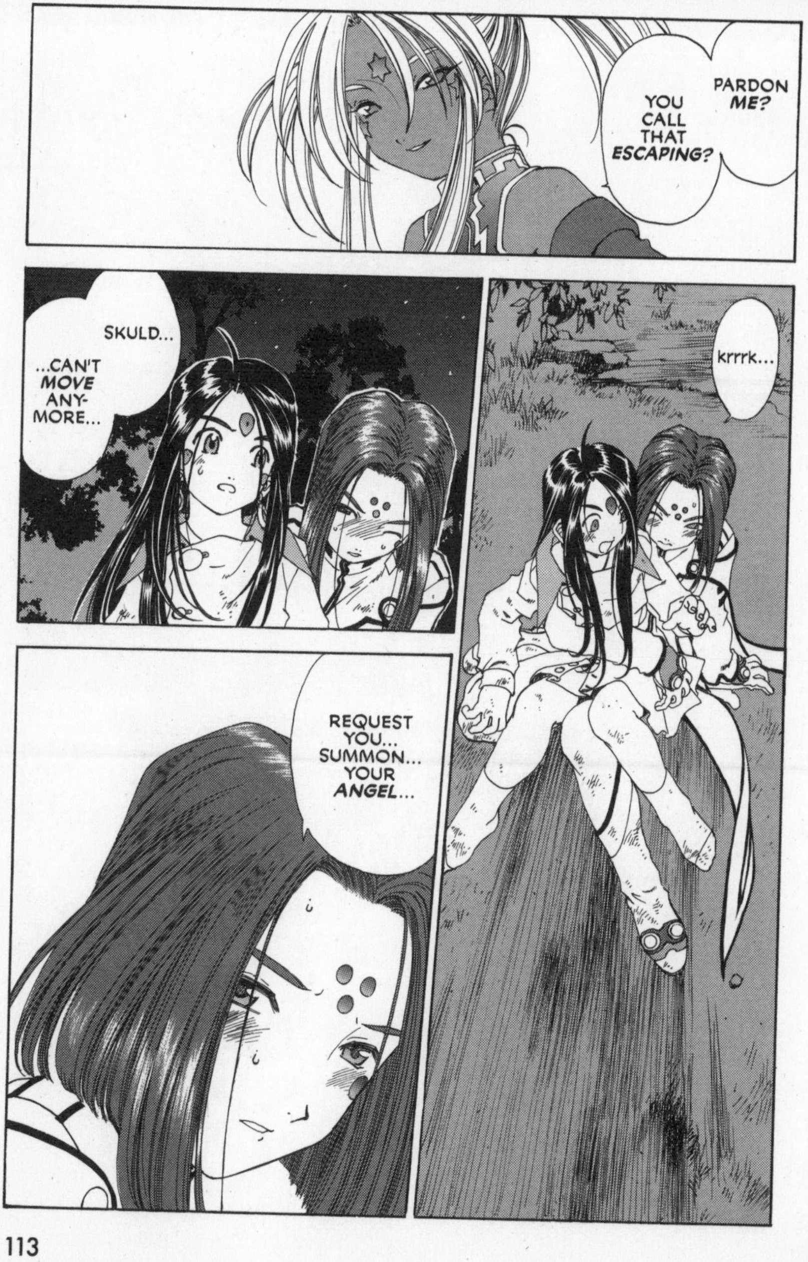
PARDON ME?
YOU CALL THAT ESCAPING?
krrrk...
SKULD... ...CAN'T MOVE ANY-MORE...
REQUEST YOU... SUMMON... YOUR ANGEL...

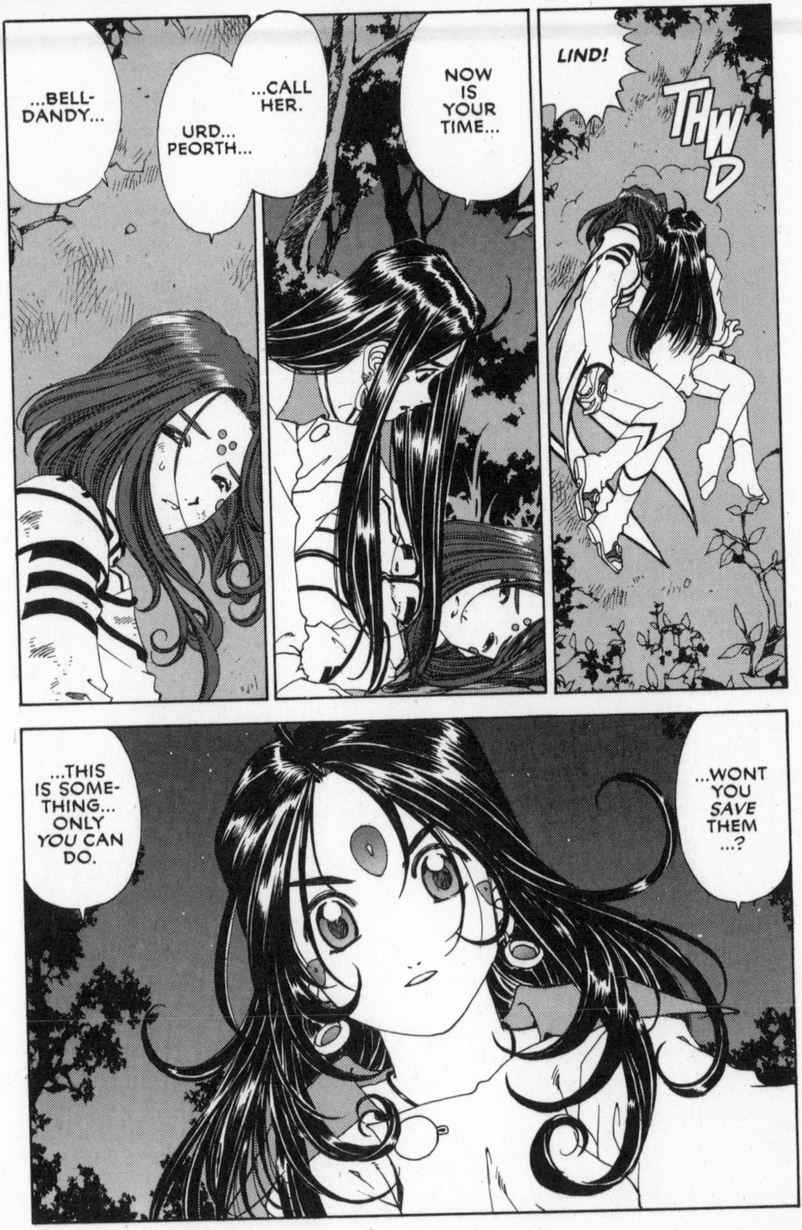
LIND!
THWD
NOW IS YOUR TIME...
...CALL HER.
URD... PEORTH...
...BELL-DANDY...
...WONT YOU *SAVE* THEM ...?
...THIS IS SOME-THING... ONLY *YOU* CAN DO.

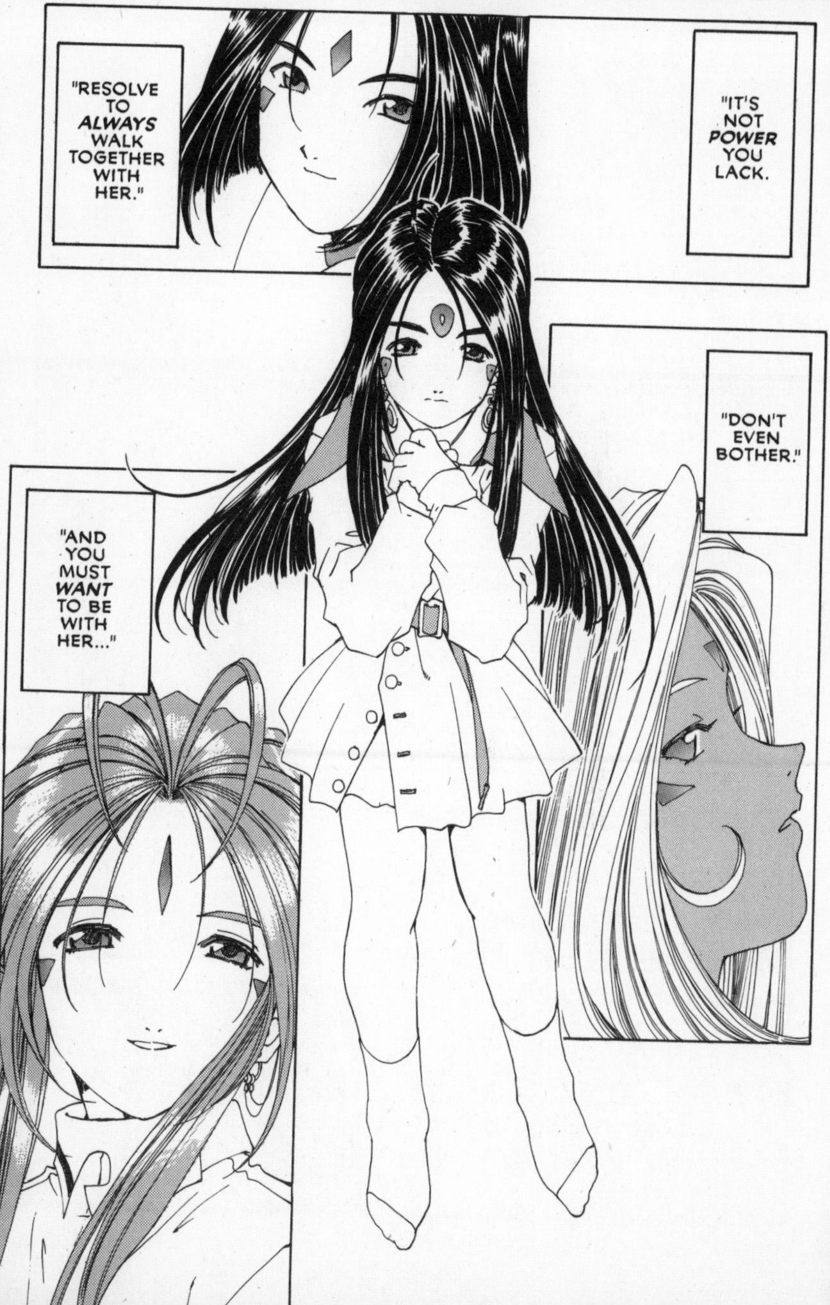
"IT'S NOT ***POWER*** YOU LACK.
"RESOLVE TO ***ALWAYS*** WALK TOGETHER WITH HER."
"DON'T EVEN BOTHER."
"AND YOU MUST ***WANT*** TO BE WITH HER..."

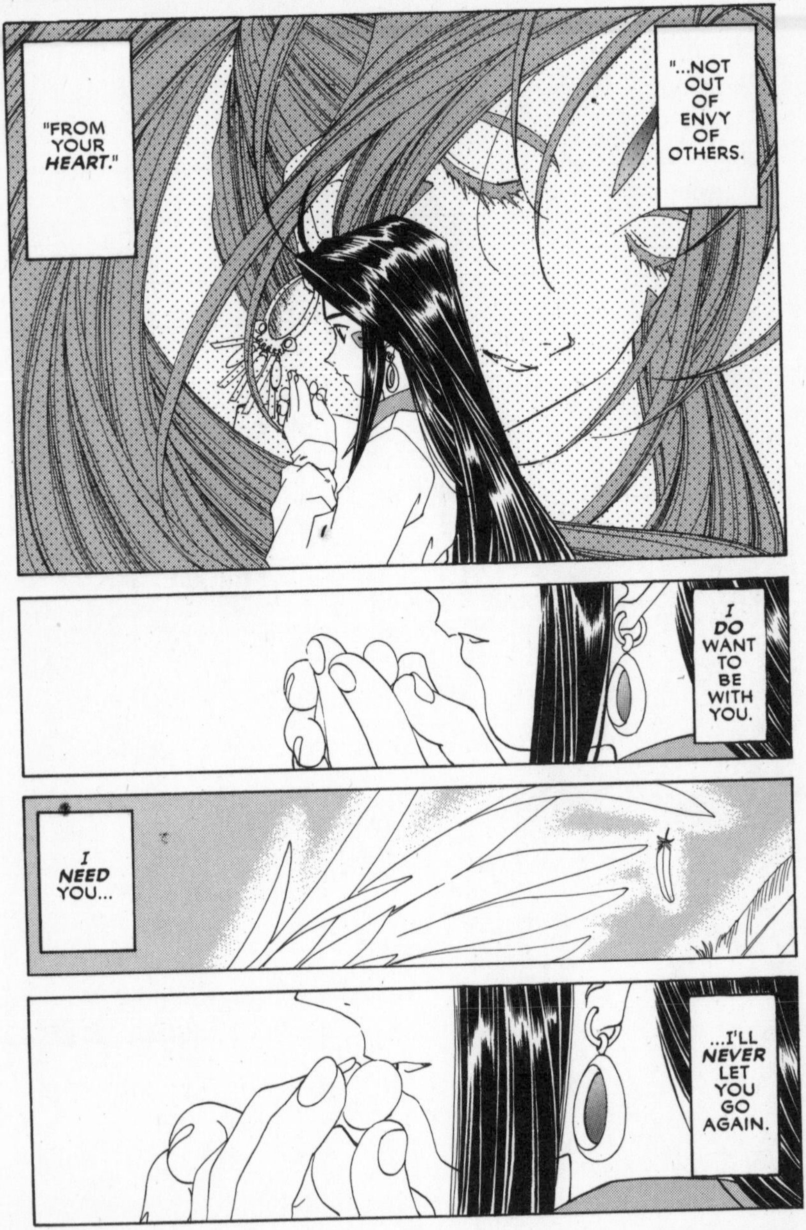
"...NOT OUT OF ENVY OF OTHERS.
"FROM YOUR *HEART.*"
I DO WANT TO BE WITH YOU.
I NEED YOU...
...I'LL *NEVER* LET YOU GO AGAIN.

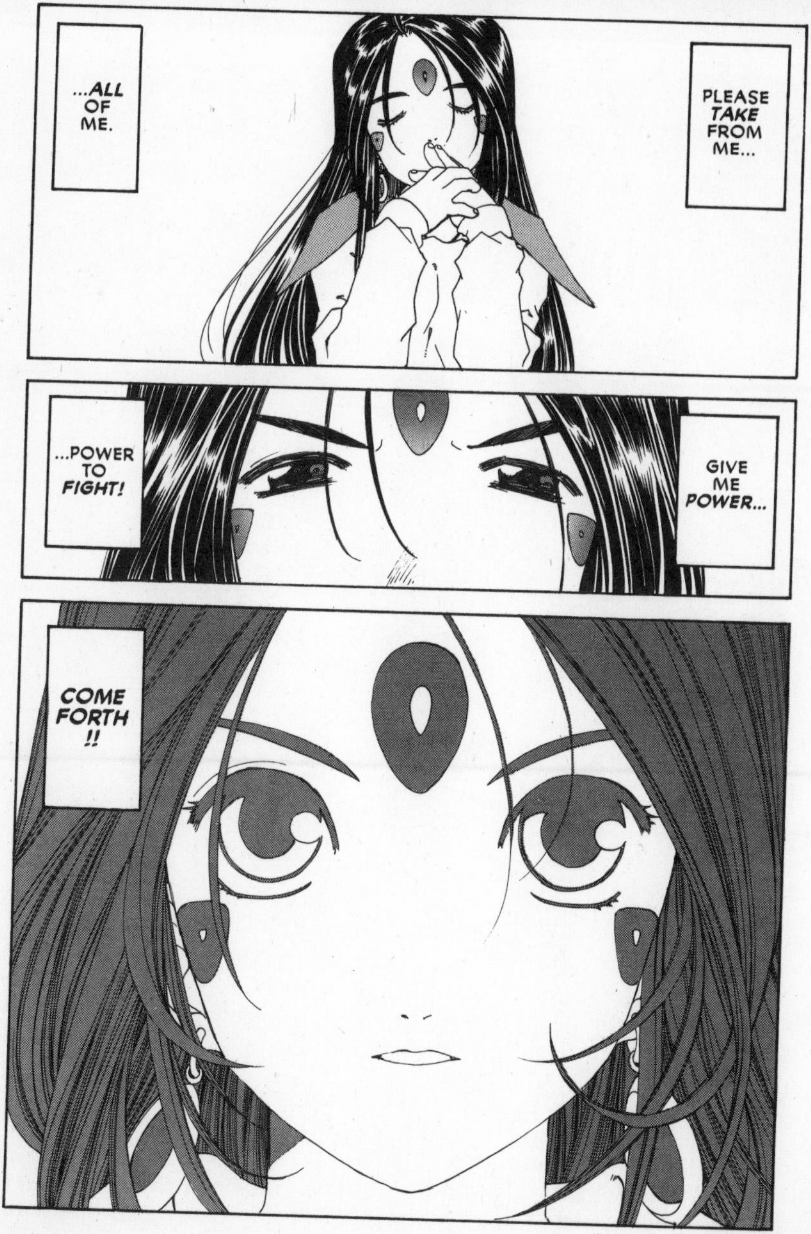
PLEASE *TAKE* FROM ME...
...*ALL* OF ME.
GIVE ME *POWER*...
...POWER TO *FIGHT!*
COME FORTH !!

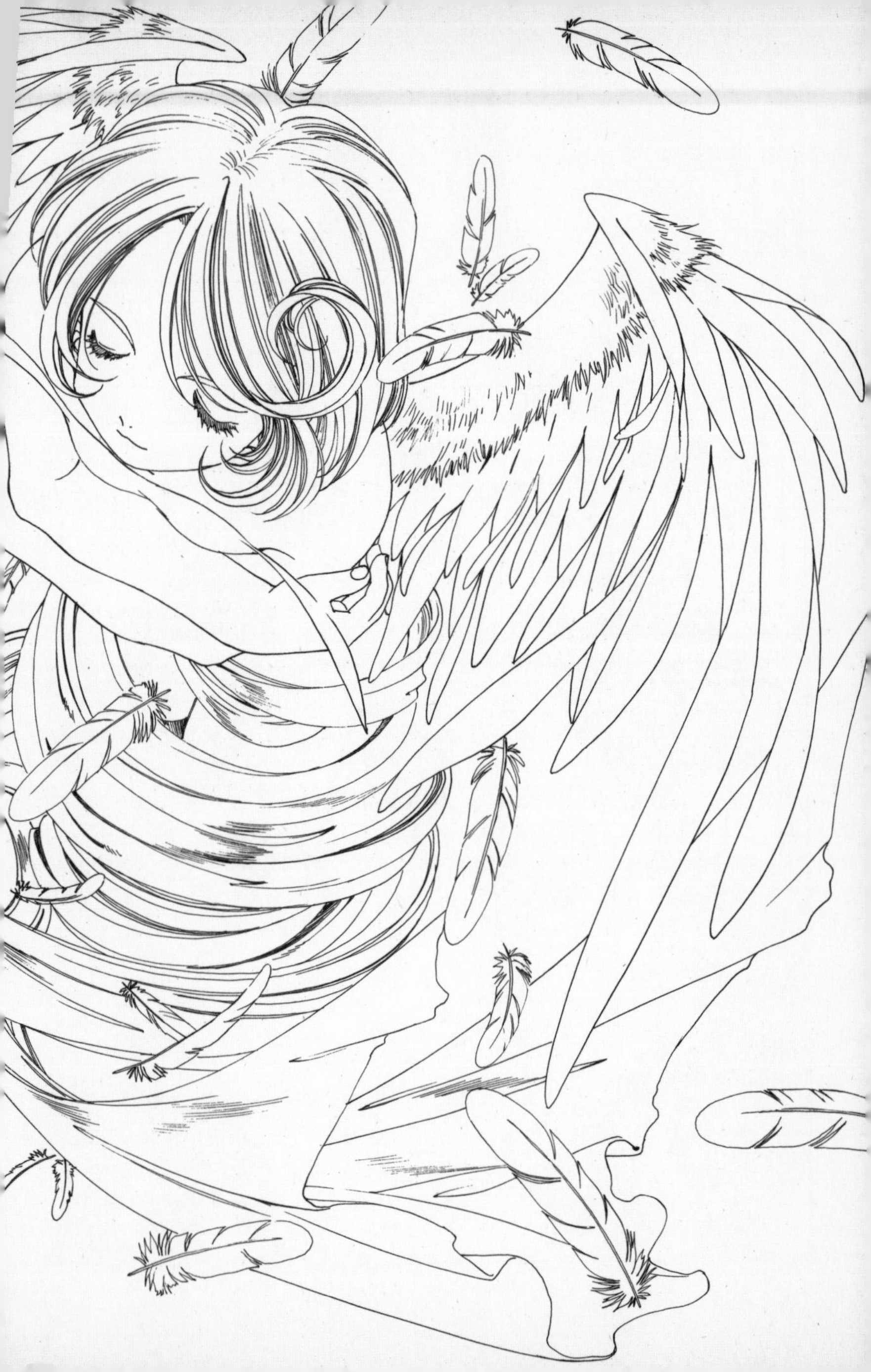

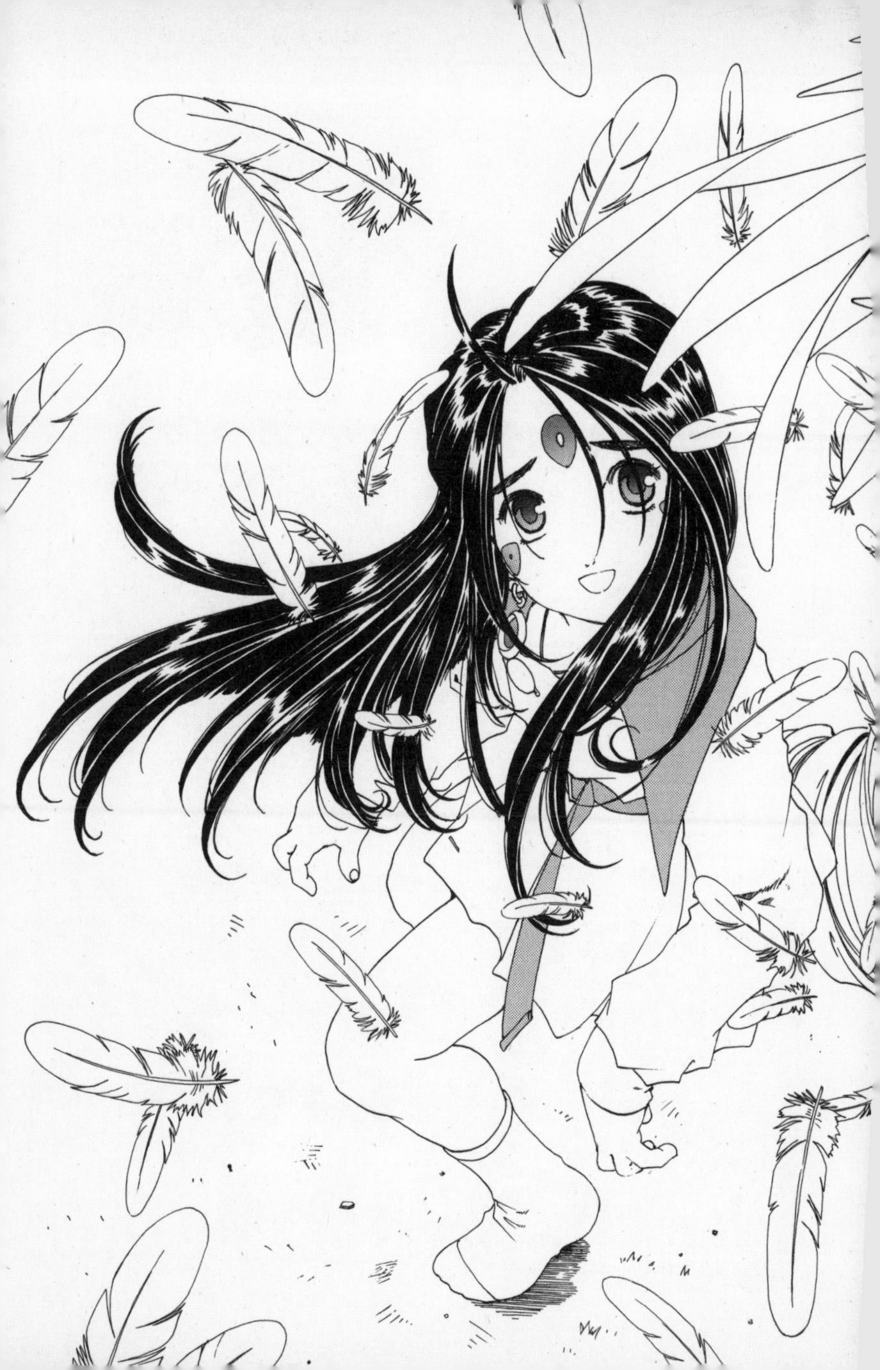

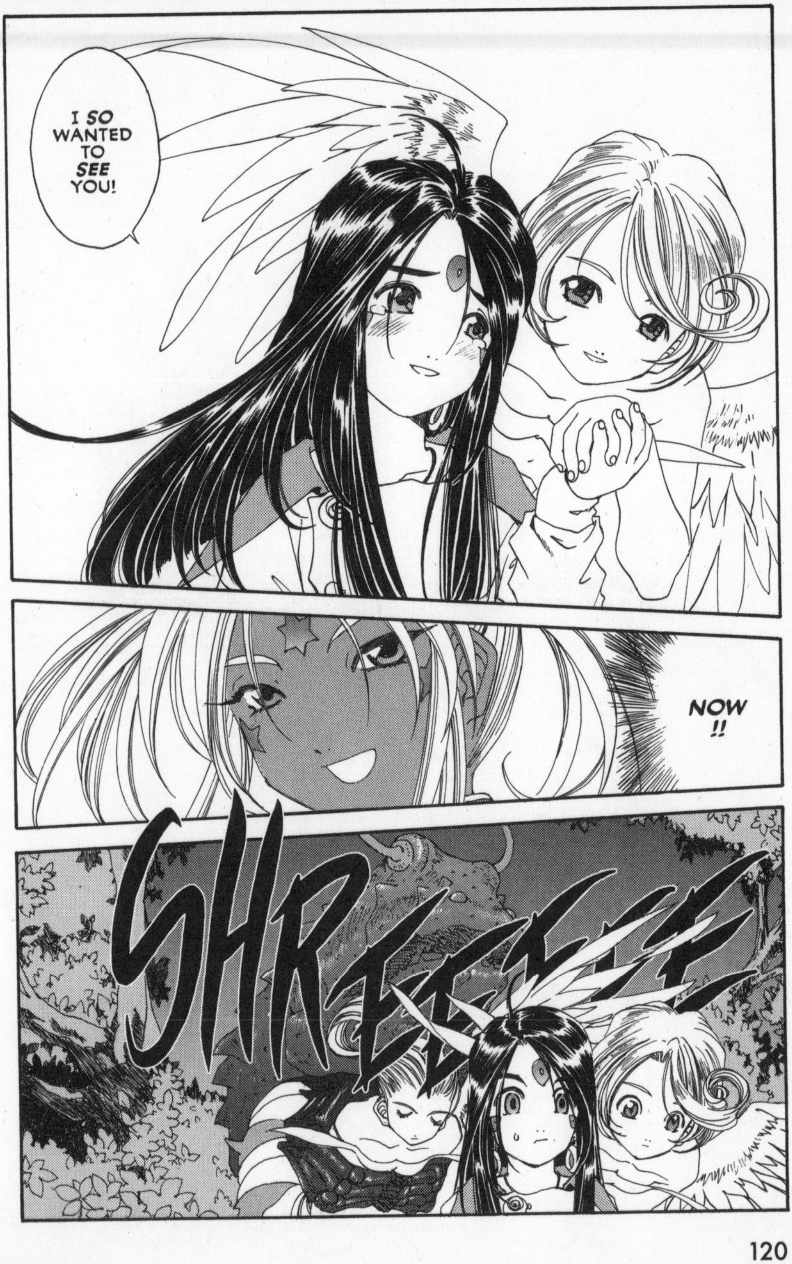
I SO WANTED TO SEE YOU!
NOW !!

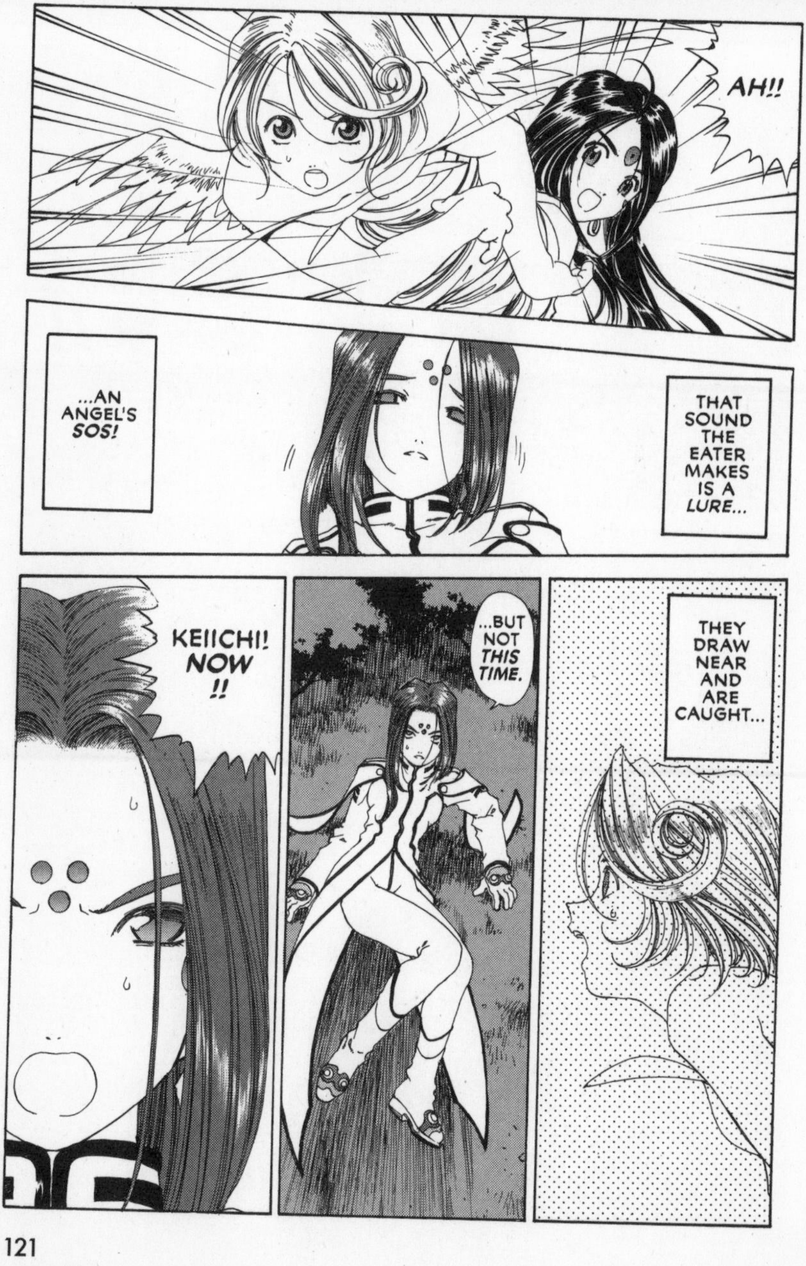
AH!!
THAT SOUND THE EATER MAKES IS A *LURE*...
...AN ANGEL'S *SOS!*
THEY DRAW NEAR AND ARE CAUGHT...
...BUT NOT *THIS TIME.*
KEIICHI! *NOW* !!

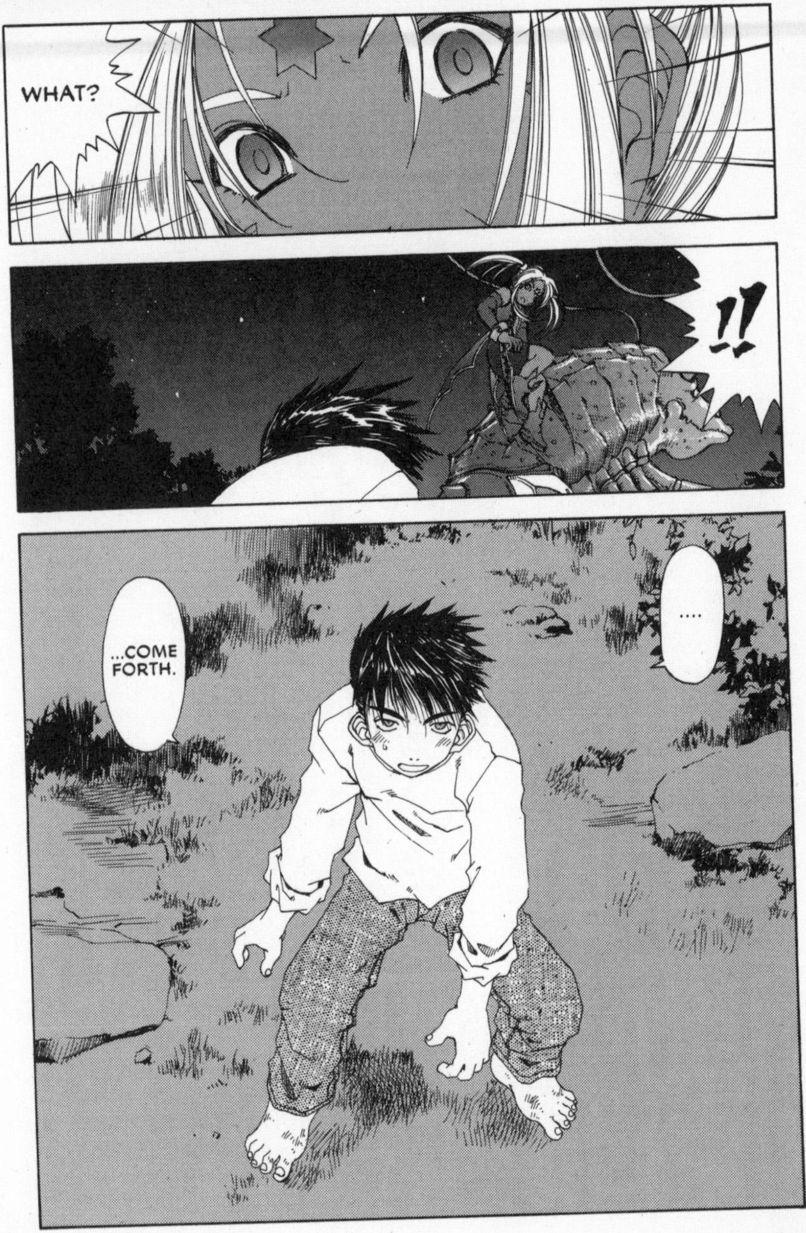
WHAT?
!!
....
...COME FORTH.

CHAPTER 161

Binary Wings

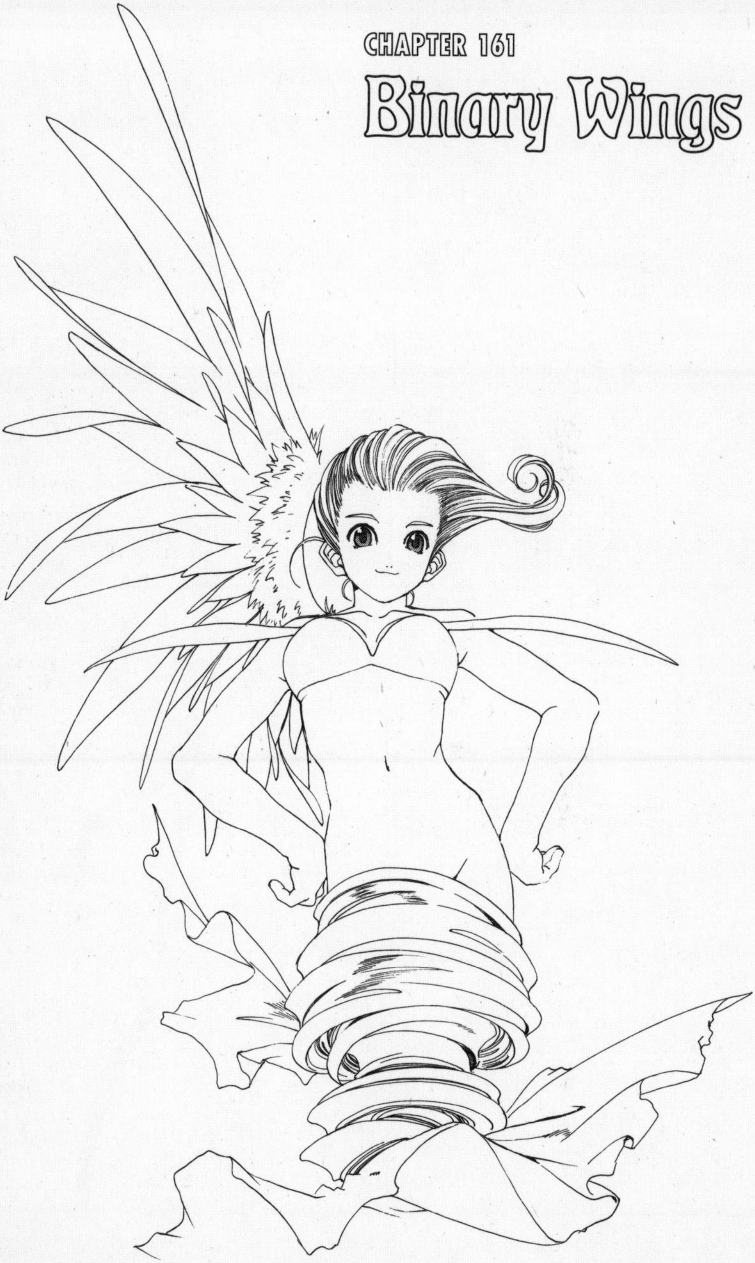

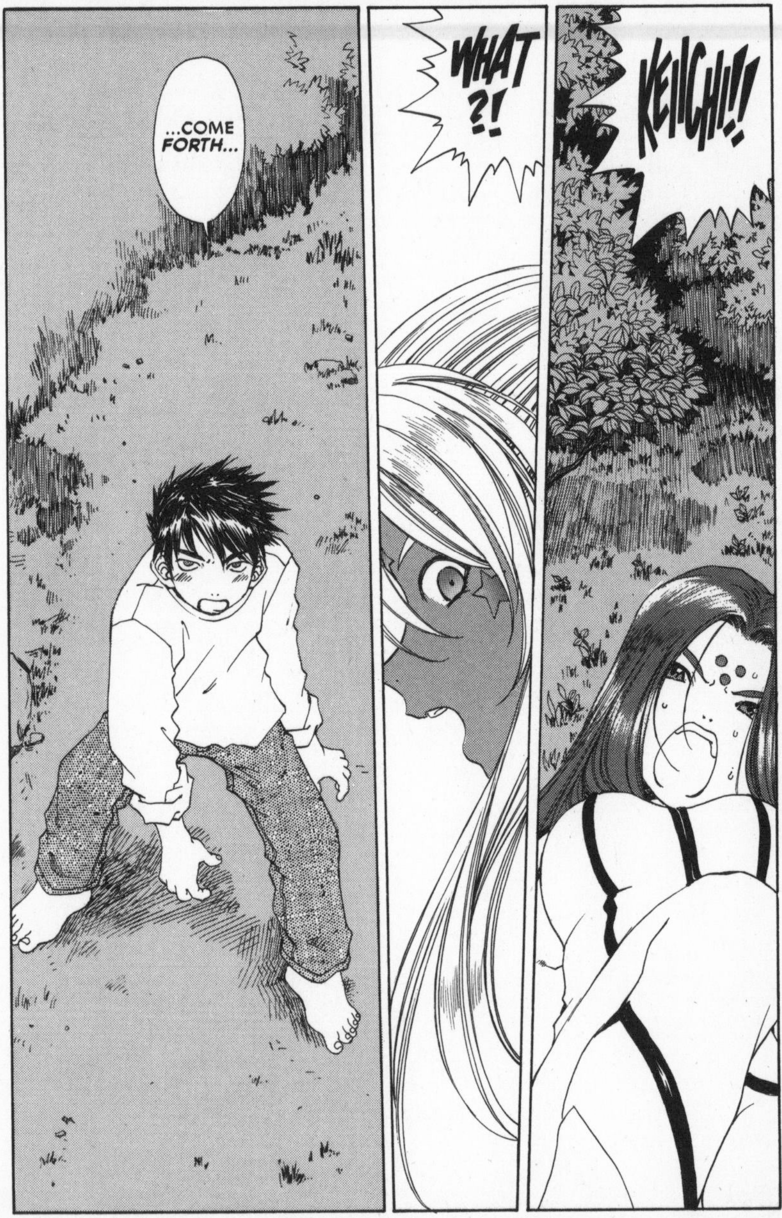
KEIICHI!!
WHAT ?!
...COME FORTH...

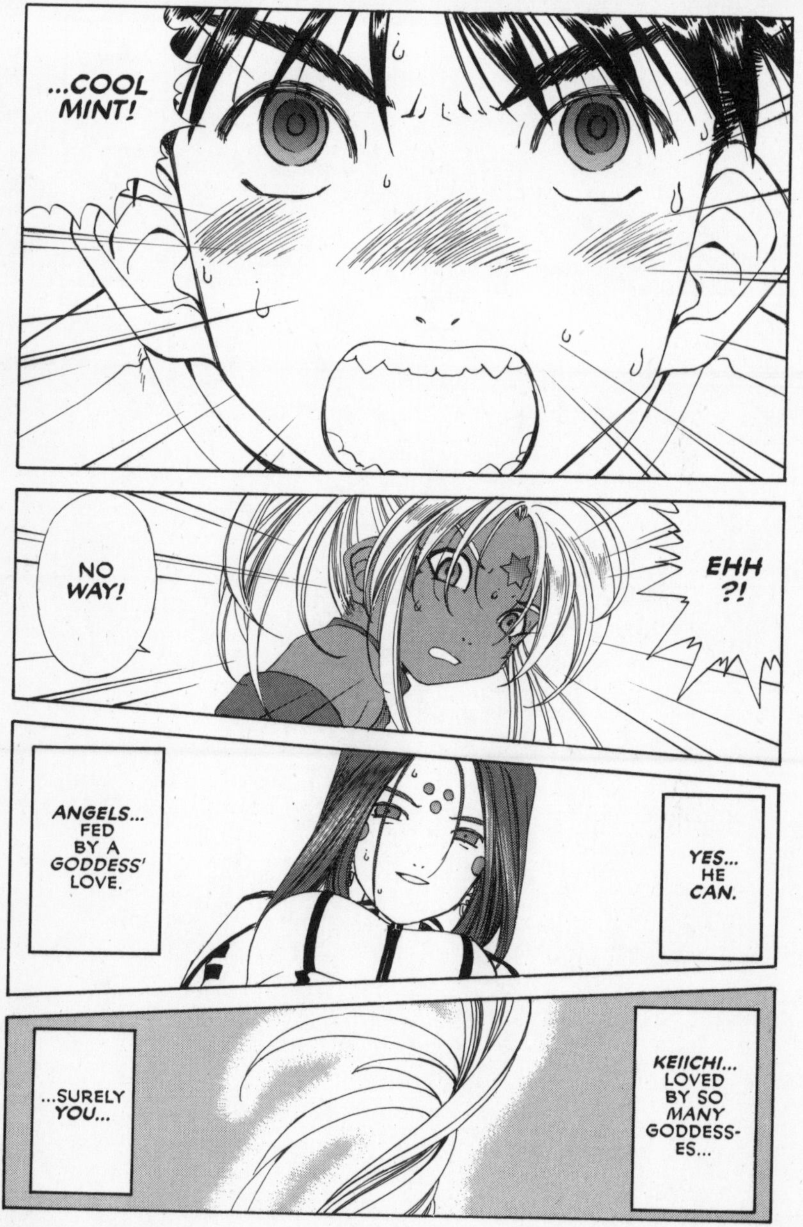
...COOL MINT!
EHH ?!
NO WAY!
YES... HE CAN.
ANGELS... FED BY A GODDESS' LOVE.
KEIICHI... LOVED BY SO MANY GODDESS-ES...
...SURELY YOU...

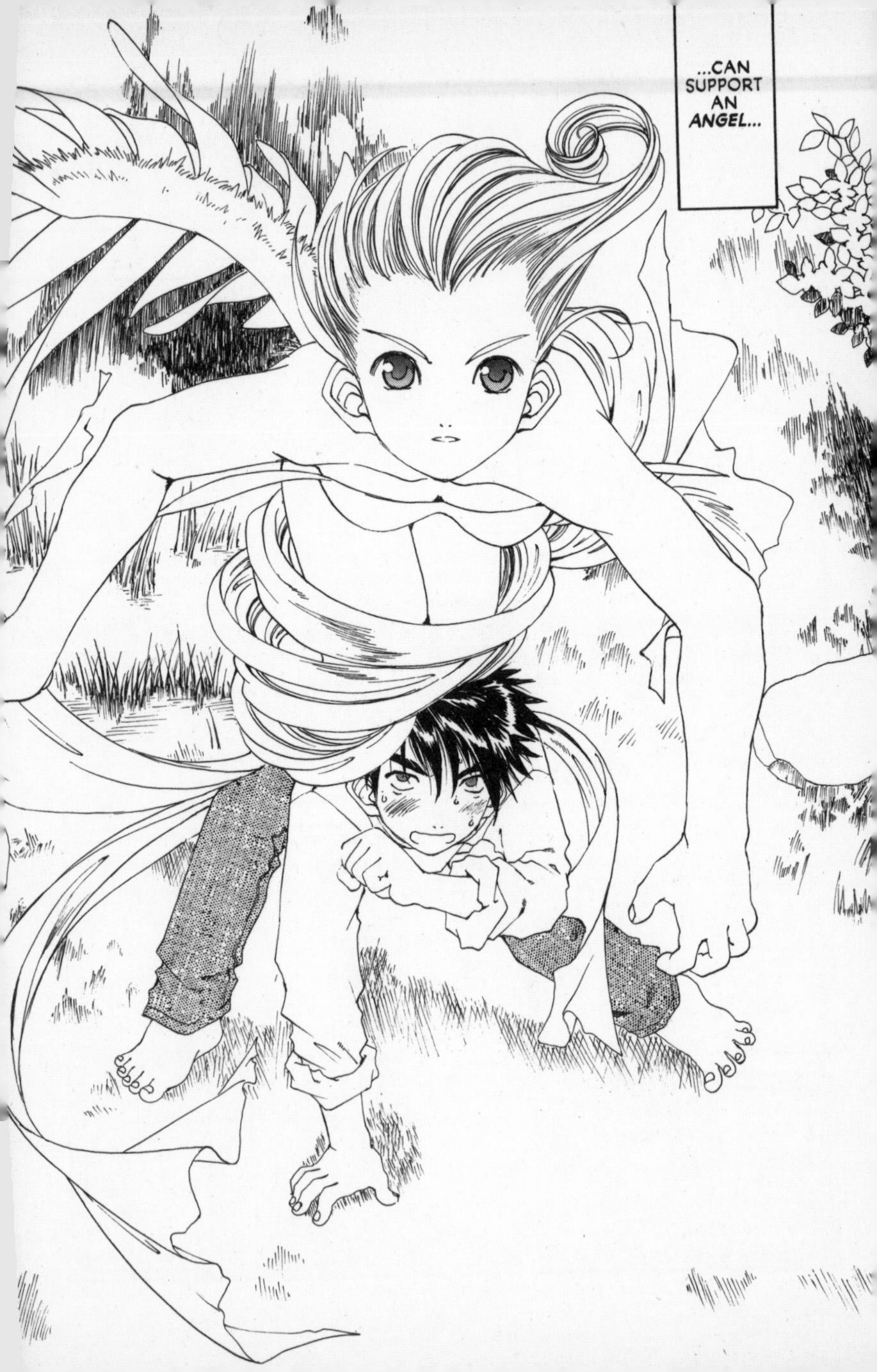
...CAN SUPPORT AN ANGEL...

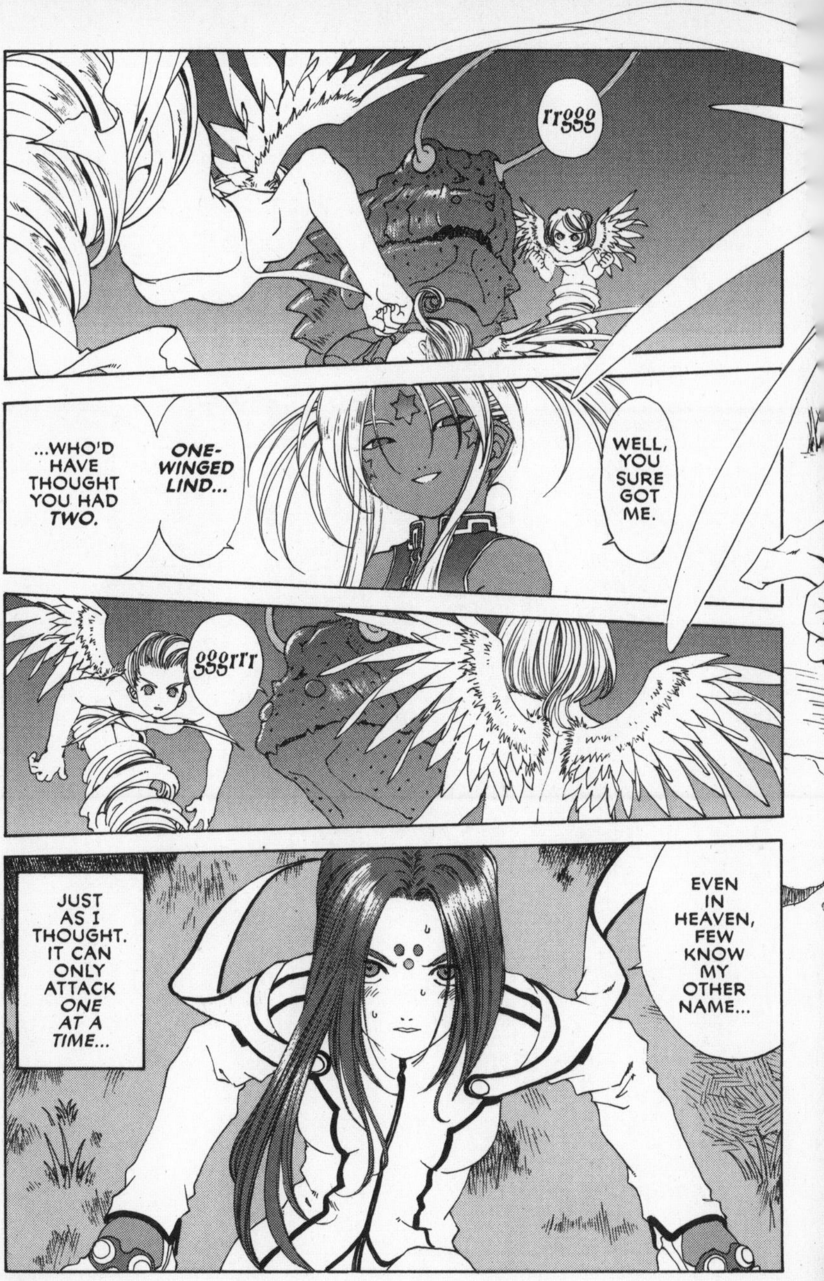
rrggg
WELL, YOU SURE GOT ME.
ONE-WINGED LIND...
...WHO'D HAVE THOUGHT YOU HAD TWO.
gggrrr
EVEN IN HEAVEN, FEW KNOW MY OTHER NAME...
JUST AS I THOUGHT. IT CAN ONLY ATTACK ONE AT A TIME...

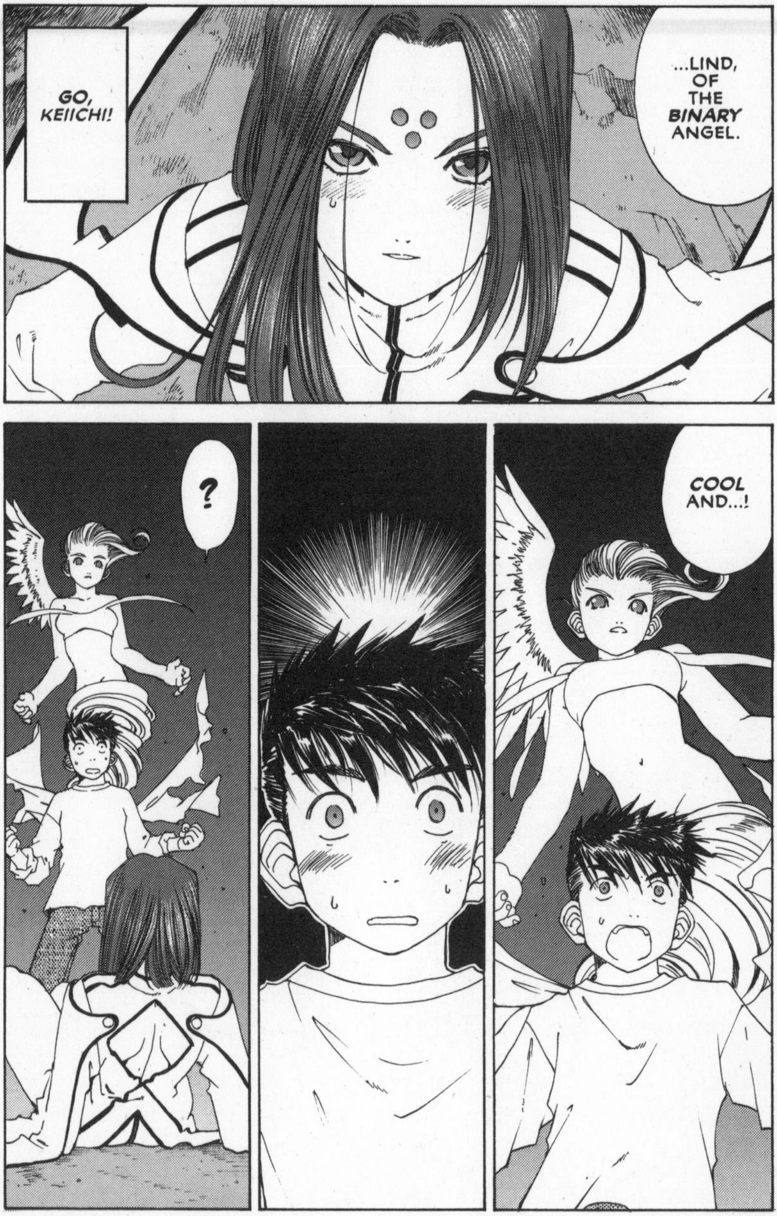
...LIND, OF THE BINARY ANGEL.
GO, KEIICHI!
COOL AND...!
?

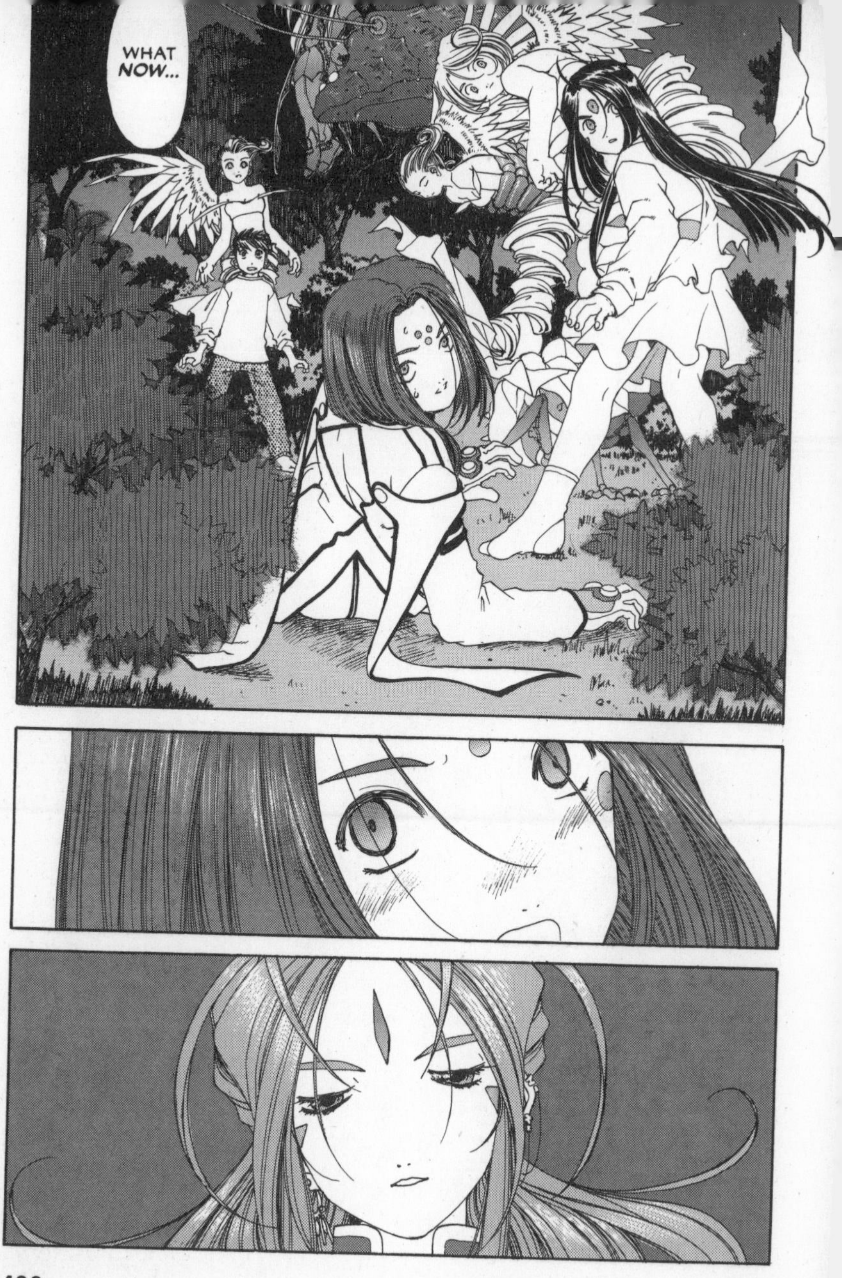
WHAT NOW...

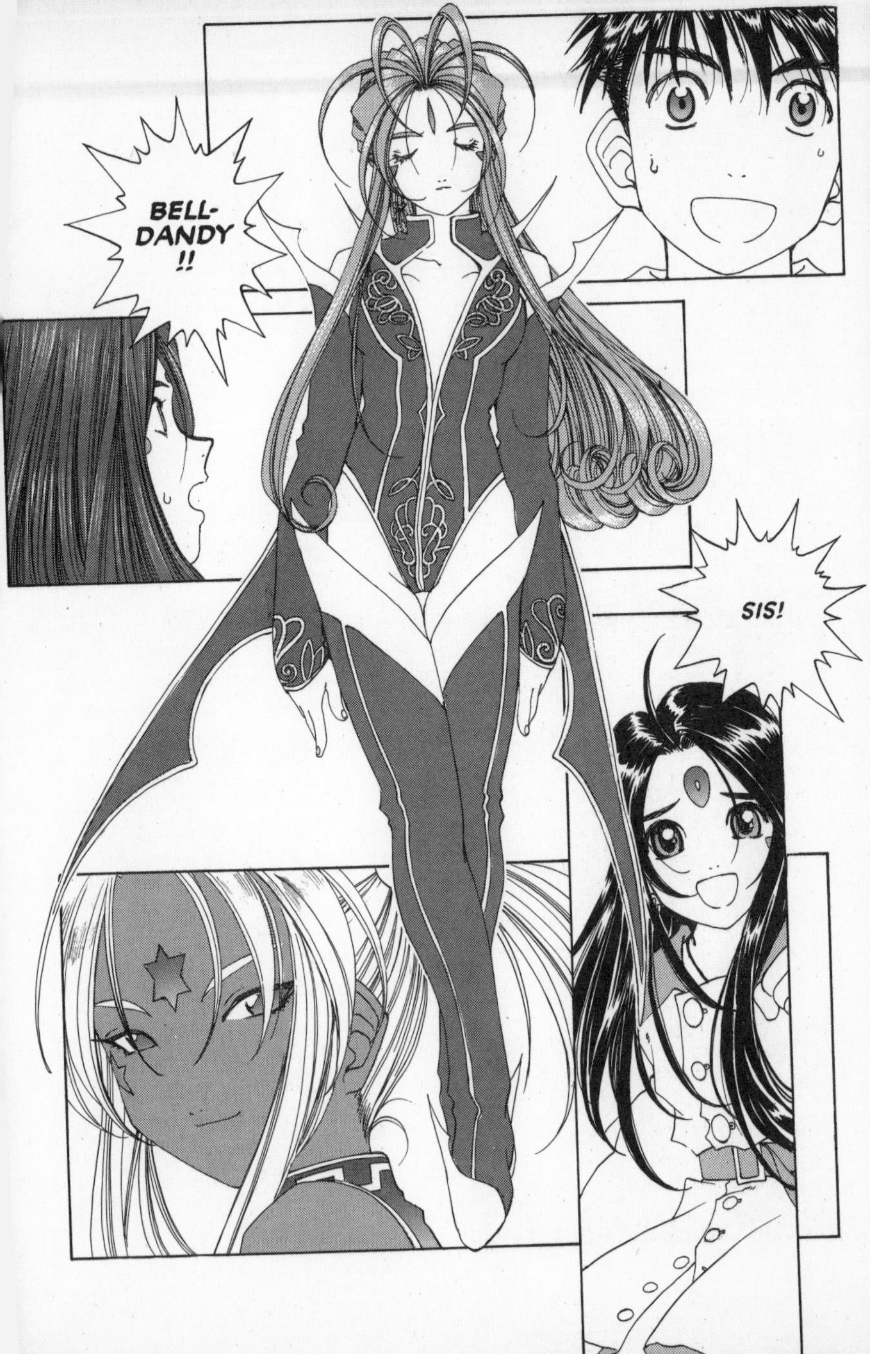
BELL-DANDY !!
SIS!

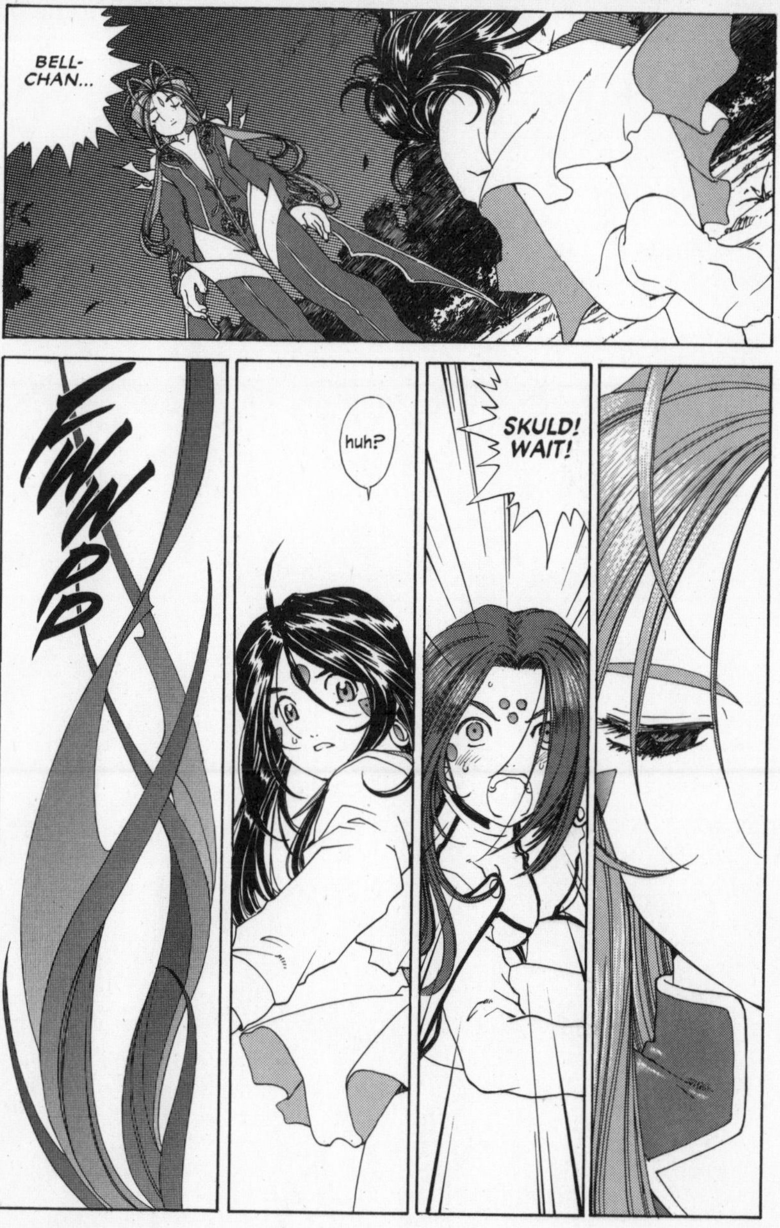
BELL-CHAN...
SKULD! WAIT!
huh?

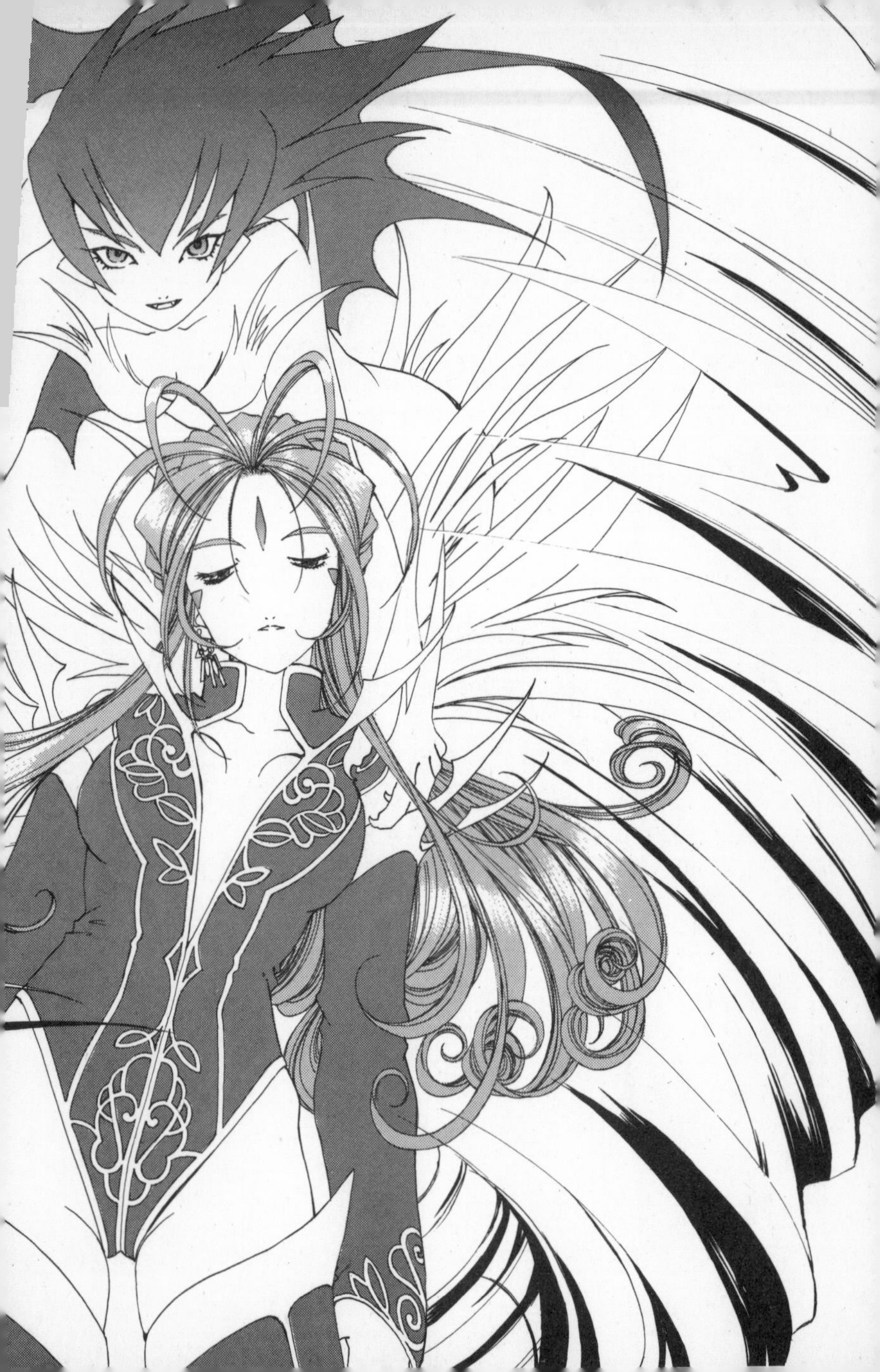

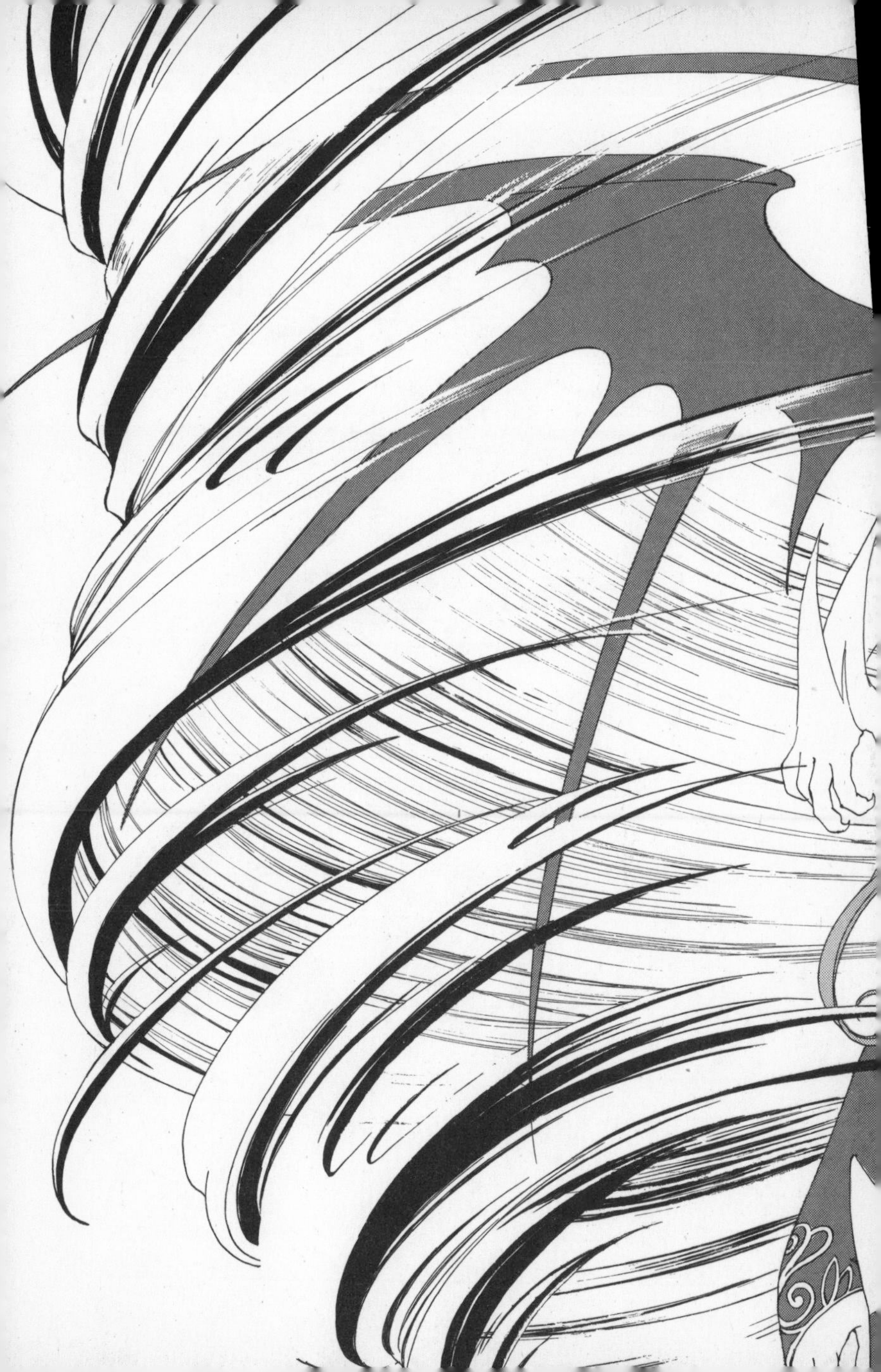

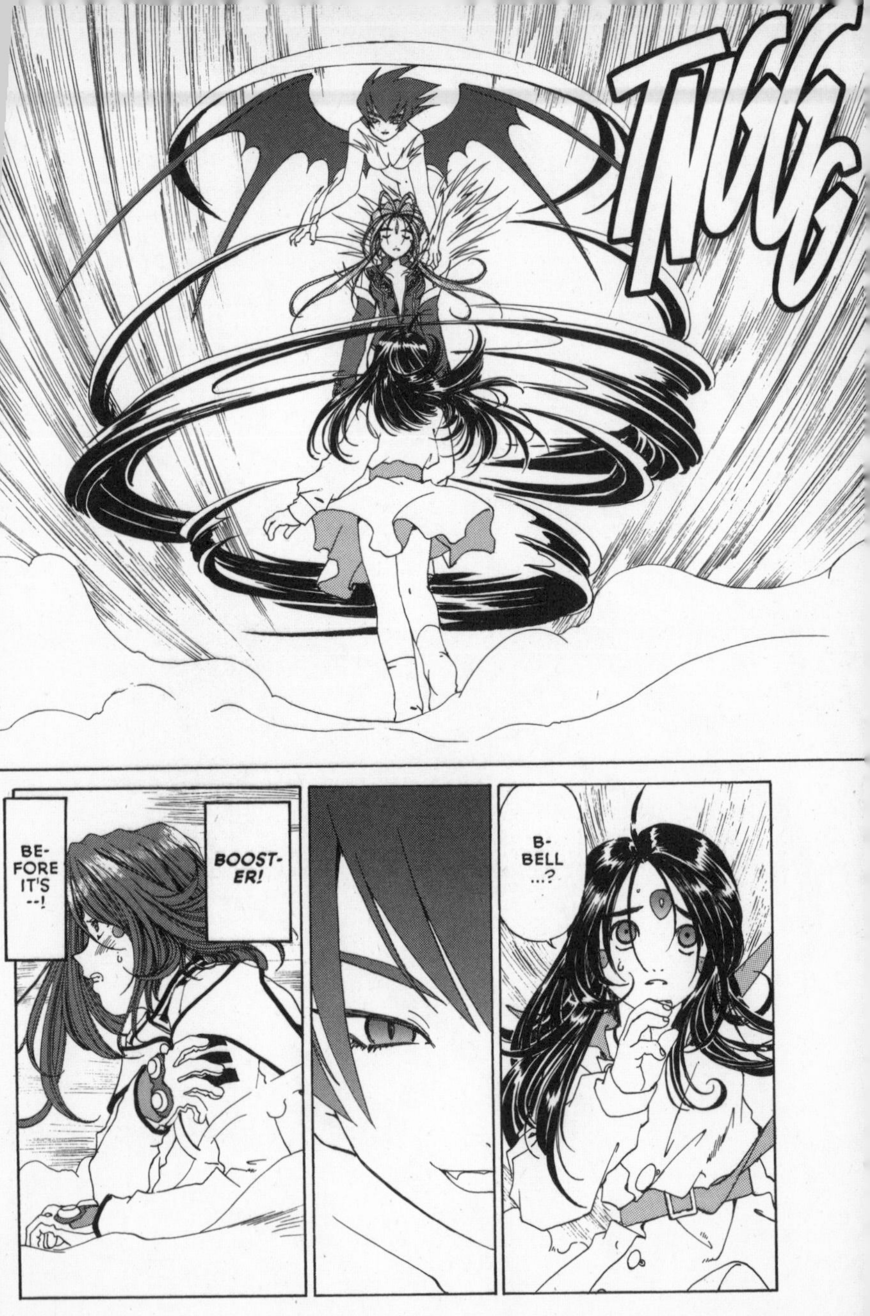
B-BELL ...?
BOOST-ER!
BE-FORE IT'S --!

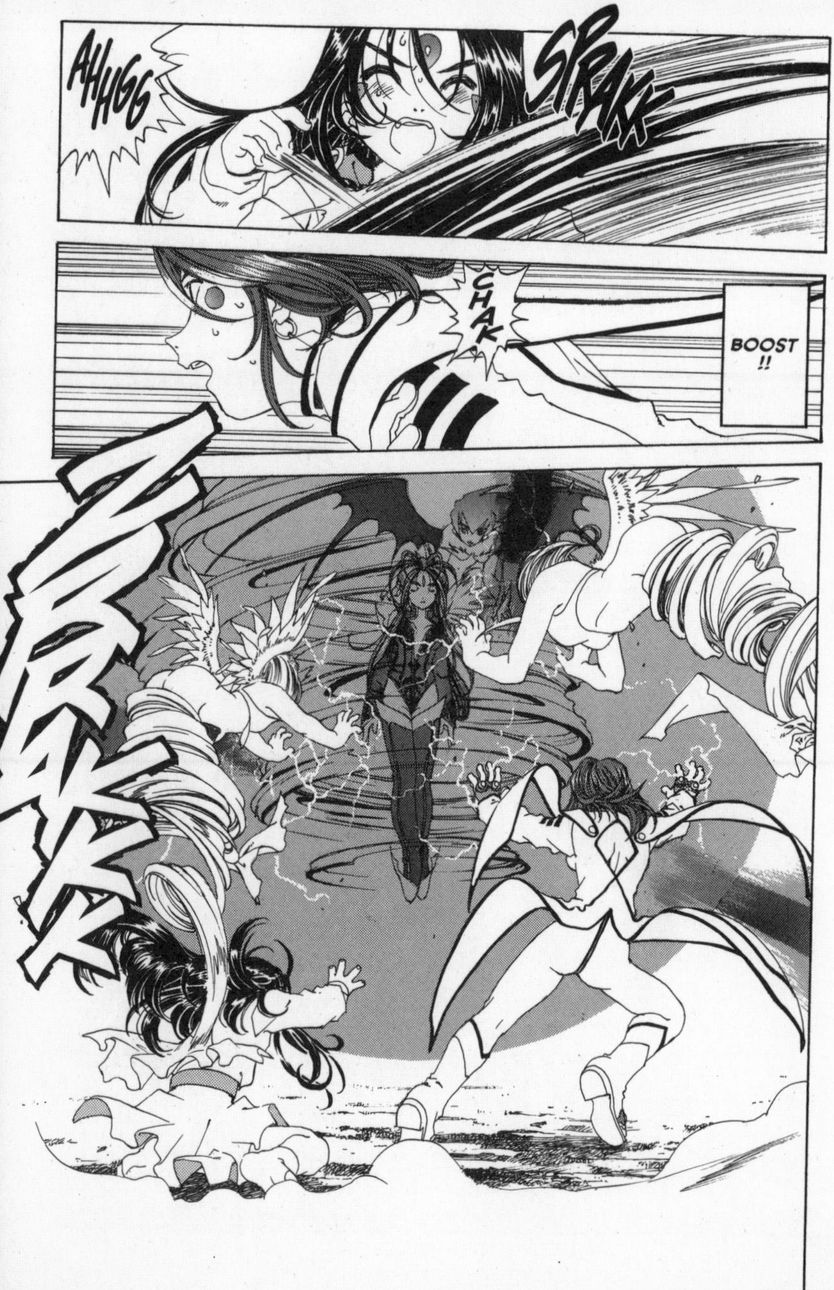
SPRAKK
AHHGG
BOOST !!
CHAK

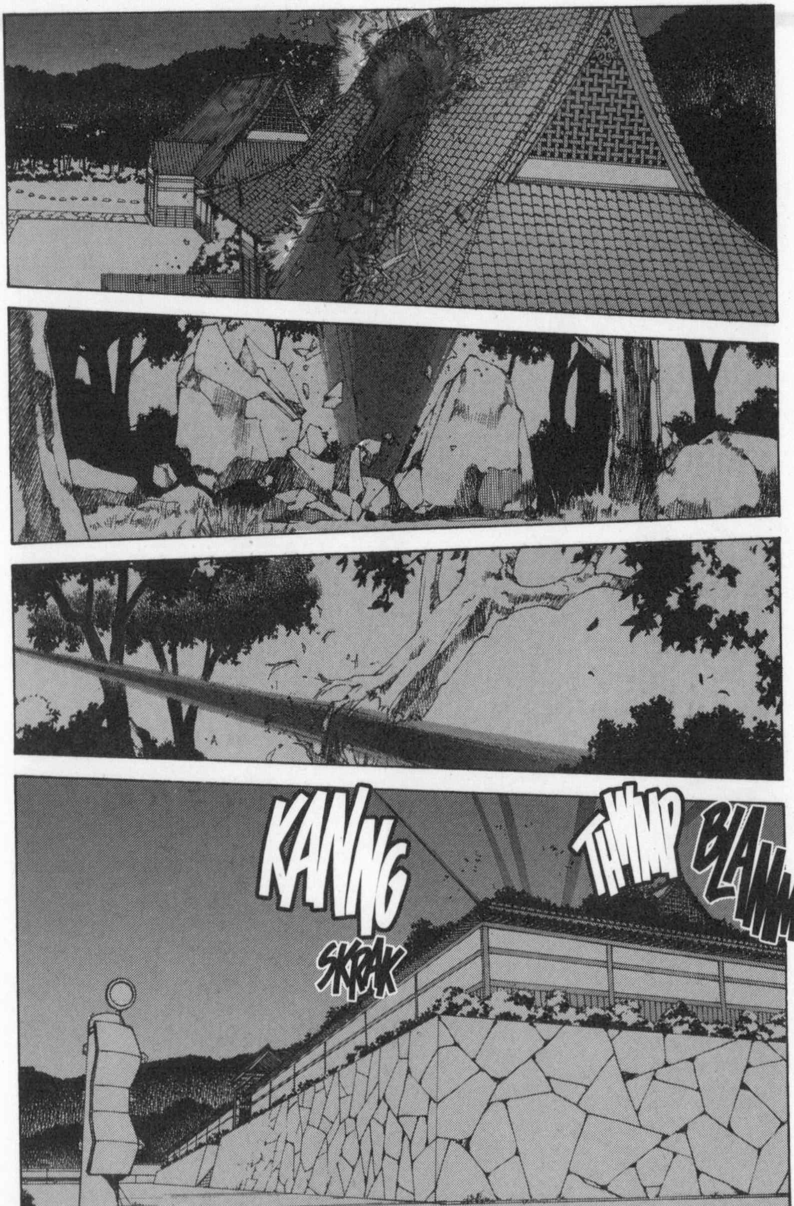
BLAMM
THWMP
KANNG
SKRAK

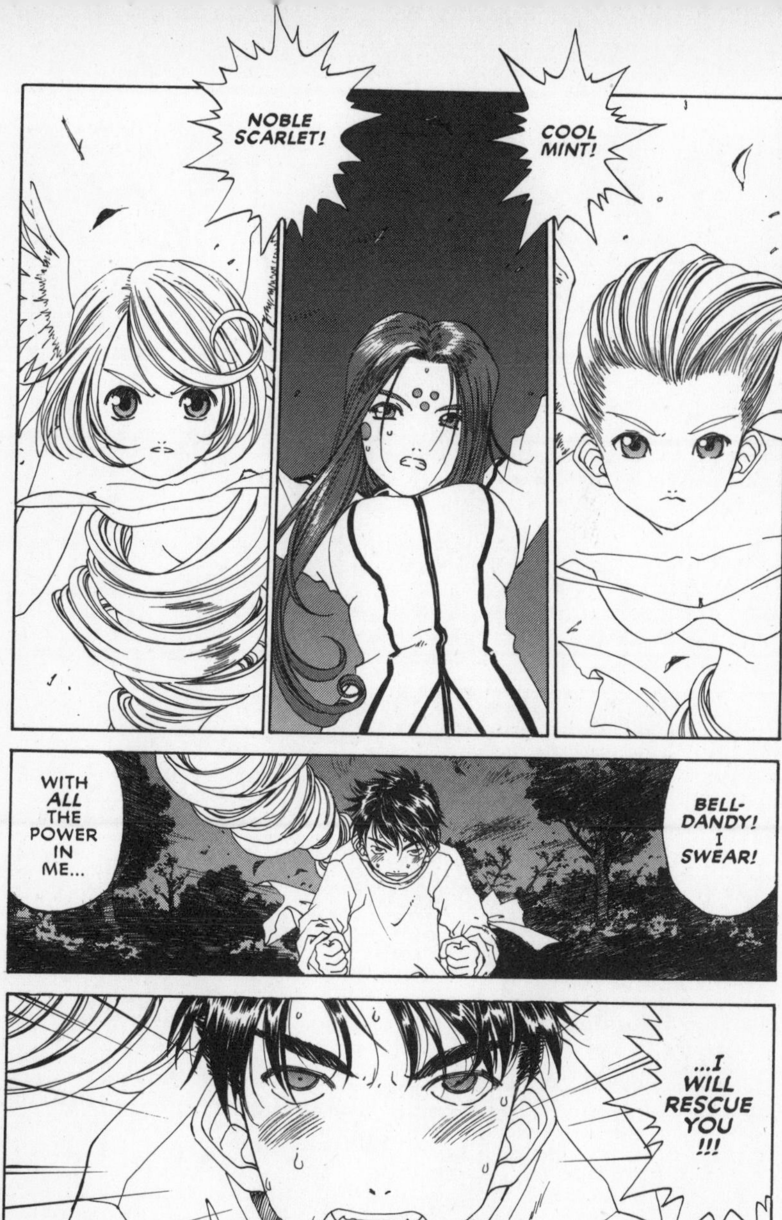
COOL MINT!
NOBLE SCARLET!
BELL-DANDY! I SWEAR!
WITH *ALL* THE POWER IN ME...
...I WILL RESCUE YOU!!!

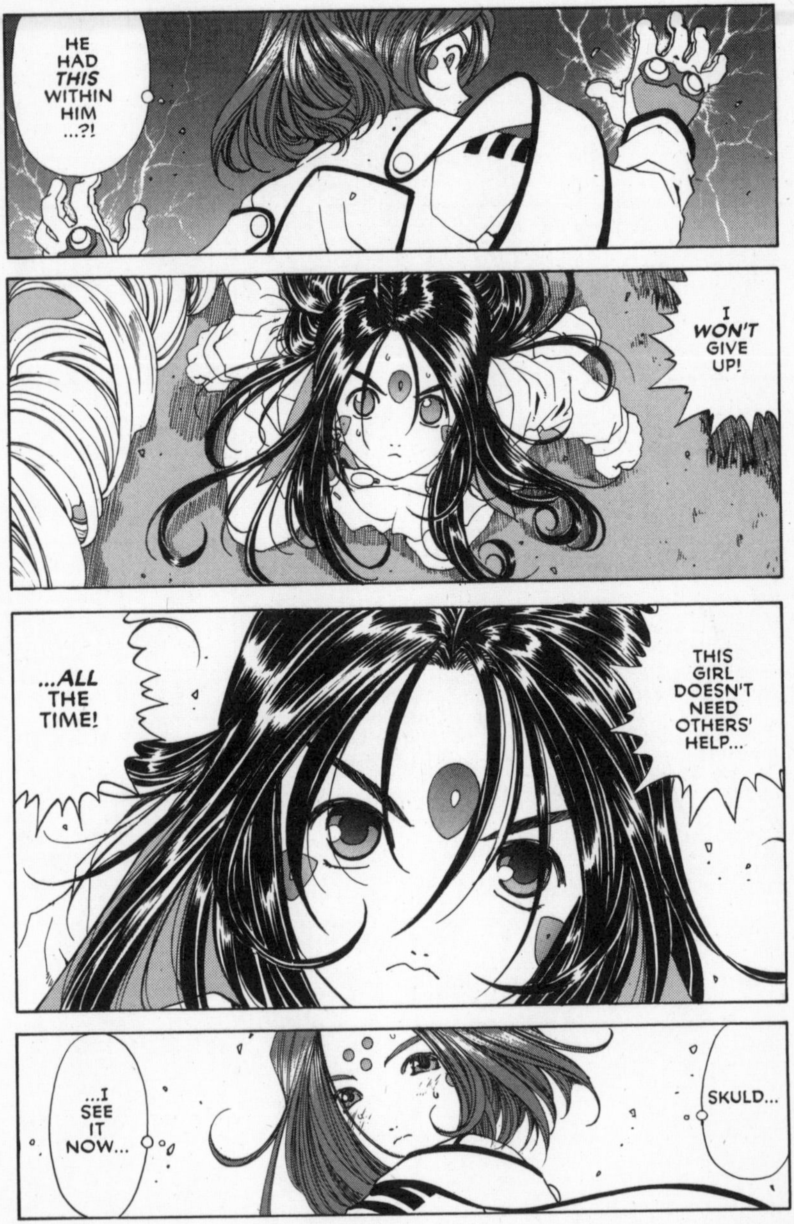
HE HAD *THIS* WITHIN HIM ...?!
I *WON'T* GIVE UP!
THIS GIRL DOESN'T NEED OTHERS' HELP...
...*ALL* THE TIME!
SKULD...
...I SEE IT NOW...

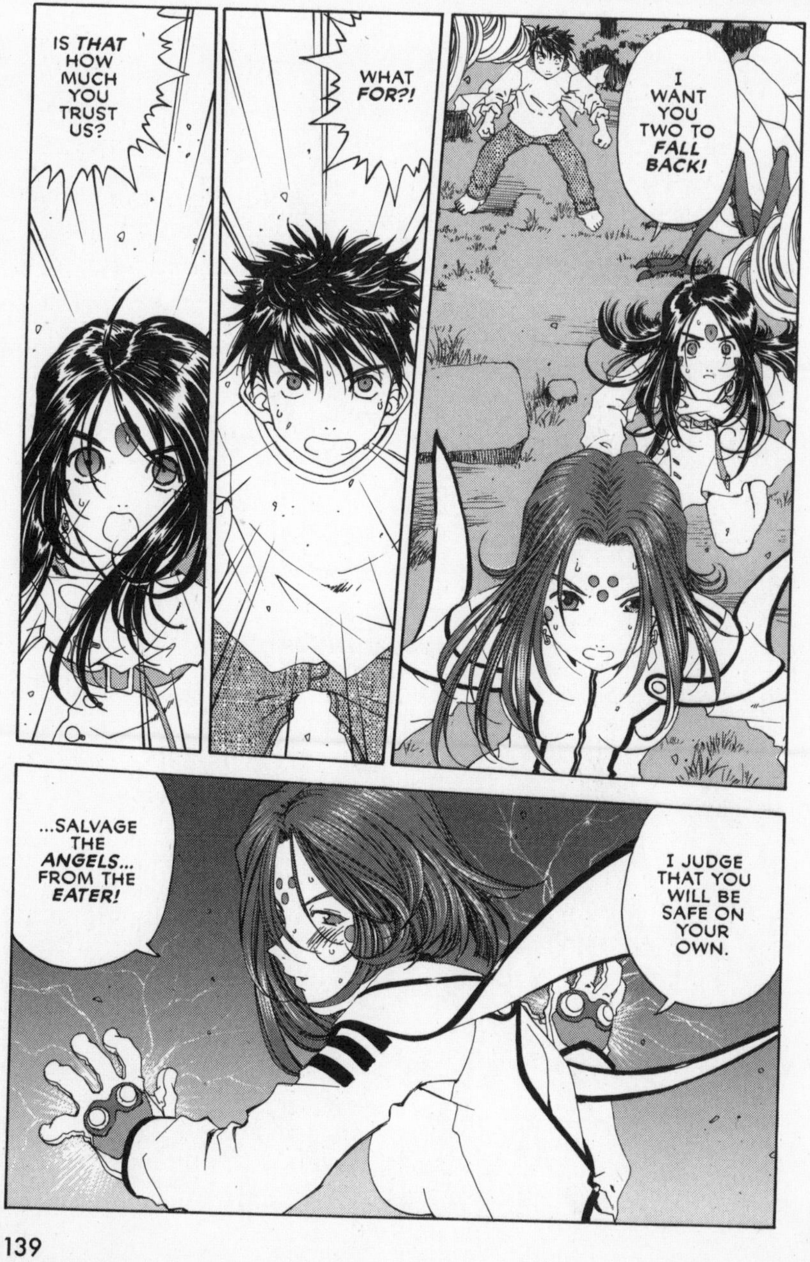
I WANT YOU TWO TO *FALL BACK!*
WHAT *FOR?!*
IS *THAT* HOW MUCH YOU TRUST US?
I JUDGE THAT YOU WILL BE SAFE ON YOUR OWN.
...SALVAGE THE *ANGELS*... FROM THE *EATER!*

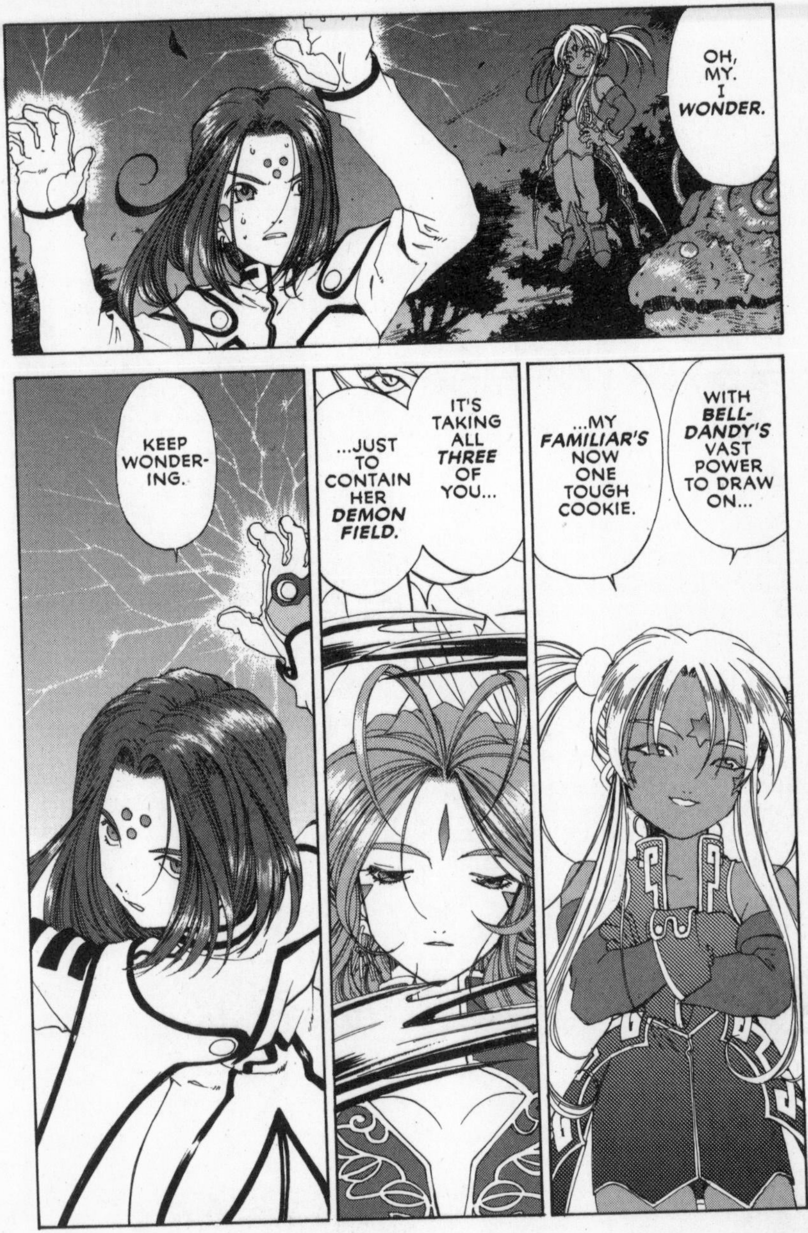
OH, MY. I *WONDER.*
WITH *BELL-DANDY'S* VAST POWER TO DRAW ON...
...MY *FAMILIAR'S* NOW ONE TOUGH COOKIE.
IT'S TAKING ALL *THREE* OF YOU...
...JUST TO CONTAIN HER *DEMON FIELD.*
KEEP WONDER-ING.

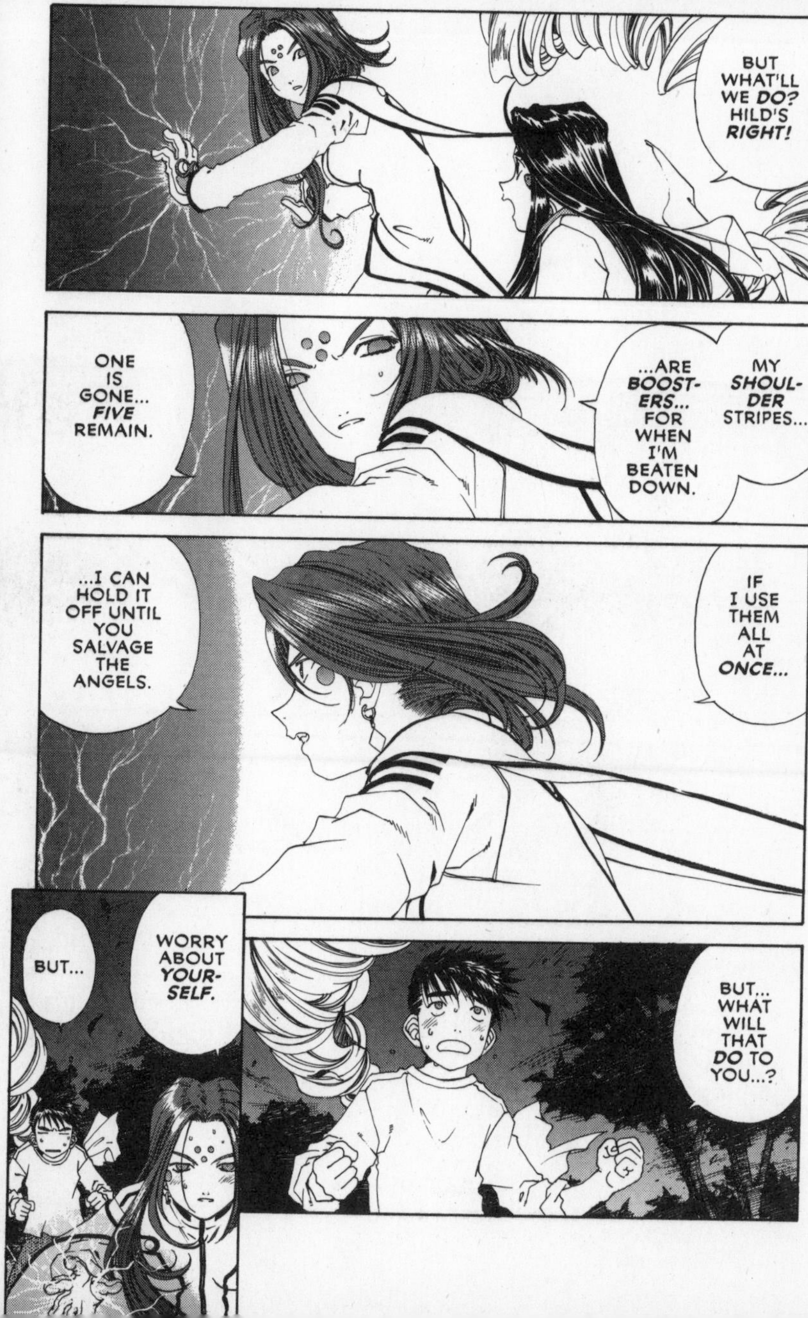
BUT WHAT'LL WE *DO?* HILD'S *RIGHT!*
MY *SHOULDER* STRIPES...
...ARE *BOOSTERS*... FOR WHEN I'M BEATEN DOWN.
ONE IS GONE... *FIVE* REMAIN.
IF I USE THEM ALL AT *ONCE*...
...I CAN HOLD IT OFF UNTIL YOU SALVAGE THE ANGELS.
BUT... WHAT WILL THAT *DO* TO YOU...?
WORRY ABOUT *YOURSELF.*
BUT...

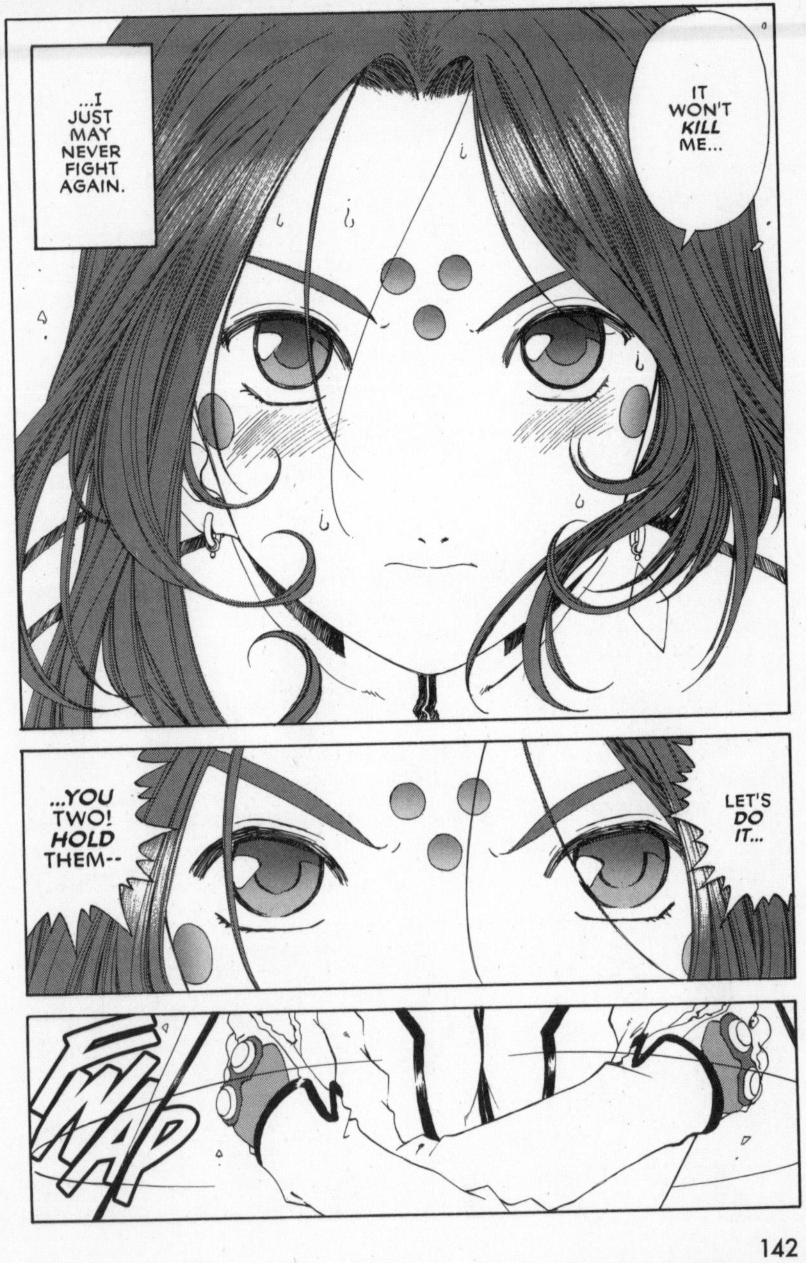
IT WON'T KILL ME...
...I JUST MAY NEVER FIGHT AGAIN.
LET'S DO IT...
...YOU TWO! HOLD THEM--
FWAP

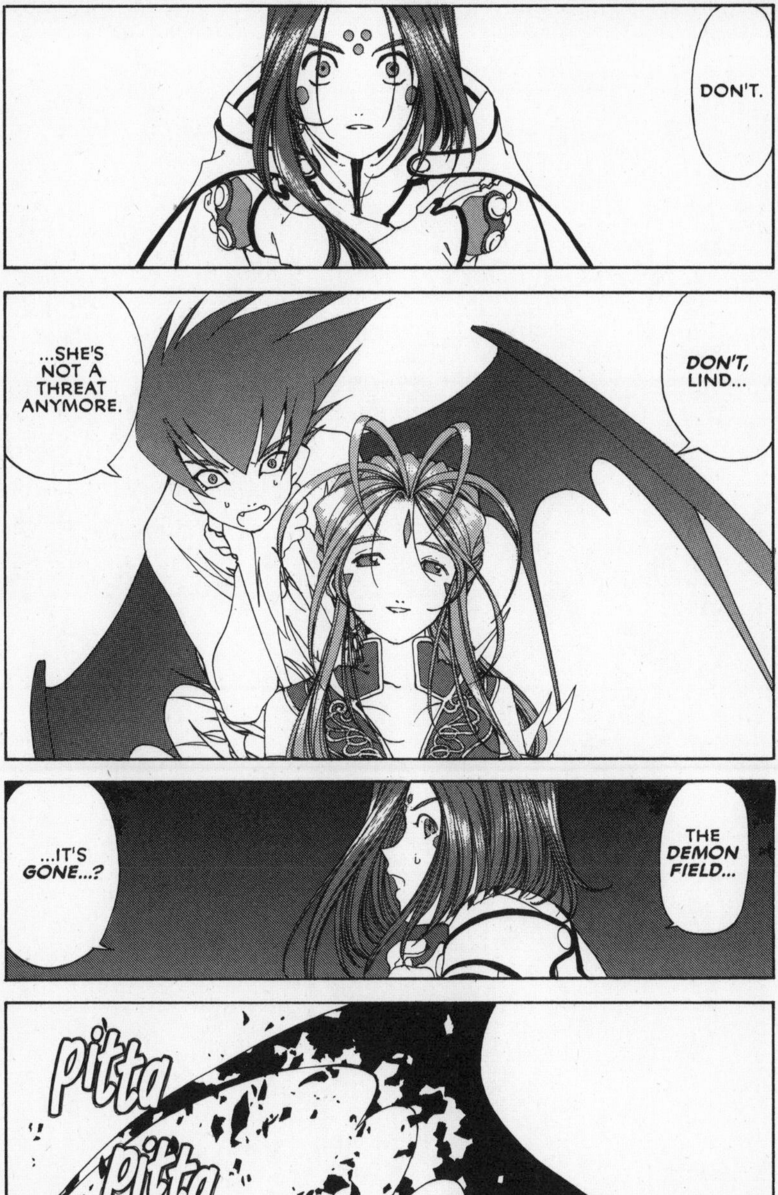
DON'T.
DON'T, LIND...
...SHE'S NOT A THREAT ANYMORE.
THE *DEMON* FIELD...
...IT'S *GONE*...?
pitta
pitta

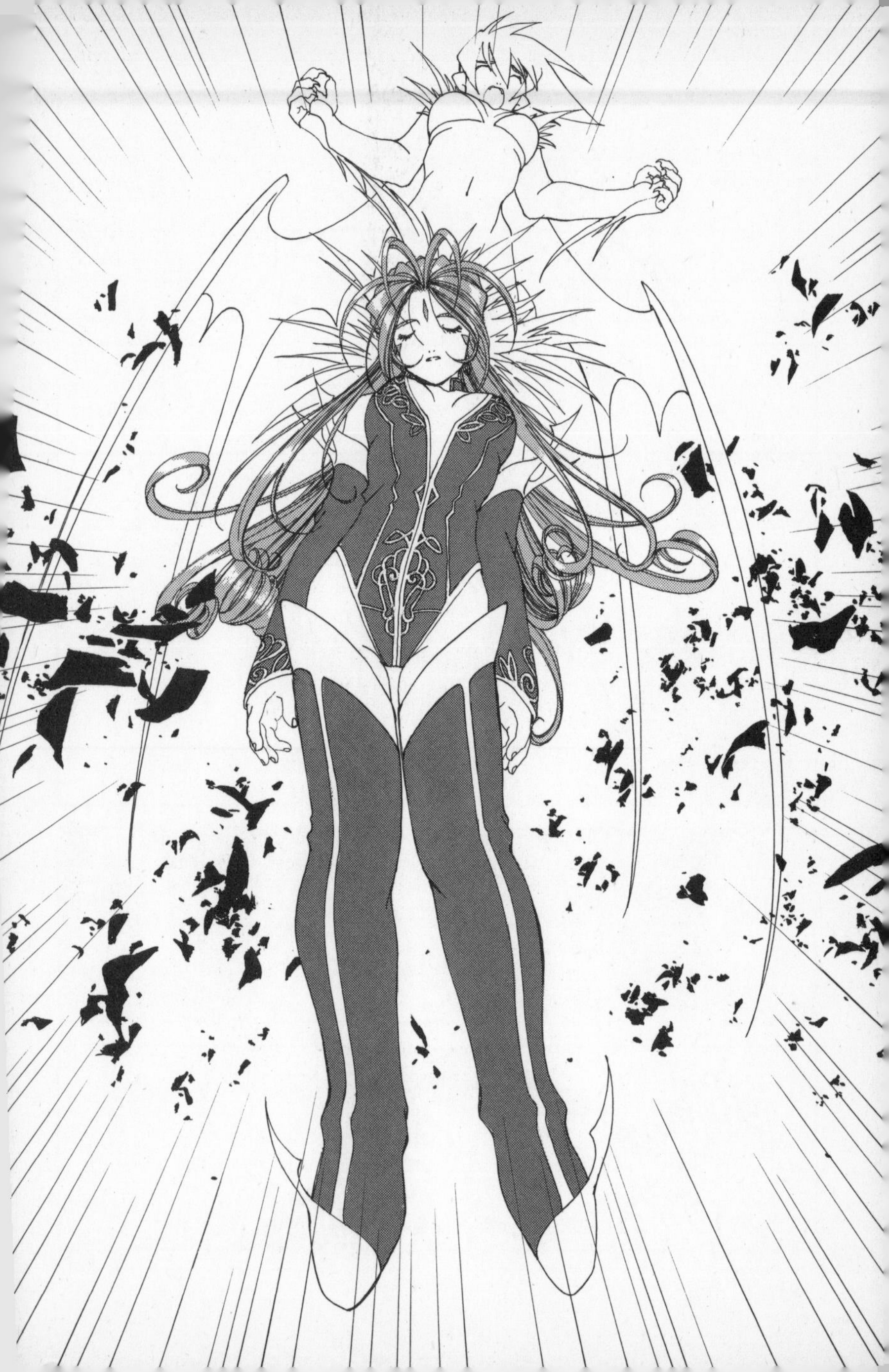

CHAPTER 162

Goddess of the Ax

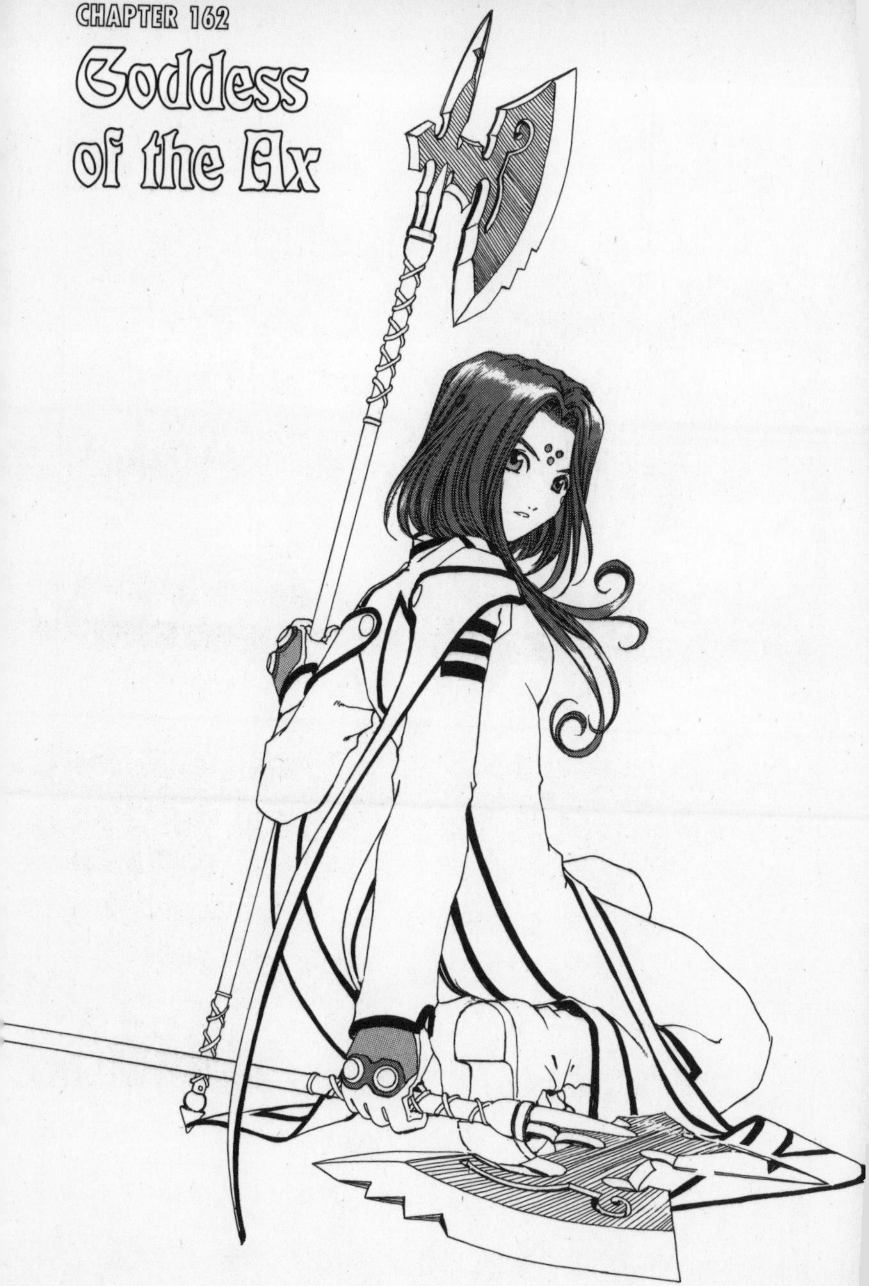

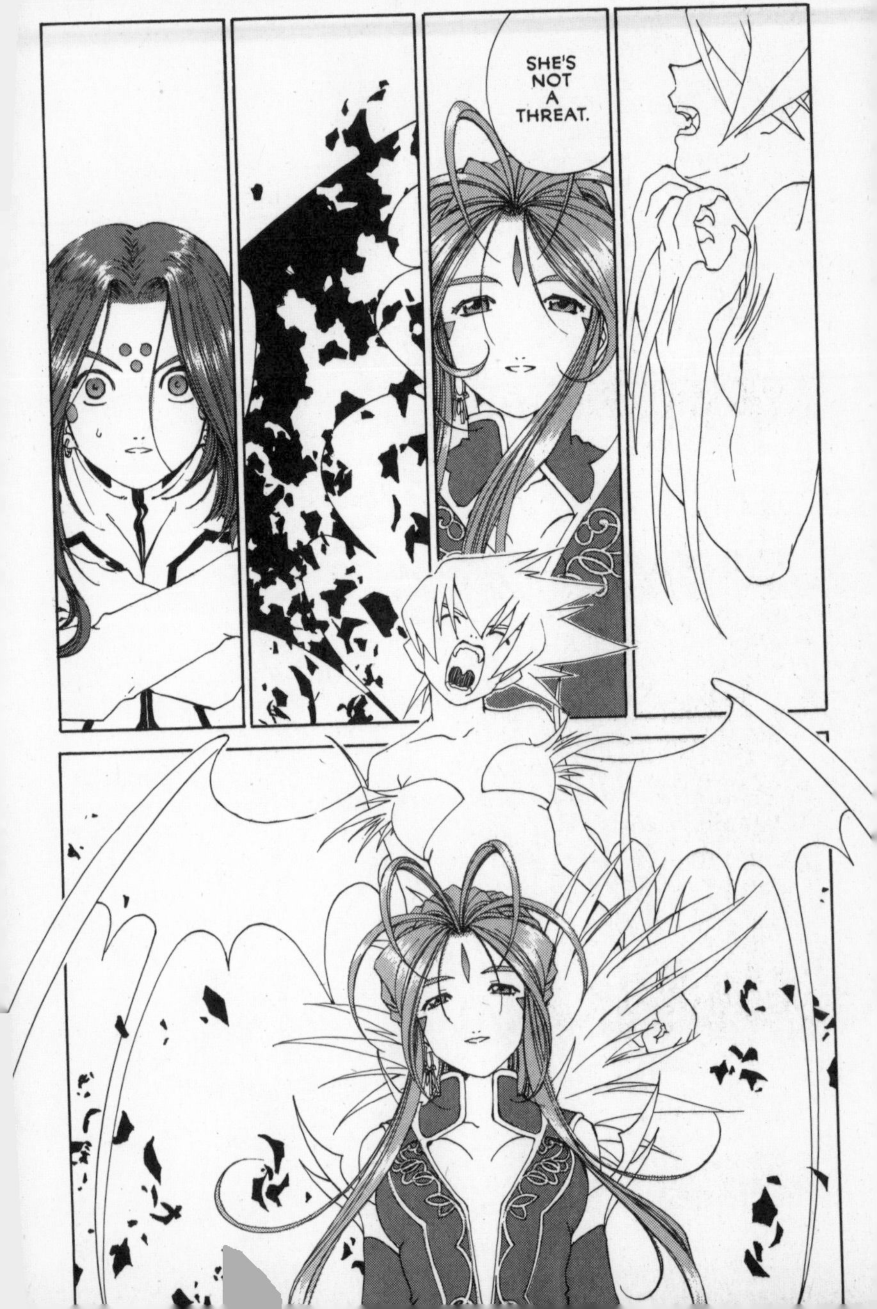
SHE'S NOT A THREAT.

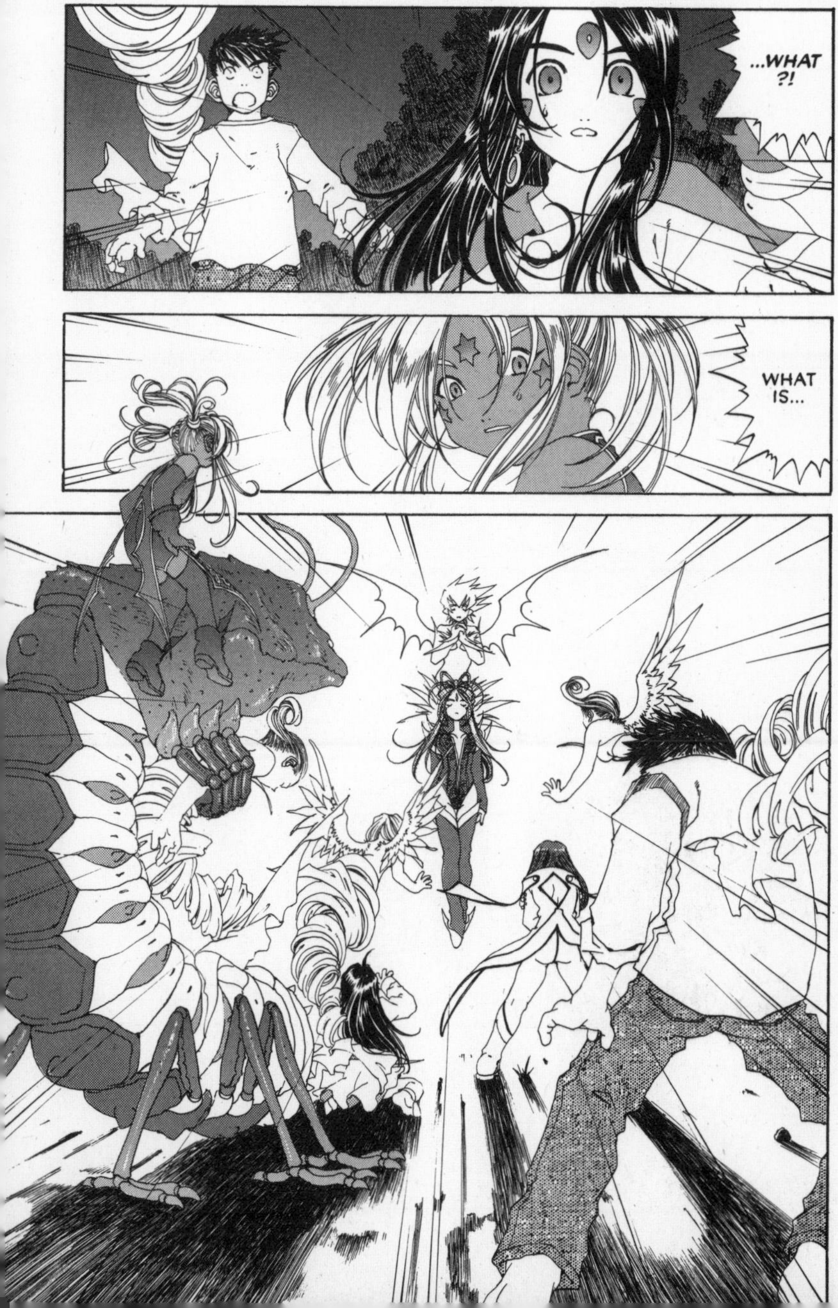
...WHAT ?!
WHAT IS...

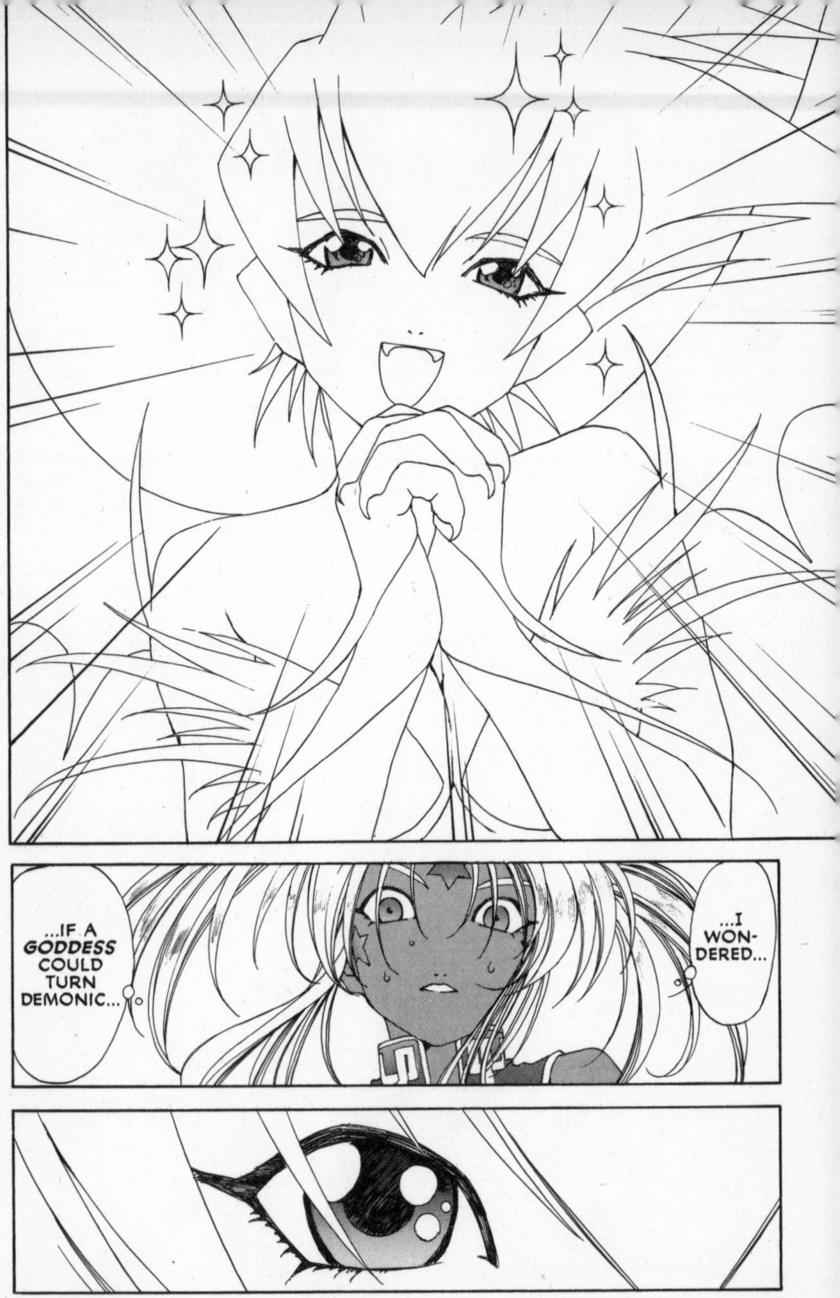
...I WON-DERED...
...IF A *GODDESS* COULD TURN DEMONIC...

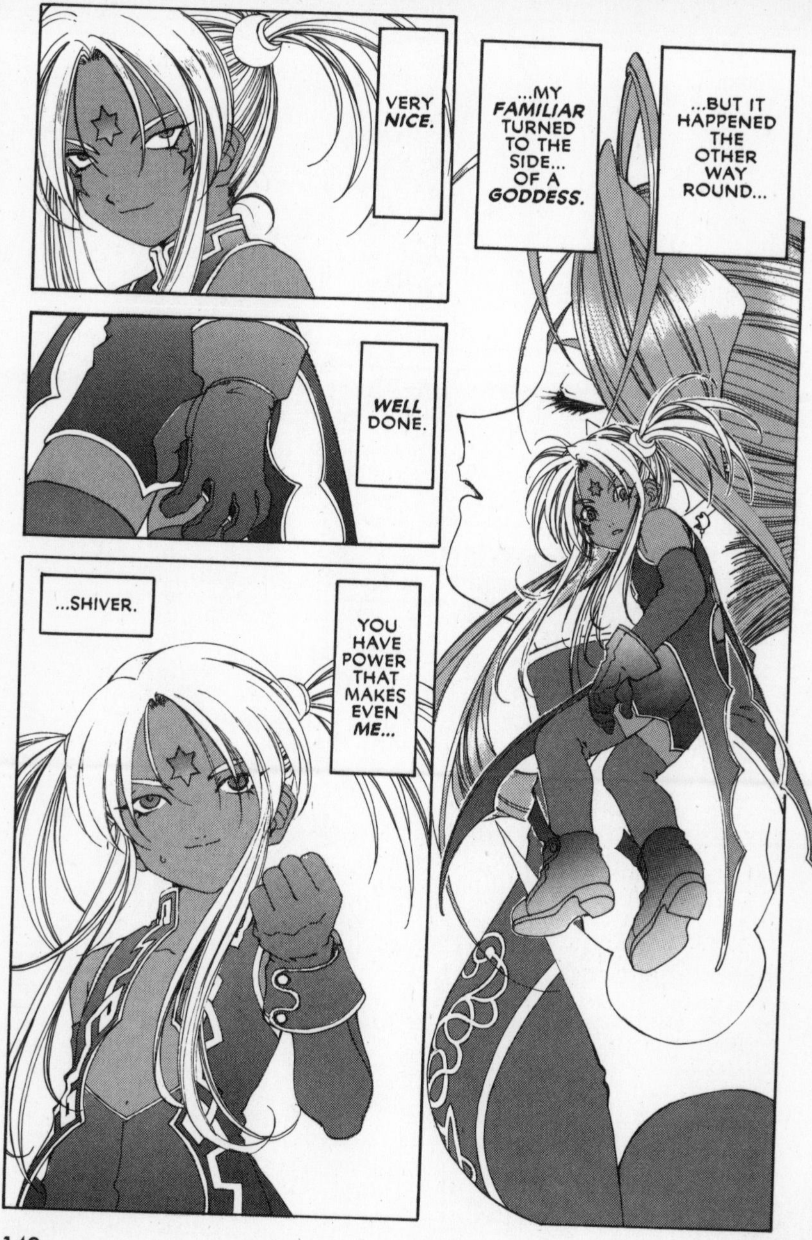
...BUT IT HAPPENED THE OTHER WAY ROUND...
...MY *FAMILIAR* TURNED TO THE SIDE... OF A *GODDESS.*
VERY *NICE.*
WELL DONE.
YOU HAVE POWER THAT MAKES EVEN *ME*...
...SHIVER.

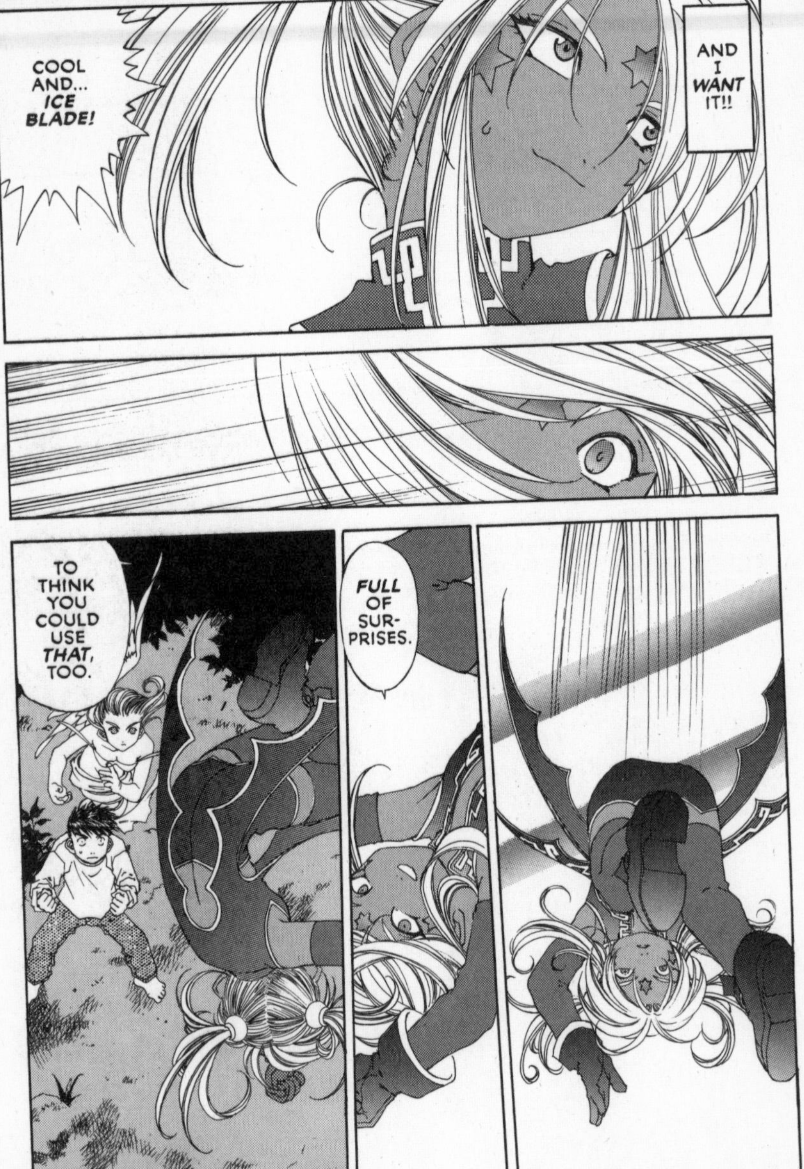
AND I *WANT* IT!!
COOL AND... *ICE BLADE!*
FULL OF SUR-PRISES.
TO THINK YOU COULD USE *THAT,* TOO.

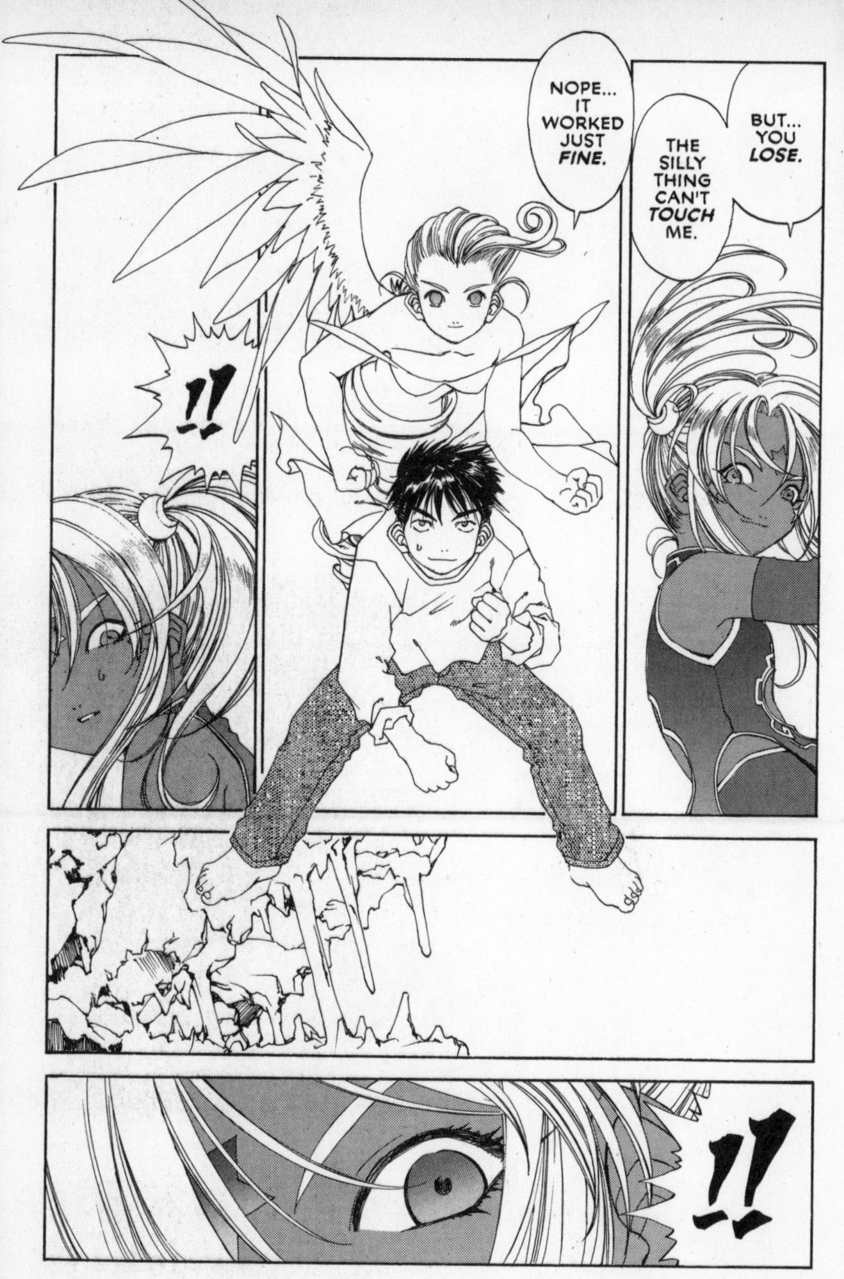
BUT... YOU *LOSE.*
THE SILLY THING CAN'T *TOUCH* ME.
NOPE... IT WORKED JUST *FINE.*
!!
!!

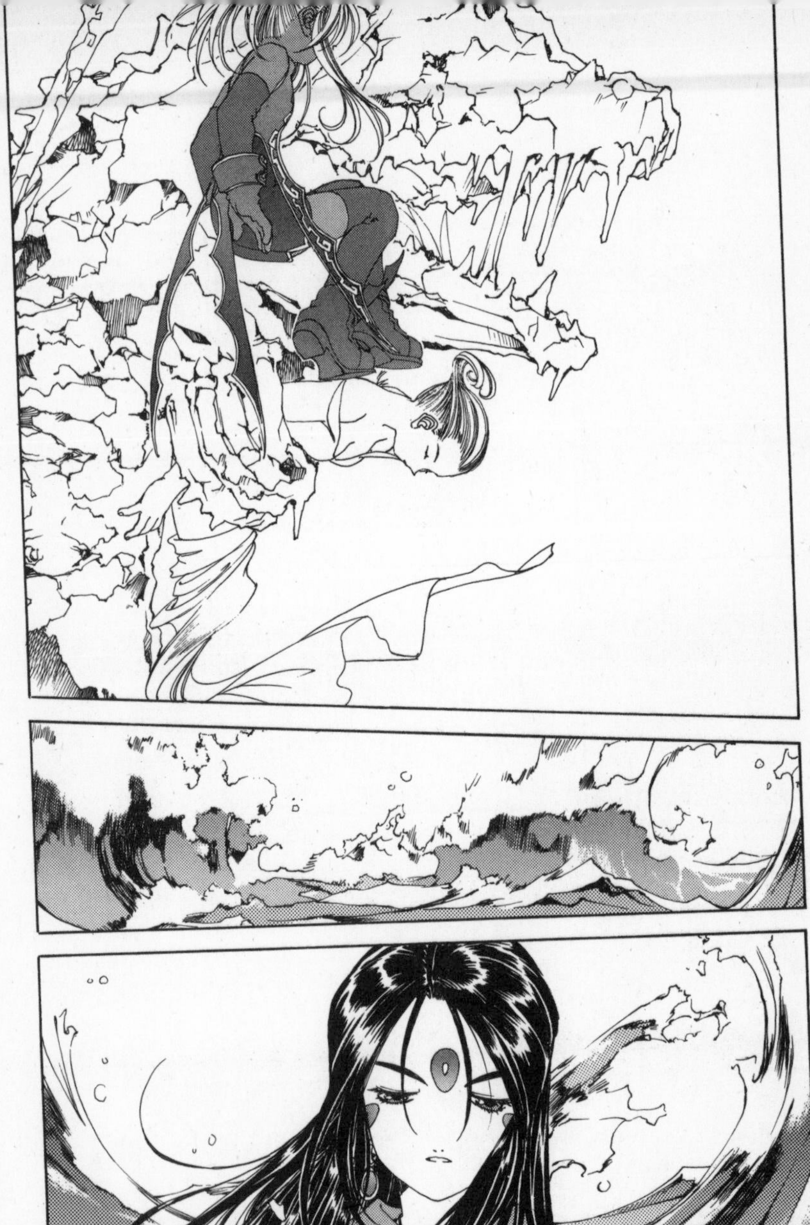

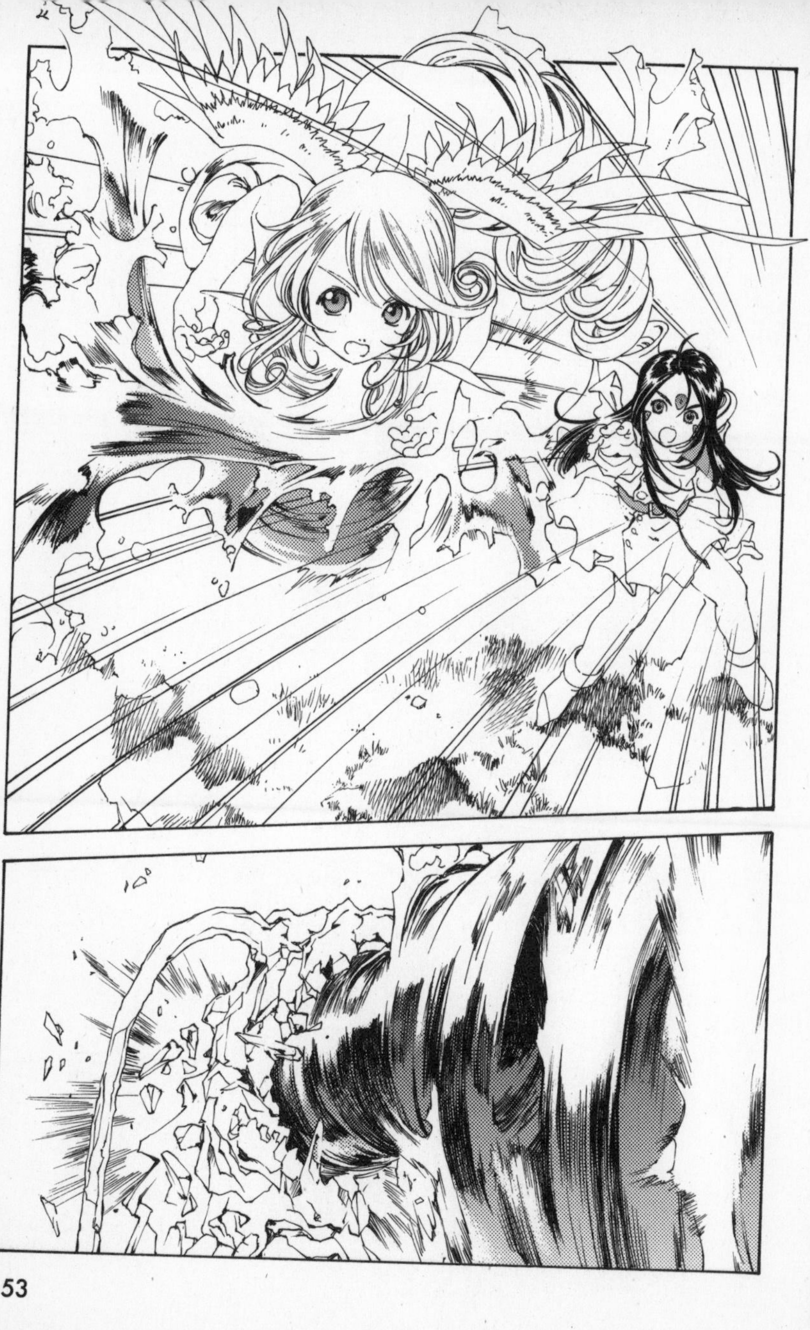

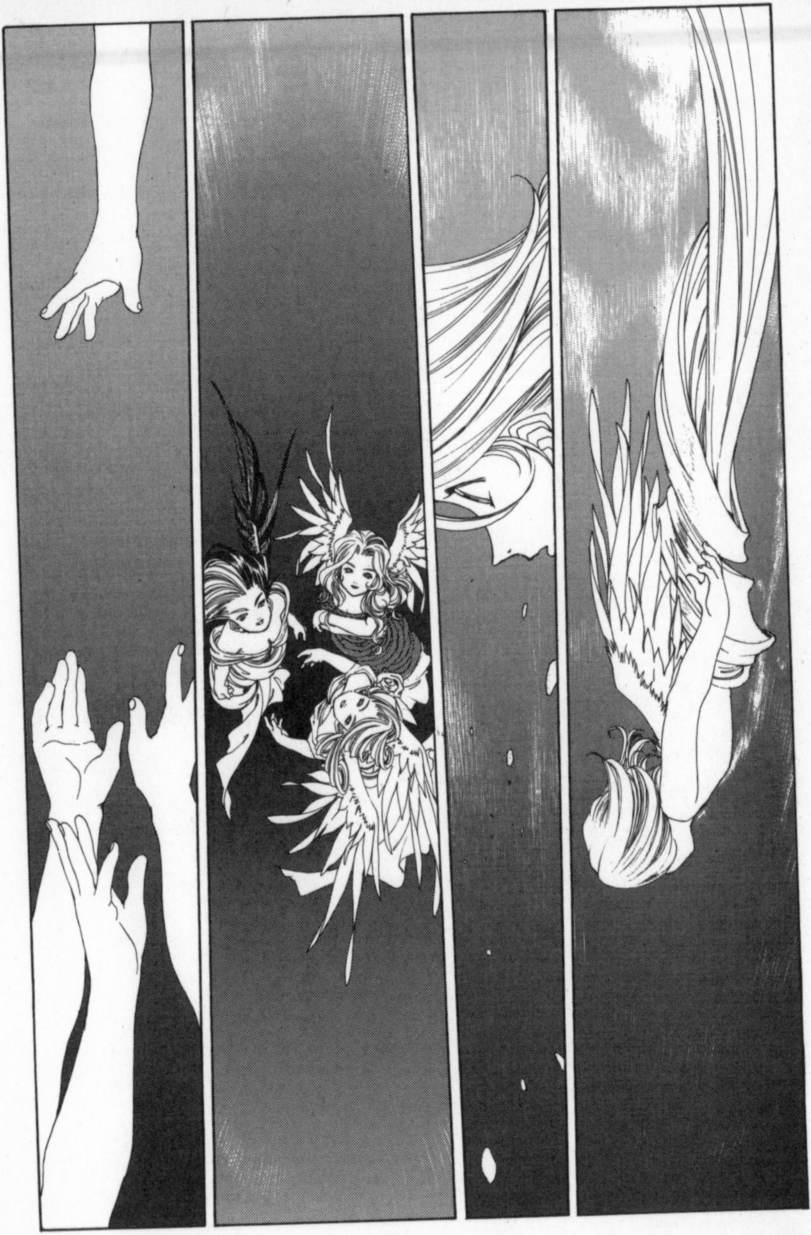

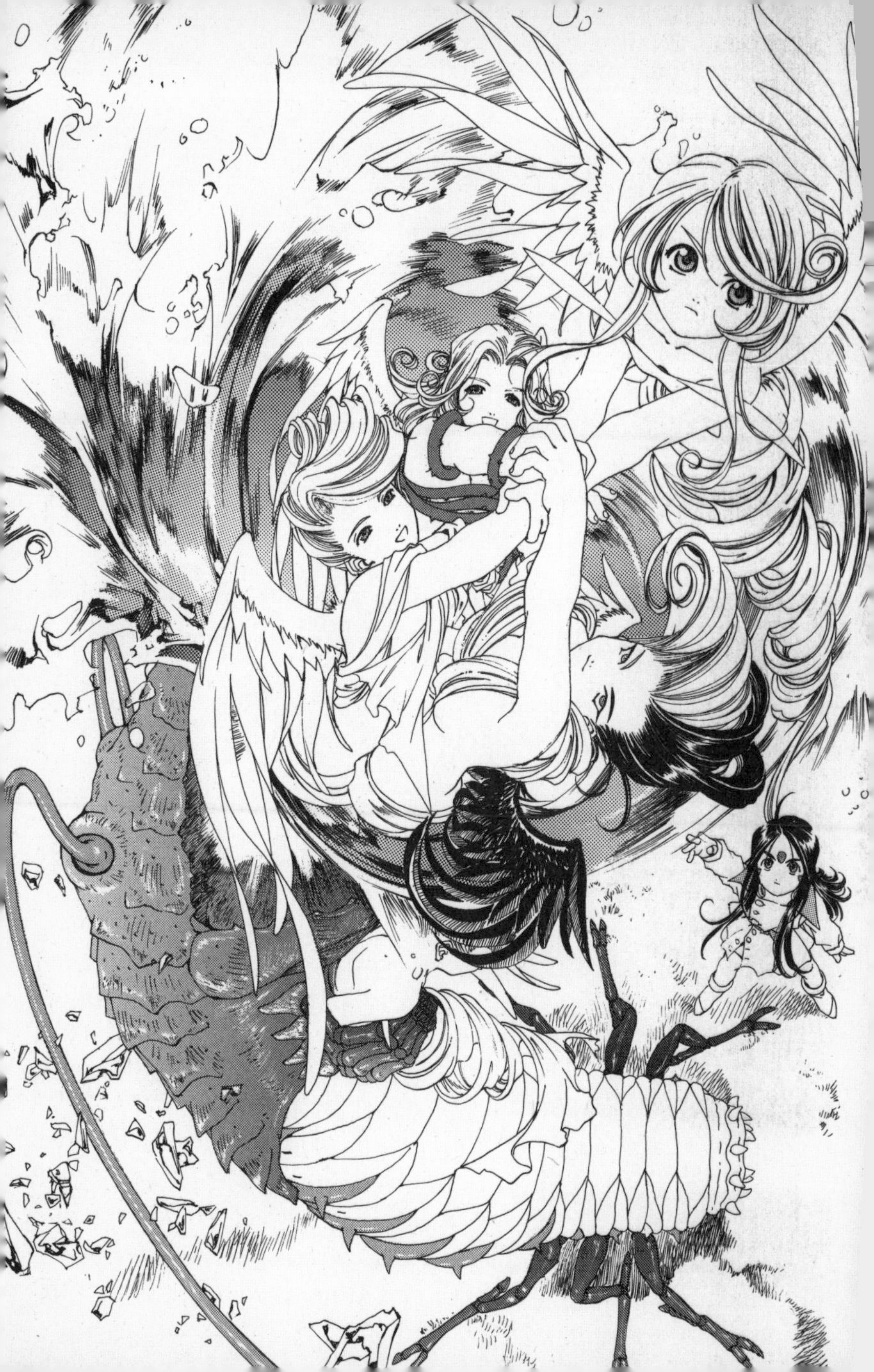

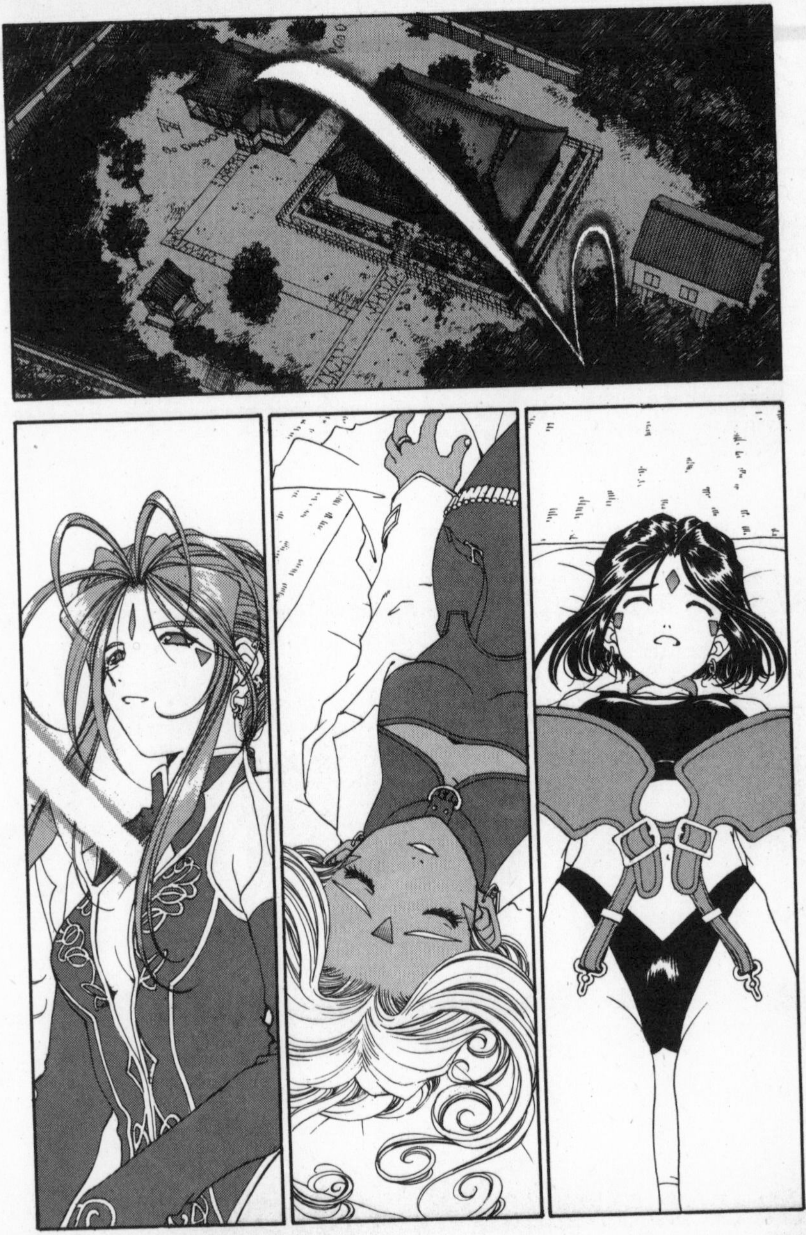

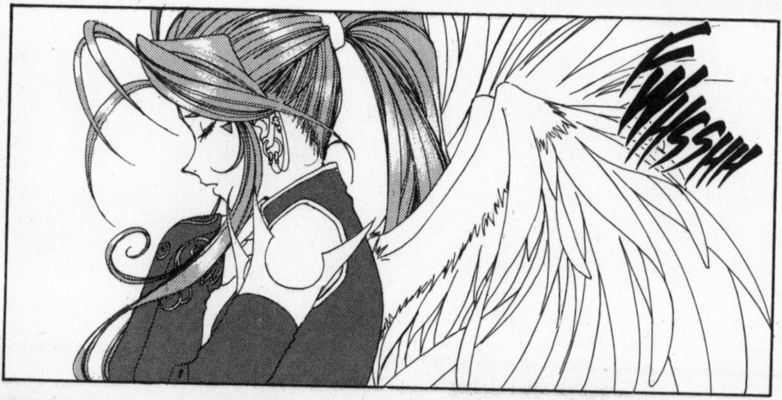
FWHSSHH

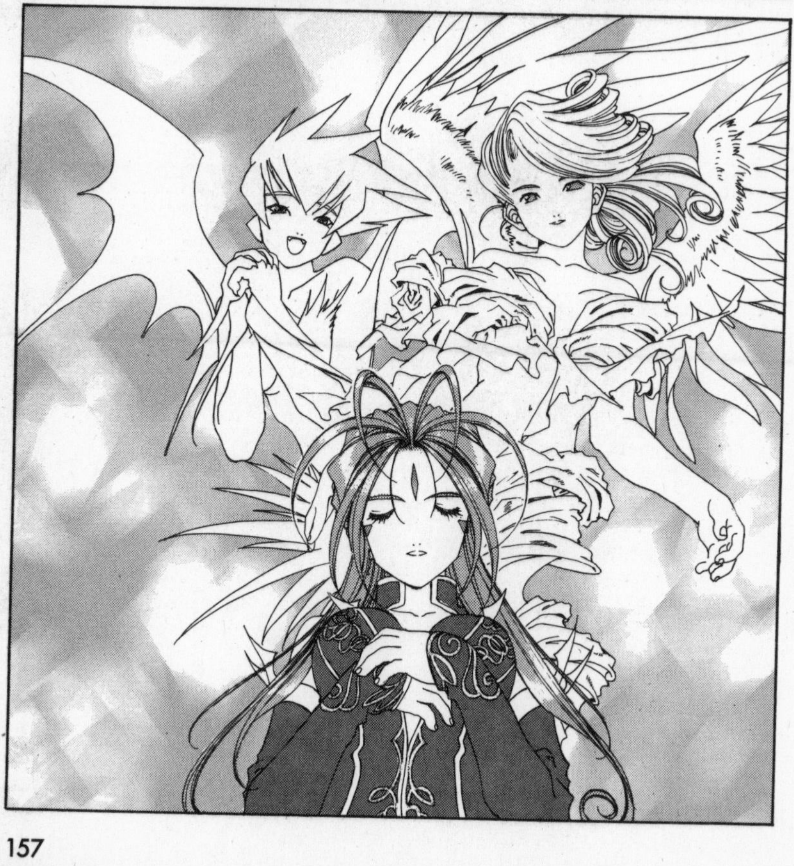

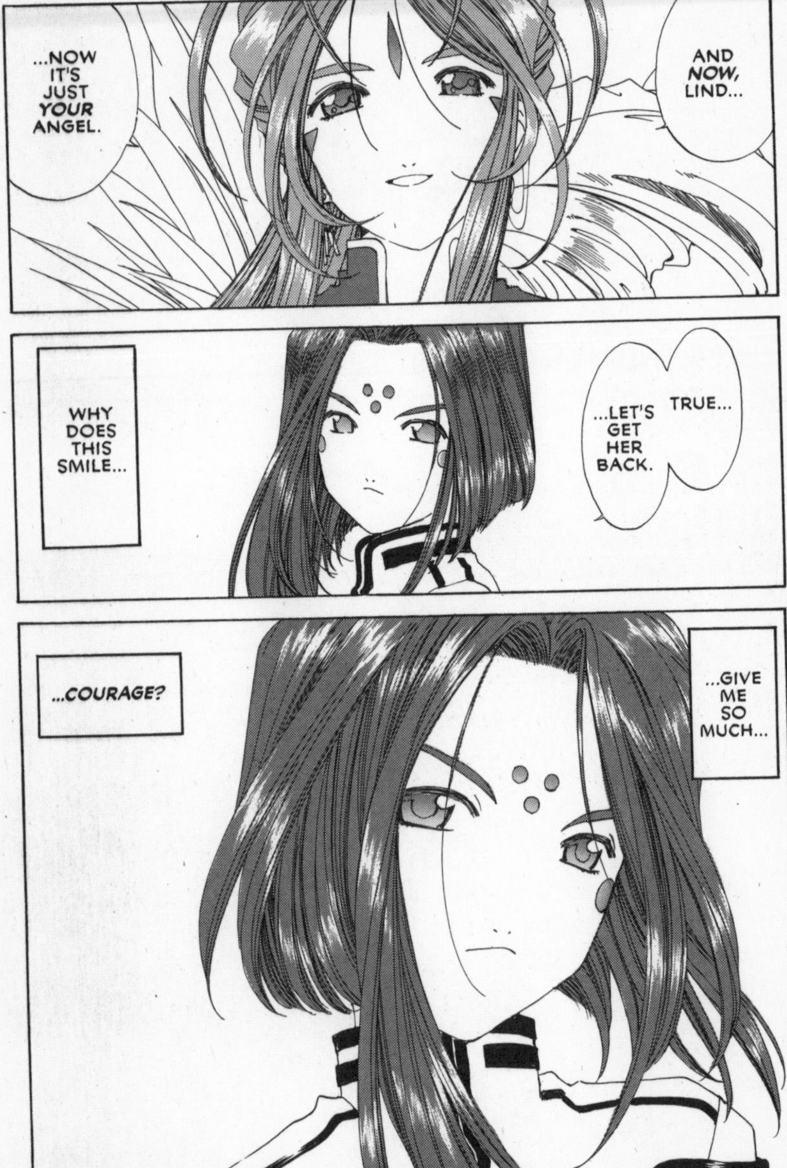
AND *NOW*, LIND...
...NOW IT'S JUST *YOUR* ANGEL.
TRUE...
...LET'S GET HER BACK.
WHY DOES THIS SMILE...
...GIVE ME SO MUCH...
...COURAGE?

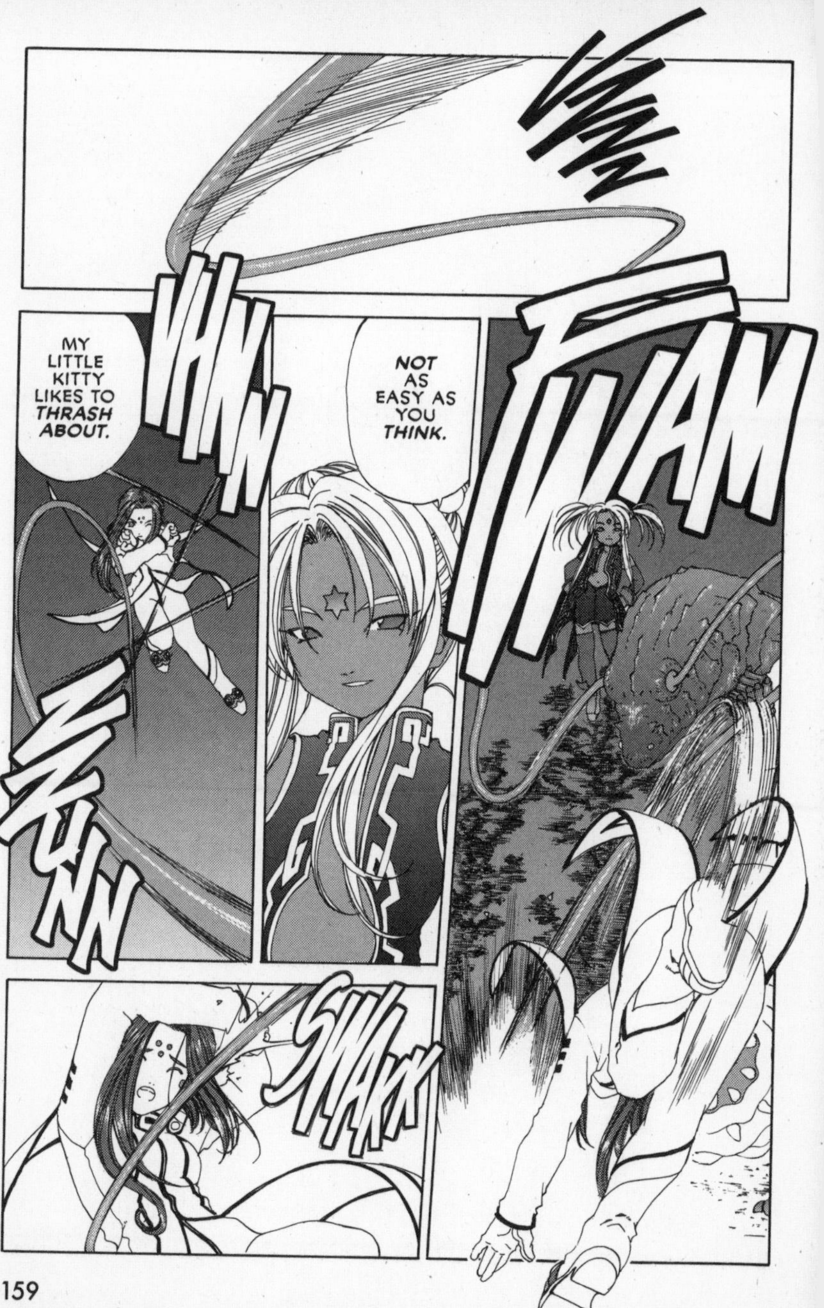
FWAM
NOT AS EASY AS YOU THINK.
MY LITTLE KITTY LIKES TO THRASH ABOUT.
VHNN
SWAKK

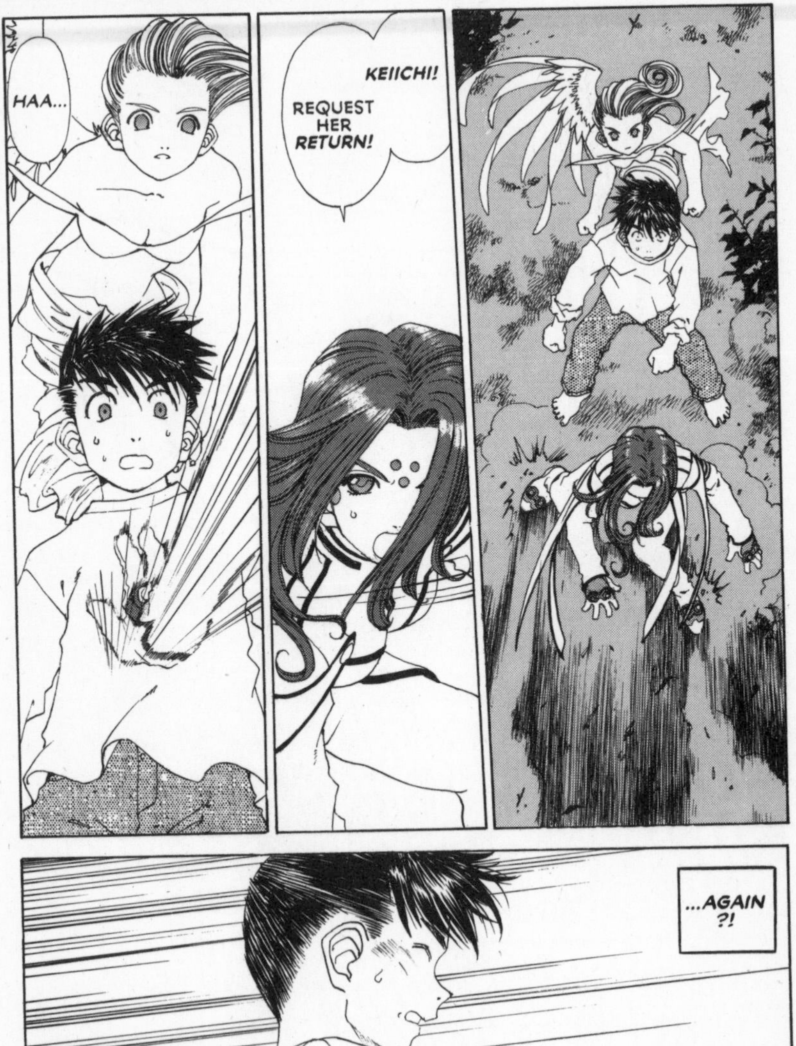
KEIICHI!
REQUEST HER RETURN!
HAA...
...AGAIN ?!

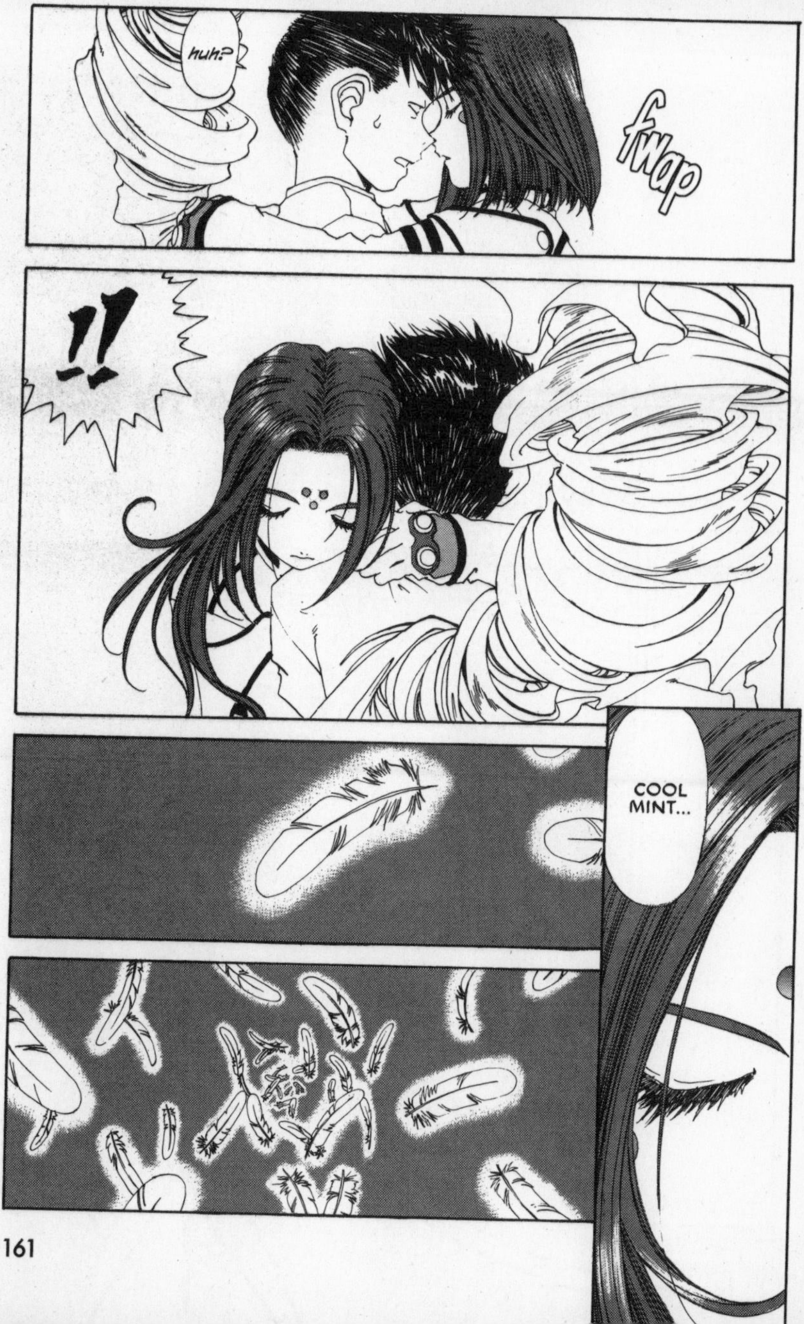
fwap
huh?
!!
COOL MINT...

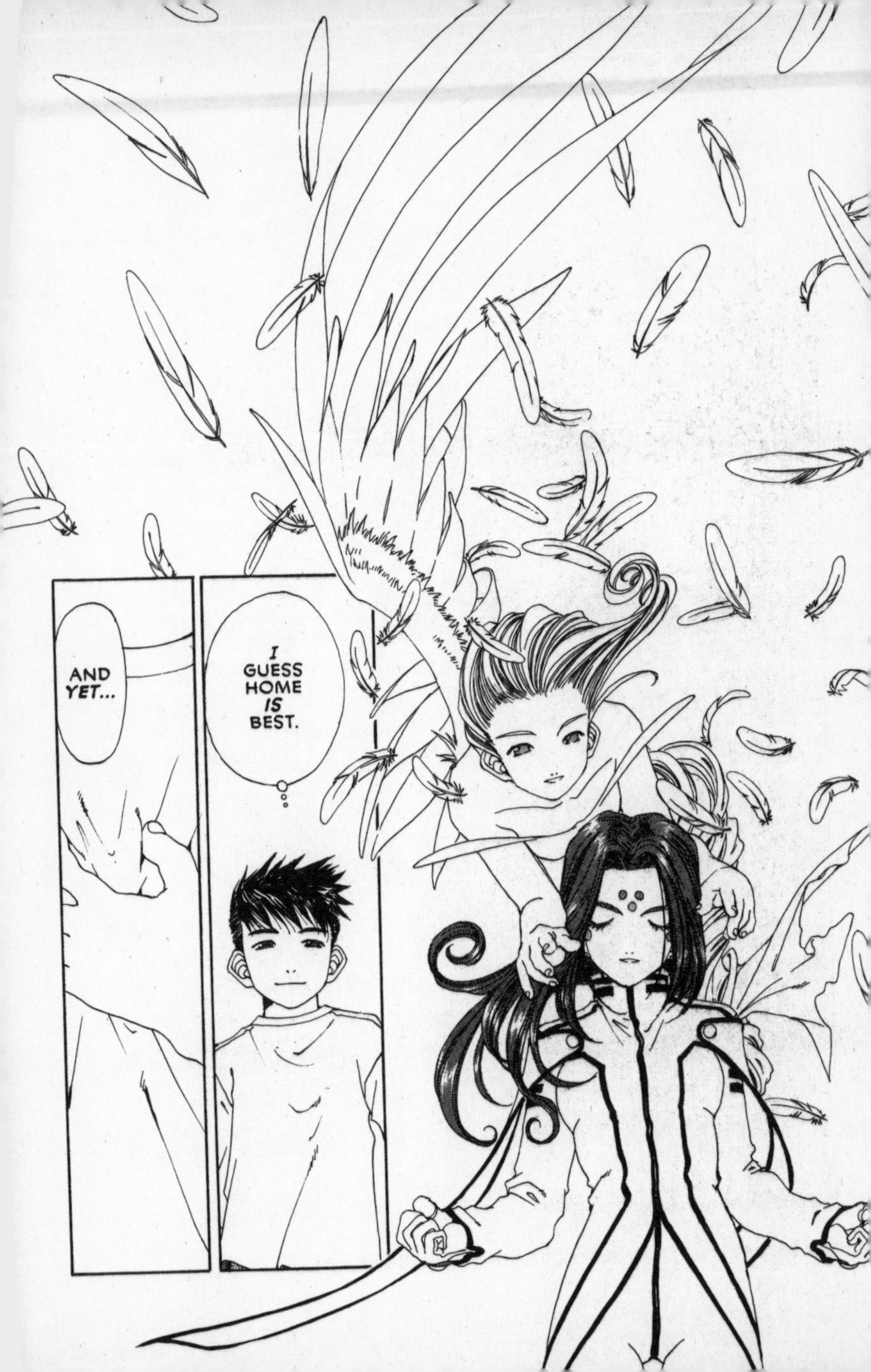
I GUESS HOME *IS* BEST.
AND *YET*...

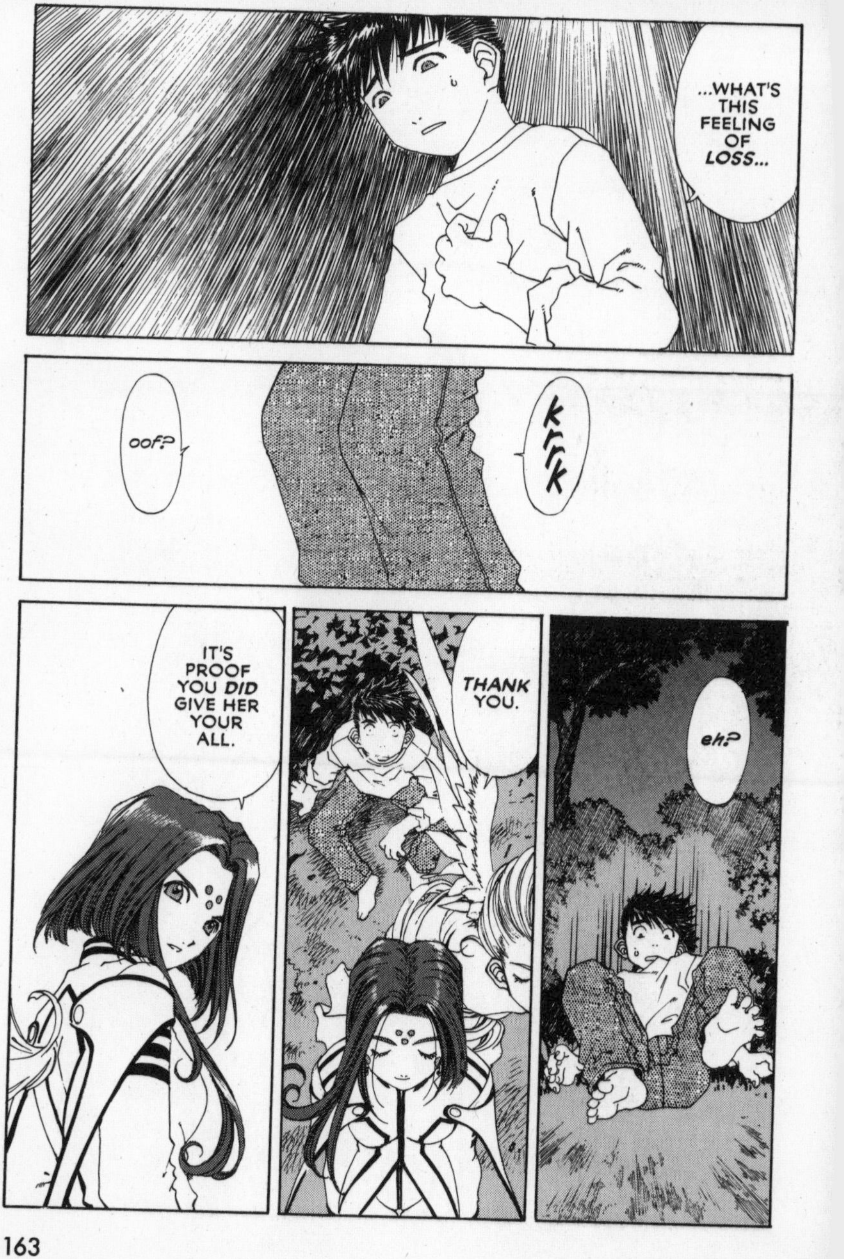
...WHAT'S THIS FEELING OF *LOSS*...
krrk
oof?
eh?
THANK YOU.
IT'S PROOF YOU *DID* GIVE HER YOUR ALL.

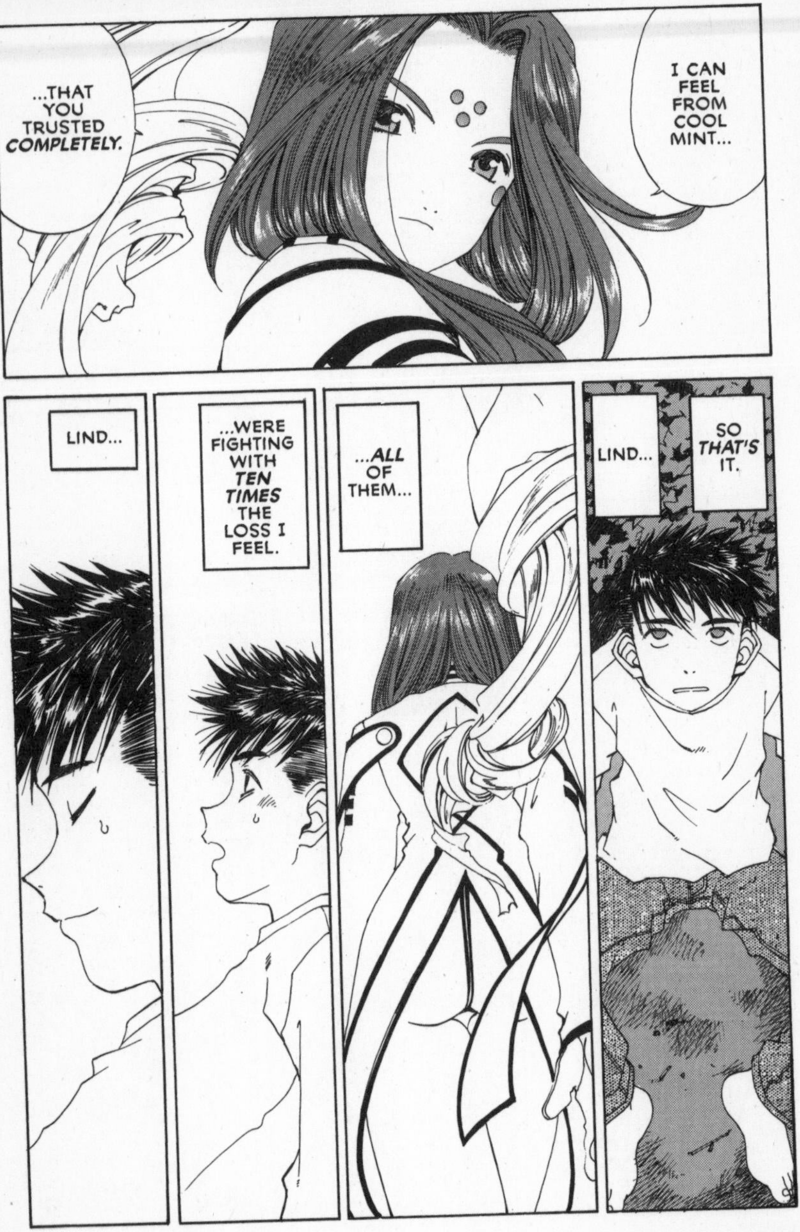
I CAN FEEL FROM COOL MINT...
...THAT YOU TRUSTED *COMPLETELY.*
SO *THAT'S* IT.
LIND...
...*ALL* OF THEM...
...WERE FIGHTING WITH *TEN TIMES* THE LOSS I FEEL.
LIND...

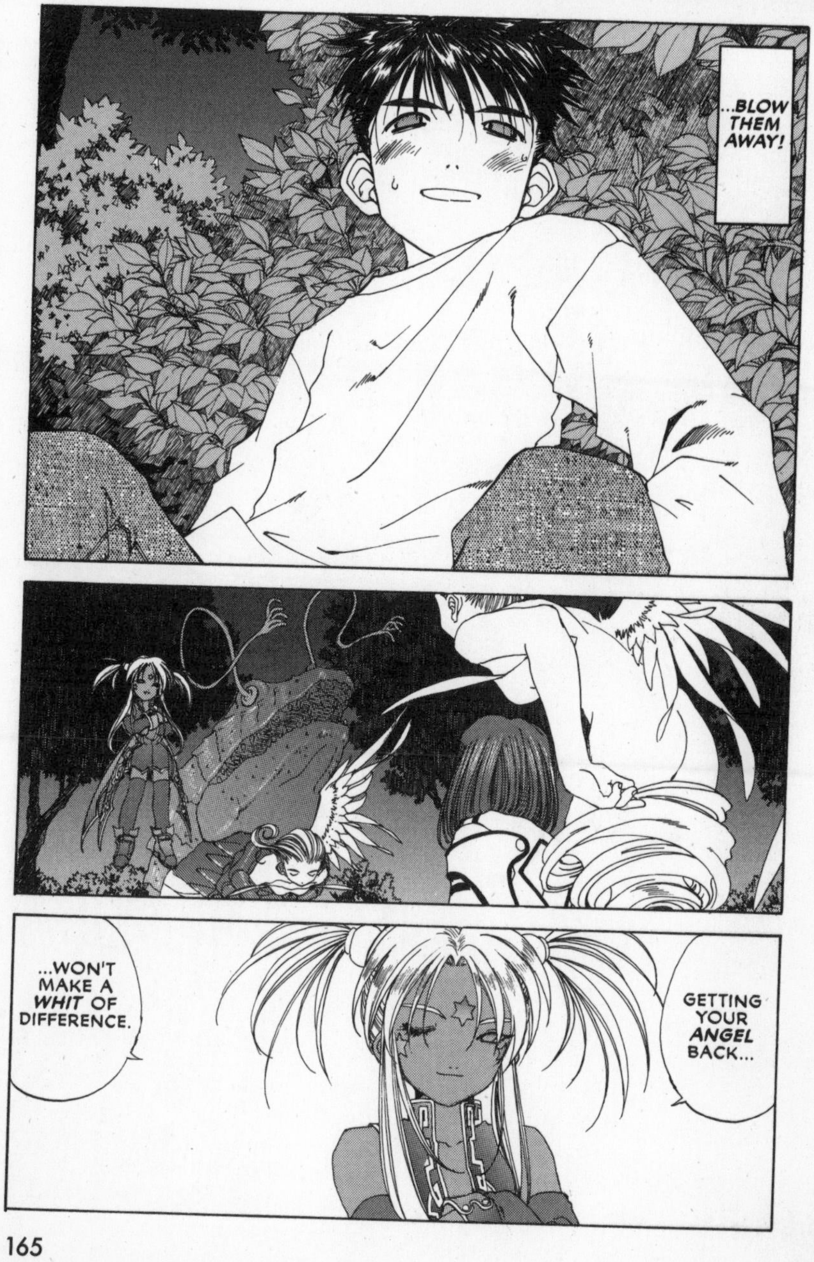
...BLOW THEM AWAY!
GETTING YOUR *ANGEL* BACK...
...WON'T MAKE A *WHIT* OF DIFFERENCE.

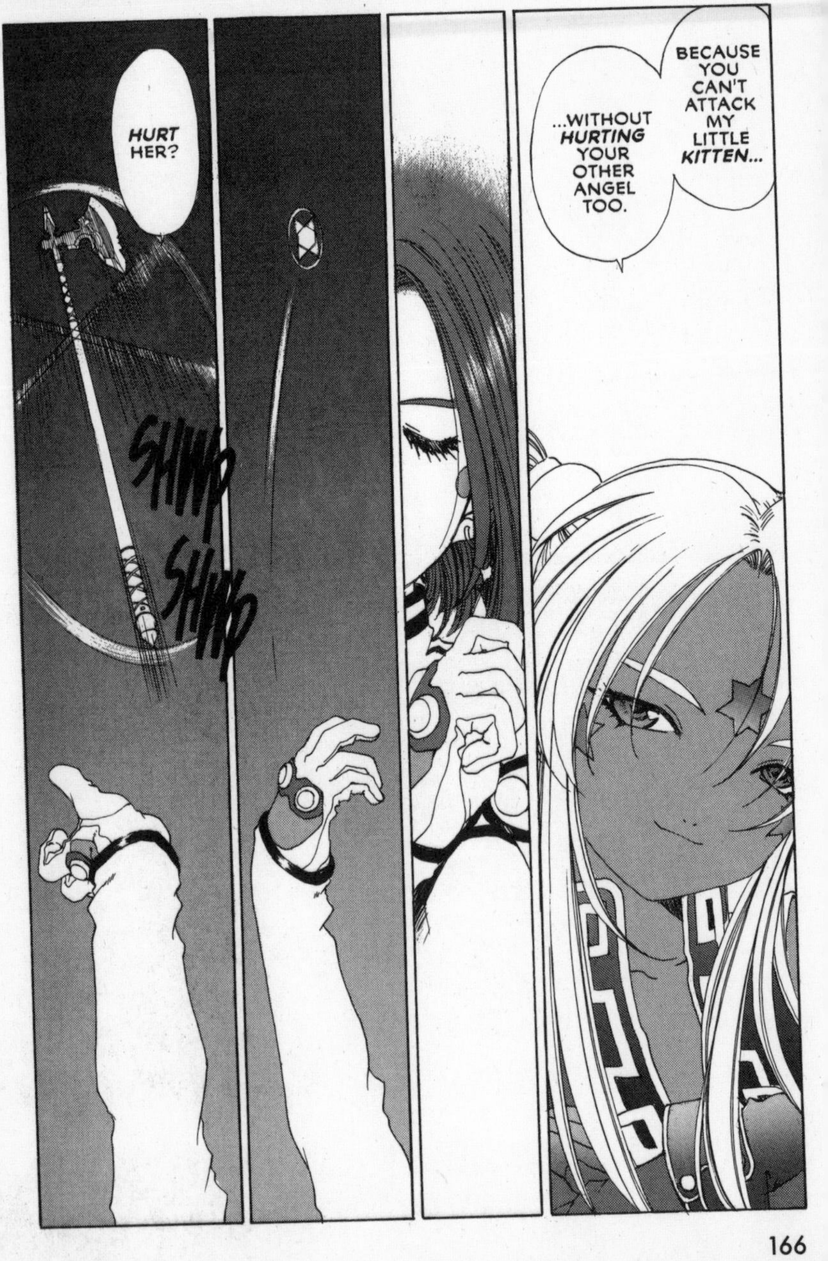
BECAUSE YOU CAN'T ATTACK MY LITTLE *KITTEN*...
...WITHOUT *HURTING* YOUR OTHER ANGEL TOO.
SHWIP
SHWIP
HURT HER?

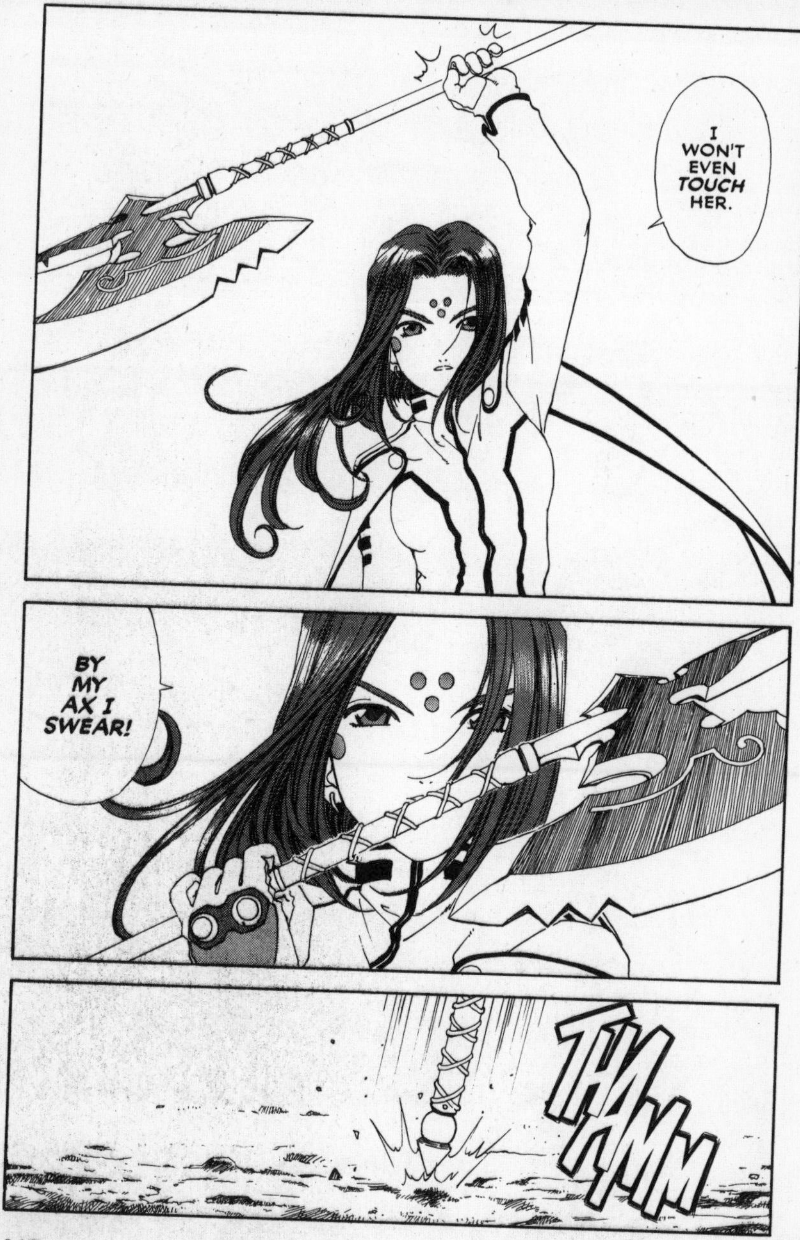
I WON'T EVEN *TOUCH* HER.
BY MY AX I SWEAR!
THAMM

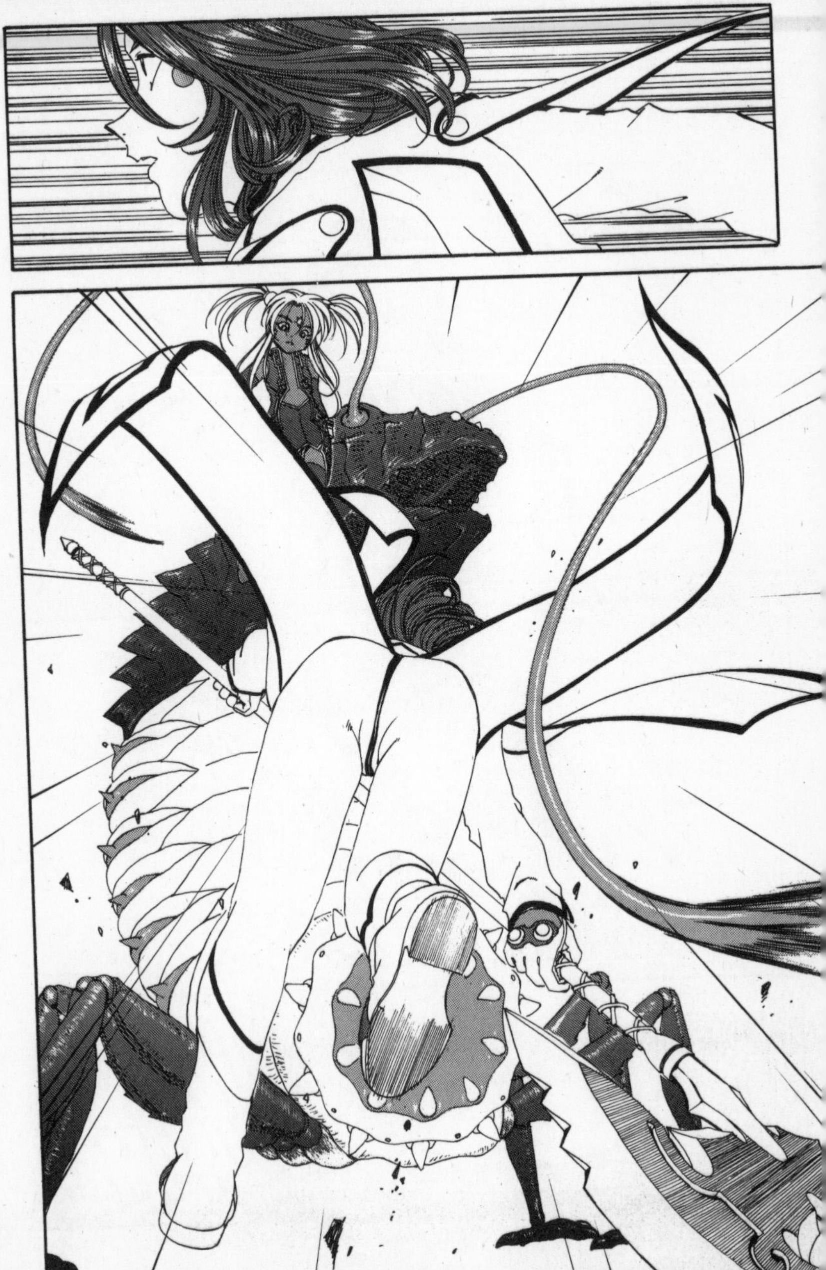

EDITOR
Carl Gustav Horn

DESIGNER
Scott Cook

ART DIRECTOR
Lia Ribacchi

PUBLISHER
Mike Richardson

English-language version
produced by Dark Horse Comics

Published by Dark Horse Manga
A division of Dark Horse Comics, Inc.
10956 SE Main Street
Milwaukie, OR 97222
www.darkhorse.com

To find a comics shop in your area,
call the Comic Shop Locator Service
toll-free at 1-888-266-4226

First edition: December 2006
ISBN-10: 1-59307-644-4
ISBN-13: 978-1-59307-644-3

1 3 5 7 9 10 8 6 4 2

Printed in Canada

letters to the ENCHANTRESS

10956 SE Main Street, Milwaukie, Oregon 97222
omg@darkhorse.com • www.darkhorse.com

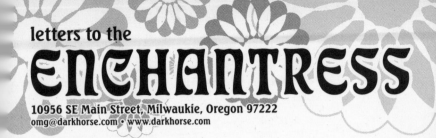

NOTE: Full addresses and e-mail addresses will not be printed, unless you ask! All fan artwork, letters, and e-mails submitted become the property of Dark Horse Comics.

Perhaps it's because this volume has an emphasis on combat and action rather than mahjong and toll roads, but there's only one note from the translator this time around—namely, her observation that although Belldandy, Urd, and Skuld are of course *named* for the Norns, as far as we all can tell, this is the first time (after more than 24 volumes) in the series Fujishima has ever actually *used* the term Norn. The editor made a quick Spotlight search through the old script archives, and could find no trace of it either; and considering that original adapter Toren Smith is cognizant of the Norse myths and their role as a motif in *Oh My Goddess!* (see his notes on naming in pp. 181-2 of Vol. 2), it's not the sort of thing likely to be removed in a rewrite.

If we don't have as much to say this time, why not go to what you've got to say? In Vol. 3 we were happy to print a number of real-life photos of the bikes of *Oh My Goddess!*, taken by correspondent Albert Sheean. Here's another letter from him:

Sir,

I discovered Keiichi and Belldandy when I'd taken my twin girls to look in the manga section at our local book emporium. The title *Oh My Goddess!* caught my eye and I began reading . . . Now I am waiting for *OMG!* Vol. 24 to arrive, and the DVDs for the next TV season to appear. While I don't particularly care if the book is flopped or not, I do wish that the books could be published in a larger format—that way more of the exquisite details in Mr. Fujishima's artwork can be appreciated. He really is quite an illustrator, with superb architectural pen and ink renderings, and faithful details in his depictions of the motor vehicles appearing in *OMG!*.

I'm an old motor head from way back, and I recognized K1's Beemer as being a "Rennsport" model with upgraded front suspension and brakes. Keima's bike is a Matchless G50, a barely civilized racer tamed for the street. I wonder what the Japanese police would say about the bellow coming from the open megaphone on his bike? Being involved in vintage motorcycle racing, I can assure you that a G50 Matchless on full is a noisy, unruly beast.

I've been enjoying the new format reissue of the earlier *OMG!* books. The color pages are fun, and going back to my older editions, I can see that the pages colorized were probably colored originally and were published in B&W anyway. Belldandy has an eye for color in her earlier "earth-bound goddess" days.

Sincerely,
Albert Sheean
Granada Hills, CA

Yes, that's right—the color pages you now see in the new format, re-issued early volumes of *Oh My Goddess!* were ones that originally ran in color in Japan, but were reproduced in black & white in the old (i.e., flopped) Dark Horse *OMG!* books. However, some of these color pages (for example, pp. 131-134 in Vol. 1) weren't reprinted in color in the *Japanese* graphic novels, either—they appeared in color only the first time the story ran in *Oh My Goddess!*'s Japanese home, *Afternoon* magazine.

Color versions of these pages have only recently become available through Kodansha's limited "Complete" editions of the early stories—it is these "remastered" files that are being used for the new format early volumes, whereas later volumes use the files of the standard Kodansha "Afternoon KC" editions. Note that only the early volumes of *OMG!* had any color pages, but it's always possible Mr. Fujishima may do some again as a special occasion. If so, we'll certainly endeavor to print them that way.

Since I'm not a rider myself, I again appreciate this commentary on the bikes of *Oh My Goddess!*, which are as essential to the manga's spirit as the Goddesses themselves are. The Goddesses, of course, can fly, but doesn't it sometimes seem as if *OMG!*'s human characters express that same sense of freedom and joy when they ride their vehicles? Belldandy appeared to recognize this in Vol. 24, and we may perhaps see this sentiment earlier, too, when she was mentoring Sora and (as her little sister had to learn to ride a human bike), Skuld, too.

Mr. Sheean also said that he hoped his bike photos are now in Kosuke Fujishima's hands, to let him know at least one of his readers recognizes the bikes he draws. As mentioned above, these photos appear in Vol. 3, and it's definitely in Mr. Fujishima's hands, as he of course receives copies of the English (and other foreign) editions. Once again, thank you!

The format in which I receive *Oh My Goddess!* is one in which I can indeed see the exquisite details—gigantic, 1200 dpi scans of the original art (sometimes the film) that are literally ten times the size of this graphic novel. It comes in especially handy when trying to decipher the teeny-tiny in-jokes that were common in the early volumes of *OMG!* (you'll recall an illustration of this in Vol. 1's "Letters to the Enchantress").

Of course, for eleven years (1994-2005), Dark Horse *did* publish *Oh My Goddess!* in a larger format—during that whole period, the book was not only translated "flopped," but published as a monthly comic book and then collected into 6" x 9" graphic novels—both the comic book and those graphic novels, of course, being larger than the 5" x 7.5" unflopped version you currently hold in your hands (unless, like certain X-Men, you have prehensile feet and/or telekinesis).

With the new format, the story is coming out faster in English (although I know that sometimes seems hard to believe), but at the loss, among other things, of the larger page size. As someone who began by editing manga in comic book format, I have definite sympathy for your viewpoint. Of course, I can remember when the "smaller" size was the 6" x 9" format—many companies, including Dark Horse, originally did their manga GNs at full comic-book size (although this was never the case with *Oh My Goddess!*, you may find some old *Outlanders* and *3x3 Eyes* graphic novels that size, as well as Shirow Masamune's works, back when he was known as Masamune Shirow ^_^).

Although the current *Oh My Goddess!* graphic novels are the same size as is the regular series in Japan (actually, the Dark Horse versions are just slightly larger), it's also true that pretty much all professional manga isn't drawn to be read at that size, but at magazine size—that is, the size of the magazine in which they appear, in *OMG!*'s case, the monthly, *Afternoon*. This means, roughly comic book size—so the abandonment of the monthly manga comic book has meant *Oh My Goddess!*'s more "authentic" format meant the abandonment in English of both its Japanese publication size and frequency. Irony, as has been observed, can be pretty ironic sometimes.

Now we'll draw you a little further into the secret world of how Dark Horse brings *Oh My Goddess!* to you. ***Behold!***

Dark Horse's Director of Asian Licensing, Michael Gombos, discovered this, the most holy shrine of the sister Goddesses, fifteen floors above Tokyo in Kodansha's towering worldwide headquarters.

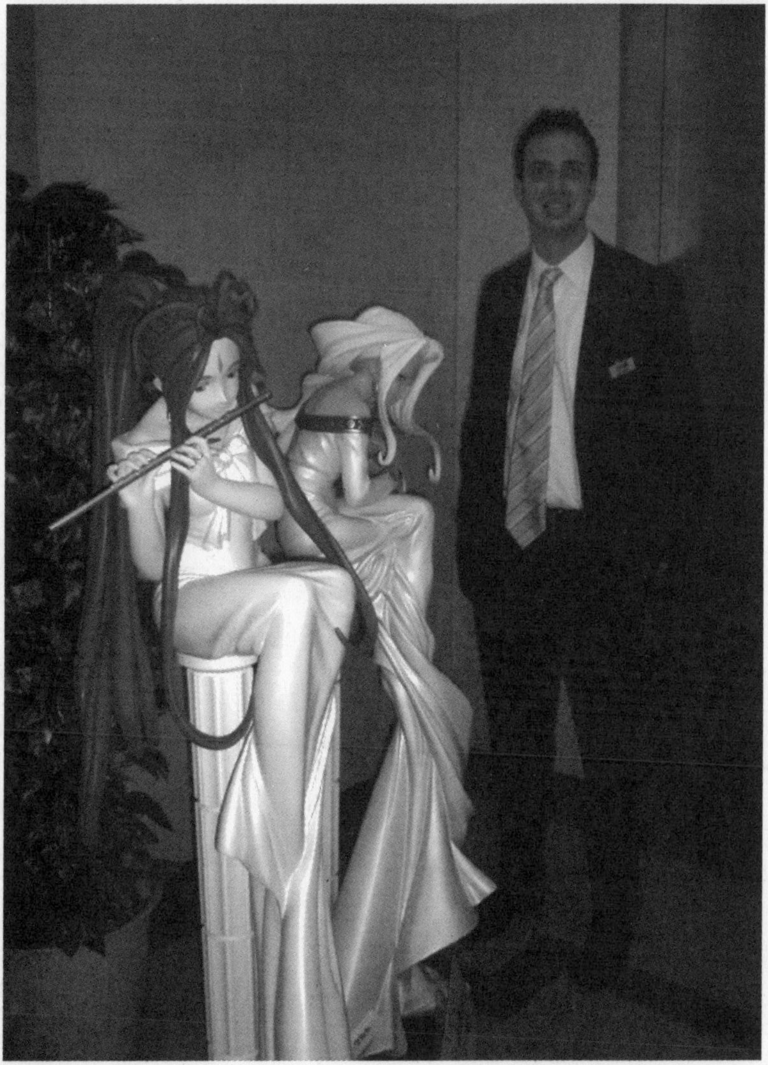

Have I mentioned before that Mr. Gombos is a really cool guy, and that I'm lucky to know him and work with him? If you study Japanese as hard as he has, perhaps you too will one day get this close to divinity.

The cruel thing is, I've been to Kodansha HQ too, but I don't remember no Goddess Trio being on hand to greet me.

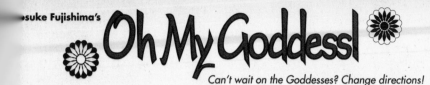

osuke Fujishima's

Oh My Goddess!

Can't wait on the Goddesses? Change directions!

Just gotten into the new unflopped editions of *Oh My Goddess!*, and found you can't wait to see what happens next? Have no fear! The first **20 volumes** of *Oh My Goddess!* are available **right now** in Western-style editions! Released between 1994 and 2005, our *OMG!* Western-style volumes feature premium paper, and pages 40% larger than those of the unflopped editions! If you've already got some of the unflopped volumes and want to know which Western-style ones to get to catch up, check out darkhorse.com's "Manga Zone" for a complete breakdown of how the editions compare!

Vol. 1: Wrong Number
ISBN: 1-56971-669-2 / $13.95

Vol. 2: Leader of the Pack
ISBN: 1-56971-764-8 / $13.95

Vol. 3: Final Exam
ISBN: 1-56971-765-6 / $13.95

Vol. 4: Love Potion No. 9
ISBN: 1-56971-252-2 / $14.95

Vol. 5: Sympathy for the Devil
ISBN: 1-56971-329-4 / $13.95

Vol. 6: Terrible Master Urd
ISBN: 1-56971-369-3 / $14.95

Vol. 7: The Queen of Vengeance
ISBN: 1-56971-431-2 / $13.95

Vol. 8: Mara Strikes Back!
ISBN: 1-56971-449-5 / $14.95

Vol. 9: Ninja Master
ISBN: 1-56971-474-6 / $13.95

Vol. 10: Miss Keiichi
ISBN: 1-56971-522-X / $16.95

Vol. 11: The Devil in Miss Urd
ISBN: 1-56971-540-8 / $14.95

Vol. 12: The Fourth Goddess
ISBN: 1-56971-551-3 / $18.95

Vol. 13: Childhood's End
ISBN: 1-56971-685-4/ $15.95

Vol. 14: Queen Sayoko
ISBN: 1-56971-766-4 / $16.95

Vol. 15: Hand in Hand
ISBN: 1-56971-921-7 / $17.95

Vol. 16: Mystery Child
ISBN: 1-56971-950-0 / $18.95

Vol. 17: Traveler
ISBN: 1-56971-986-1 / $17.95

Vol. 18: The Phantom Racer
ISBN: 1-59307-217-1 / $17.95

Vol. 19/20: Sora Unchained
ISBN: 1-59307-316-X / $18.95

Adventures of the Mini-Goddesses
ISBN: 1-56971-421-5 / $9.95

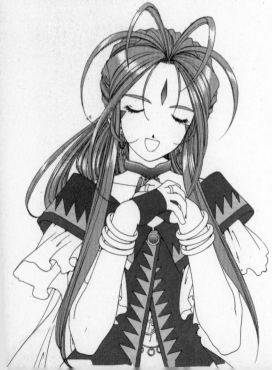

AVAILABLE AT YOUR LOCAL COMICS SHOP OR BOOKSTORE
*To find a comics shop in your area, call 1-888-266-4226

For more information or to order direct:
- On the web: darkhorse.com
- E-mail: mailorder@darkhorse.com
- Phone: 1-800-862-0052 Mon.-Fri. 9 A.M. to 5 P.M. Pacific Time.

DARK HORSE MANGA

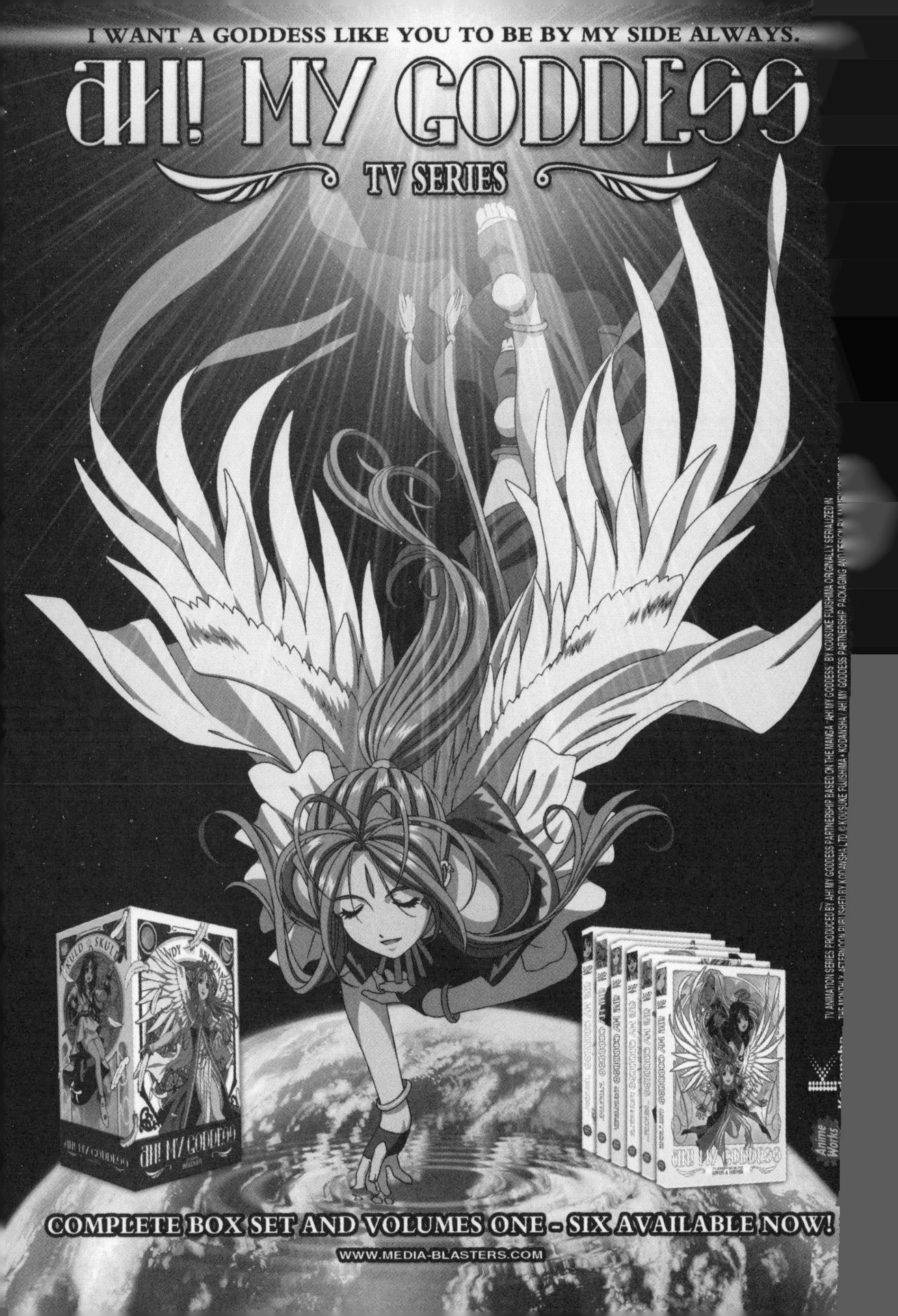
I WANT A GODDESS LIKE YOU TO BE BY MY SIDE ALWAYS.
AH! MY GODDESS
TV SERIES
TV ANIMATION SERIES PRODUCED BY AH! MY GODDESS PARTNERSHIP BASED ON THE MANGA "AH! MY GODDESS" BY KOUSUKE FUJISHIMA ORIGINALLY SERIALIZED IN
THE MONTHLY AFTERNOON PUBLISHED BY KODANSHA LTD ©KOUSUKE FUJISHIMA • KODANSHA AH! MY GODDESS PARTNERSHIP PACKAGING AND DESIGN BY
Anime Works
COMPLETE BOX SET AND VOLUMES ONE - SIX AVAILABLE NOW!
WWW.MEDIA-BLASTERS.COM

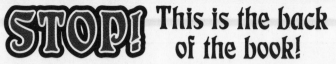

STOP! This is the back of the book!

This manga collection is translated into English, but arranged in right-to-left reading format to maintain the artwork's visual orientation as originally drawn and published in Japan. If you've never read comics this way before, take a look at the diagram below to give yourself an idea of how to go about it. Basically, you'll be starting in the upper right-hand corner, and will read each word balloon and panel moving right-to-left. It may take a little getting used to, but you should get the hang of it very quickly. Have fun! If this is the millionth manga you've read this way, never mind. ^_^

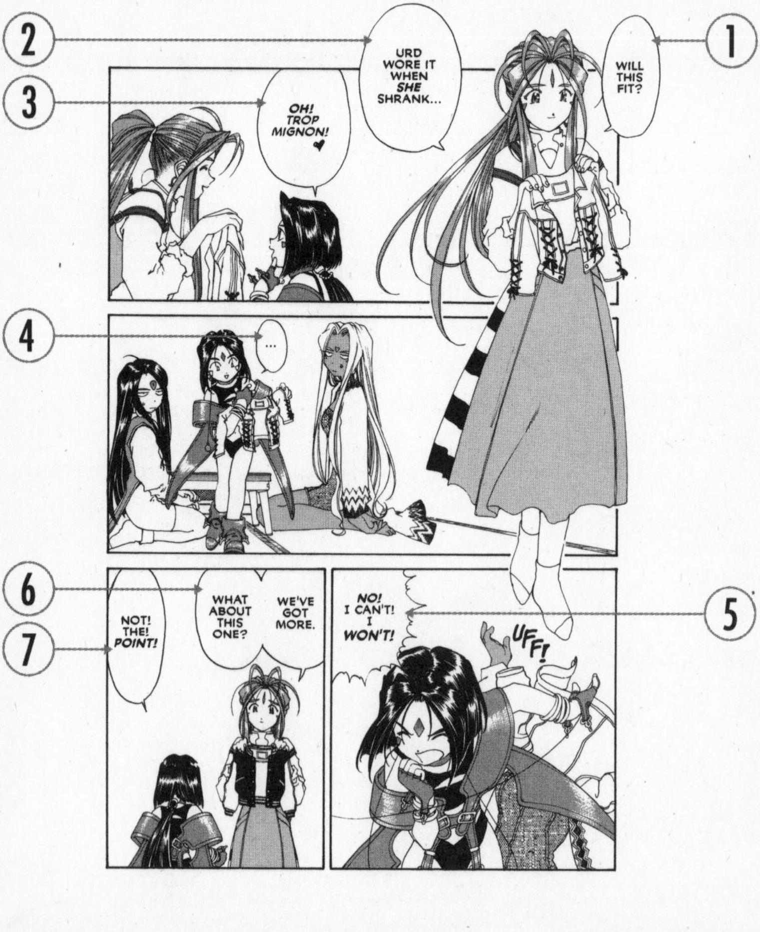
1
WILL THIS FIT?
2
URD WORE IT WHEN SHE SHRANK...
3
OH! TROP MIGNON!
4
...
5
NO! I CAN'T! I WON'T!
UFF!
6
WE'VE GOT MORE.
WHAT ABOUT THIS ONE?
7
NOT! THE! POINT!